# GETTING SCREWED

# GETTING

*Sex Workers and the Law*

# SCREWED

*Alison Bass*

ForeEdge

ForeEdge
An imprint of University Press of New England
www.upne.com
© 2015 Alison Bass
All rights reserved

Manufactured in the United States of America
Designed by April Leidig
Typeset in Adobe Caslon by Copperline Book Services, Inc.

Library of Congress Cataloging-in-Publication Data
Bass, Alison.
Getting screwed: sex workers and the law / Alison Bass.
pages cm
Includes bibliographical references and index.
ISBN 978-1-61168-634-0 (cloth: alk. paper)
ISBN 978-1-61168-845-0 (ebook)
1. Prostitution. 2. Prostitution—Law and legislation. I. Title.
HQ118.B37 2015
306.74—dc23    2015010963

5 4 3 2 1

*For Carmen Rudy*
*and all the other sex workers*
*whose murders remain unsolved.*

# CONTENTS

# PREFACE

I hadn't given much thought to the largely hidden world of sex work until a student met with me one day to go over the draft of her profile assignment. She had chosen to write about a young activist who helped defeat an ordinance that would have made it illegal for homeless people to panhandle on the streets of Northampton, a progressive but increasingly gentrified city in western Massachusetts. My student had heard this twenty-seven-year-old woman speak at a town meeting and, impressed by her passion for helping those less fortunate than herself, had interviewed her for the profile. But my student was having trouble bringing her subject to life on the page, and as we discussed how to do that, she suddenly blurted out, "She's also a sex worker." How interesting, I thought. I told my student that this information would be intrinsic to any profile she wrote about this woman. Two other interesting facts leaped out at me: the young woman's middle-class background and her volunteer work with the Freedom Center, a Northampton-based advocacy group that offers support and alternative treatment for people with mental illness. She had apparently struggled with depression at a teenager, and after being heavily medicated, she had chosen to stop taking psychoactive drugs and use alternative methods of treatment. At the time, I was writing a weekly blog about the side effects of antidepressants (the topic of my first book), so I decided to interview this woman about her work with the Freedom Center.

I met Jillian at a café in Northampton, and during that initial interview, the topic of how she earned a living (so she could spend most of her time volunteering) came up. "I enjoy being a middle-class escort," she said, as if what she did was just an ordinary job. "I provide a girlfriend experience for an hour. I create a persona, and in that persona I can connect and bond with someone. It's fun."

Over the next months, I met with Jillian (her professional name) several times, and she opened up a fascinating window onto the reality of being a sex worker in the twenty-first century. When I expressed an interest in writing about prostitution, she put me in touch with other sex workers around the country. The stories that Jillian and her compatriots told me clashed with the popular narrative of prostitutes as drug-addicted, victimized women who were invariably forced into the sex trade by abusive pimps and traffickers. Research by respected academics also contradicted this narrative and pointed to a very different story: that laws criminalizing prostitution not only are largely ineffective in curbing the sex trade but also create an atmosphere that encourages the exploitation of sex workers and violence against all women. A growing body of research showed that antiprostitution laws in the United States and other countries only make it more difficult for sex workers to protect themselves—from physical harm and sexually transmitted diseases such as HIV infection.

The more I delved into this issue, the more I realized that in many respects, history was repeating itself. The historical record shows that during periods in the United States when prostitution was either legal or operating under a de facto system of decriminalization, there was less violence toward sex workers and working conditions were safer. Until the latter part of the nineteenth century, for example, an atmosphere of relative tolerance prevailed, and many sex workers operated openly, particularly in the American West, where they were often respected as entrepreneurs (more on this in Chapter 1) By contrast, during times when the U.S. government actively tried to suppress prostitution with restrictive laws—in the run-up to both World Wars—sex workers were at greater risk of violence and harassment from clients and police.

As the sexual revolution of the '60s began eroding moralistic views about casual sex, it created a paradoxical surge in demand for commercial sex (despite the promise of all that free love). Yet even with the more permissive attitudes toward sexual experimentation and the emergence of the modern sex workers movement in the '70s, laws against prostitution in the United States continued to wreak havoc on women's lives (Chapter 2).

More recently, conservative groups allied with some feminists have used the rubric of sex trafficking to create public alarm and opposition to prostitution, even when it's clearly consensual. While there is no question that some foreign-born women are being smuggled into the United States and forced into the sex trade, most references to sex trafficking today reflect a new attack on an old problem: the exploitation of teenagers from dysfunctional homes in their own communities (Chapter 5).

In the last decade, antitrafficking proponents have wielded inaccurate and highly inflated statistics to persuade state and local authorities to pass ever more restrictive laws against prostitution. At a time when the rest of the developed world—most of Europe, Australia, New Zealand, even parts of South America—has moved toward decriminalizing commercial sex, the United States has lurched in the opposite direction: toward increasingly punitive measures against prostitution. Yet such laws have done little to curb either trafficking or the exploitation of runaway teenagers. Nor have these measures reduced the numbers of women and men engaged in prostitution.

In fact, as shown in Chapter 3, the demand for commercial sexual transactions here and abroad has soared in the last three decades, in large part because of globalization and the growth of the Internet. What sociologist Barbara Brents calls the "pornographication of culture" extends beyond traveling businessmen; it permeates every facet of American society, spread by mass media (advertising, television shows, YouTube, Snapchat) that encourage voyeurism and sexual experimentation. "This 'sexed-up' nature of contemporary society forms the backdrop for understanding the prevalence and visibility of sex venues in Western society," Brents and coauthor Teela Sanders write in a 2010 essay for the *Journal of Law and Society*.[1]

As Brents and Sanders note, sexuality has become a central component of late-capitalist consumer culture, despite the moralistic tone the mainstream media take whenever a well-known politician or official gets caught with a sex worker. Prostitution continues to flourish under new guises, blurring the lines between what is legal and what is not. Escort services, strip clubs, private lap-dance parties, and pornography—all legal—constitute a multibillion dollar industry, and that doesn't include the millions of dollars that hotel chains such as Marriott, Holiday Inn, and Hyatt make each year from supplying adult films to their guests and renting hotel rooms to people in the sex trade. Nor does it include the millions that giant telecommunications companies earn from phone sex or cell phones used by sex workers to screen clients and arrange liaisons. Indeed, the sex industry here and abroad has largely converged with other mainstream service industries. In 2006, Americans spent $13.3 billion on adult videos, DVDs, live sex shows, strip clubs, cable films, phone sex, and X-rated magazines, according to one researcher, who counted about 3,500 strip clubs in the United States.[2] The same year, $97 billion was believed to have been spent on pornography globally.[3] The money spent on the illegal sex trade (the actual exchange of money for sex) is harder to gauge precisely because it is still illegal in some countries. In the late '90s, the illegal sex industry in the United States was estimated to generate about $18 billion annually.[4] The global sex industry was estimated at between $30 and $50 billion per year, according to another study.[5]

In areas of the United States where prostitution is legal (such as rural areas of Nevada) and in European countries such as Germany and the Netherlands, commercial sex is treated as a commodity like any other service and has become increasingly dominated by mainstream corporate entities that sell escapism, adventure, and specially tailored fantasies (Chapters 7 and 10). The same corporations that run upscale brothels in Nevada also own restaurants, nightclubs, and hotels.

Yet the actual individuals who work in this increasingly mainstreamed industry remain marginalized by social stigma and are often exploited. As freelance contractors, rather than employees, the women who work in legal brothels here and abroad have very few rights to protect themselves from labor abuses. The situation for women and men who work in the illegal sector is much worse. While antiprostitution laws have done little to stem the thriving industry in recreational sex, they exact a high price on public health and safety. Although violence is not intrinsic to the sex trade (Chapter 4), many sex workers fear getting arrested if they report violent clients or exploitative pimps. Hence, criminalization allows killers and others to prey on women with impunity. Predators target prostitutes precisely because they are less likely to go to the police, and nonprostitutes are victimized as well when killers go unchecked (Chapter 6).

As shown in Chapter 8, laws criminalizing prostitution also foster corruption among some police officers, who harass sex workers for free sex in exchange for not arresting them. In addition, recent antitrafficking measures that dispense money from stiff fines and fees to police and prosecutors create a financial incentive for law enforcement to go after adults engaged in consensual prostitution and make the problem of trafficking look worse than it actually is.

This stands in stark contrast to the situation in countries where prostitution is legal and prostitutes work with police to curb crime and sex trafficking. The red-light districts in the Netherlands, where prostitution has been decriminalized since the 1970s and has been legal since 2000, are safe places to live and walk around in (Chapter 10).

Laws criminalizing prostitution likewise make it difficult for many sex workers, particularly those who are homeless or addicted to drugs, to practice safe sex and gain access to health care that could stem the spread of HIV infection and other sexually transmitted diseases (Chapters 10 and 11). More recent antitrafficking laws in many states prevent women from working together as a safety measure, since they face an increased risk of being arrested and charged with trafficking each other (Chapter 12). Antitrafficking proponents have also been successful in shutting down Internet sites where sex workers advertise their services, making it more difficult for them to work off the street in safer indoor locations (Prologue and Chapters 10 and 11).

Such policies are not only dangerous and disingenuous; they are a colossal waste of taxpayers' money. As shown in Chapter 8, the overwhelming majority of prostitutes who are arrested are not prosecuted or imprisoned, and most are back on the street within hours. At the same time, police often fail to distinguish between women and men who do sex work by choice and those who are forced into it against their will. Despite laws that classify the latter group as trafficking victims, these women are usually treated as criminals, and if found to be in the country illegally, they are deported against their will (Chapters 9, 10, and 12).

As I hope to show in this book by weaving together the true stories of sex workers and the latest research, many of the problems associated with prostitution in the United States would diminish if sex work were decriminalized and regulated to some degree. The most successful approach from a public health and safety standpoint can be found in New Zealand. In 2003, government officials there removed all prohibitions against adult consensual prostitution (retaining laws against child prostitution and trafficking). At the same time, the government required brothels, escort agencies, and other commercial sex venues to be licensed. New Zealand's hybrid law allows for periodic inspections of such venues and gives local officials the authority to shut them down if violations are found. However, unlike sex workers in Nevada's brothels and those in Germany, New Zealand's sex workers are not required to register with the authorities, thus reducing the social stigma these women experience. As shown in Chapter 10, New Zealand's semilegal approach has vastly improved working conditions for both indoor and street workers, not only reducing the risks of violence from clients, pimps, and police but also curbing the spread of HIV infection and other sexually transmitted diseases.

As I argue in this book, federal and state authorities in the United States would do well to consider a similar approach toward adult consensual prostitution. Under such a scenario, brothels and other venues engaged in commercial sex could be taxed and regulated as businesses. Adult sex work would be decriminalized, making it easier for women and men who are doing sex work by choice to protect themselves from violence and disease. A hybrid approach that decriminalizes and regulates sex work would free law enforcement to go after real criminals, such as rapists, violent predators, and men who traffic in vulnerable children.

# GETTING SCREWED

# PROLOGUE

## *The "Friendliest" Brothel in Manhattan*

**J**ulie Moya is running late again. A Manhattan madam, Julie was once a working girl herself, a sought-after escort who could command thousands of dollars for a few hours of her time. Now fifty-five, she runs two busy brothels in midtown and has arranged to meet me at her "office" on 46th street and take me to one of the brothels. As I walk from Penn Station to her office (the taxi line stretched around the block), she calls me twice, apologizing for her tardiness. (This is our third get-together, and Julie has been at least fifteen to twenty minutes late each time.) When I finally arrive at 31 W. 46th Street, soaked in sweat from the 90-degree heat, Julie is still not there. But Corrine, one of her long-time managers who asked to be identified by her first name only, buzzes me into the second-floor office. There is a full-size bed in a spare front room, filing cabinets in the back room, and one small desk in the large, mostly empty middle room. That is where Corrine, a forty-two-year-old former schoolteacher, stripper, and sex worker who has worked for Julie on and off for eleven years, sits and fields calls from prospective customers. The three cell phones on the desk are constantly buzzing, each with a different ringtone. It is lunchtime, and the clients are hungry.

Corrine, who wears her light-brown hair in long braids and looks like she would fit right in at a Woodstock-style love-in, answers one phone and says, "We have Gabriela, she's new, a lovely South American girl, twenty-three. She has a tight ass and flat abs. I also have Denny, Ava, Toni, and Sophia. Daisy comes in at 5 p.m. Okay, just call back." She answers another phone, listens, and replies: "Sweetie, you can't talk to Roxy; you can make an appointment to see her. I can give you all the information you need. No, you can't talk to Roxy. I can help you." She listens for a beat and then says: "For two clients, it's $480. Can I put you on hold?" She answers another phone and listens. "At 2 p.m. I have Raquel available, and at 2:15 p.m. I have Raquel and Sarah," she says. "Sarah's donation is $300 for the hour and $200 for the half-hour." She tells yet another caller, "Sweetie, Indira is only there on weekends. We don't book ahead; you have to call the same day." To another caller, she says, "The donation is $250 for an hour; $160 for a half-hour. Can you hold?" At one point, Corrine is working all three cell phones simultaneously.

When the phones stop buzzing for a second, Corrine turns to me and explains that she doesn't book ahead because sometimes the girls don't show up. She shrugs. "Sometimes the men don't show up either." Most of the clients calling in today, she explains, are regulars; they already have a pin number, so Corrine can bill their credit cards automatically. All clients have to have a pin number, and before they get that number, they go through a vetting process, to establish that they are who they say they are and that their credit cards work.

For security reasons, Corrine never gives out the exact addresses of the brothels when she sets up the appointments. She tells the men to call back when they arrive at the closest intersection and then she will direct them to the right address. When a new client arrives at the designated apartment building, one of the women who work as security goes downstairs to greet him in the lobby and offers to give him a blow job on the spot. Or she will ask him to take out his penis. "Let's see what you got," the woman will say. If the man refuses either request, that is a tip-off. "It's an l.e. [law enforcement] check. Cops won't do it," Corrine says. "It was Julie's idea, and it works really well."

Corrine picks up another ringing phone; it's a client named John, who has arrived at the brothel on 28th Street. She quickly picks up another phone and punches in some numbers. When the woman on the other end answers, she says: "John for Roxy right now." Another regular, named Doug, calls, and Corrine says, "Right now I don't have anyone available. I think it will be ten to twenty minutes." Doug hangs up, and finally there's a moment of silence. Corinne puts her head down in her hands and groans, "Aargh."

A few minutes later, Julie Moya rushes in and gives me a hug, apologizing again for being late. She's wearing a low-cut pink top with ruffled sleeves and tight blue jeans. She looks hot and frazzled, her straight blond hair damp at the edges. She heads for the bathroom. "I need to dry off," Julie says. "It's a stinker out there."

After lunch at a quiet Italian restaurant next door, Julie drives me to one of the brothels, located in a narrow apartment building on 28th and Madison. She says she moves their locations every year or so to keep the brothels under police radar. Just eighteen months ago, there was a crisis involving one of her girls, a pretty Korean whom she calls Minna. Minna had a millionaire lover on the side who was so entranced by her that he paid for her boob job and the rental on her Manhattan apartment, Julie says. But when Minna broke up with him, the millionaire was furious. He hired a bunch of private investigators who posed as cops and started harassing the brothel, which was then located in "a very nice building" at 24th Street, Julie says. She was forced to fire Minna and move her entire operation almost overnight.

When we arrive at the brothel's current location on 28th Street, Erin, the woman in charge of security, buzzes us in, and Julie and I walk up to the third floor. Erin meets us at the door; she is a hard-faced woman in her forties or fifties who looks as if life has roughed her up a bit. The long hallways are painted a bordello black, and the bedrooms are New York apartment–style small. A double bed takes up much of the space in one room; it is draped with a burgundy bedspread, colorful throw pillows, and canopy netting designed to make the room look like somebody's idea of a sultan's harem. We find four of Julie's working girls lounging in a common room down the hall; they are in between assignations. All in their twenties, they wear slinky off-the-shoulder tops cut low to reveal cleavage, tight miniskirts, and sexy high-heeled sandals. When one of the girls sits down, I can see she is not wearing underwear. Erin introduces me to them, using their working names, not their real ones.

Sarah, a tiny spit of a blonde wearing a short shiny-silver skirt, speaks up first. She is Israeli, she says, originally from Russia, and has been living in New York for the last three years. "I'm studying art history at Hunter College," Sarah says. "I want to do art authorizations—you know, check for counterfeits." When I ask if her family, still in Israel, knows she is doing sex work, Sarah says, "N.O. I say my ex-boyfriend helps me." Sarah confides that the first couple of times she was assigned a client, she "chickened out." Corrine had to tell Sarah's prospective customers, who were cooling their heels outside the brothel, waiting to be buzzed in, that she had become unavoidably ill. Corrine was terribly sorry; would they be willing to party with someone else?

A tall, voluptuous blonde strolls into the lounge, and Sarah grins. "Natasha loves sex," she says teasingly. "She's from Russia too." Natasha says that she came to New York two years ago on "vacation," and has been here ever since. The other women titter and Sarah winks, implying that her Russian friend is here on an expired visa. Seated at the other end of the sofa is Rachel, a pretty, light-skinned twenty-one-year-old with soft features, dark hair, and a curvaceous figure. She has been working at Julie's for only three weeks. "It took me a while to figure out the rules and everything," Rachel says. "Not everybody makes you feel comfortable." It is clear she is referring to her clients; it is equally clear that with Erin hovering in the background, she doesn't feel comfortable saying anything more. Next to her, knees pressed primly together, sits "Paris," a slender brunette with large breasts who lives in New Jersey and attends Rutgers University.

Paris says that when she graduates, she'd like to work with children. "This helps me pay for school," she says. She views sex work as a "normal job," and when she isn't in class, she drives in from Jersey and parks in a garage nearby. When I ask how much parking costs, she says, "$40 a day" and shrugs, as if to say, that's nothing compared with what she can make in a few hours here.

When I ask the women if they like what they do, Sarah says, "Sometimes you have good days; sometimes you have bad days." Her coworkers giggle knowingly. While we're talking, Julie wanders into the lounge and admonishes Erin about a stain she found on one bedspread. "You need to wash this before the next client comes," she says. "It's so unprofessional."

Before coming to New York, I had heard there was going to be a protest against the *Village Voice*, the alternative weekly that owned backpage. com, a classified ad website that includes ads for sex workers. The Coalition against Trafficking in Women (CATW) and several religious groups had mounted a campaign to shut down backpage.com on the premise that it encourages underage prostitution by allowing traffickers to solicit clients for minors. The New York chapter of Sex Workers Outreach Project (SWOP), a national advocacy group for sex workers, was going to stage a counter-rally at the protest, which was slated to be held in front of the *Village Voice*'s offices in Cooper Square the same day as my visit to New York. When I told Julie about the event, she immediately offered to accompany me.

Earlier that day over lunch, Julie had a lot to say about the folly of trying to shut down websites that allow sex workers to advertise their services. "If they ditched backpage, I think it would put more people on the street," she says, picking at her salad. "It doesn't make sense."

In 2010, after the murders of several sex workers who advertised on Craigslist, public pressure (and the threat of lawsuits by several state attorneys general) forced Craigslist to shut down its adult classified section. But Julie says sex workers still advertise on Craigslist; they simply migrated to other sections, such as the therapeutic and casual encounters sections. "They just write in code. They say, 'I love 200 roses.' What they mean is, I charge $200," Julie says.

Advertising online, Julie says, allows sex workers to screen potential clients more carefully and practice safe sex. Julie herself requires all her workers to use condoms, and more than once, she or one of her security personnel has had to remove a client who was insisting on "bareback sex."

Back at the brothel, several of the sex workers insist that they would never have sex without condoms, and Sarah tells a story about how she found a rash on one man's "pee pee." That threw her into a panic. "I called Erin, and she checked in and said I should ask him to put a cover on it even for a blow job," she says. "But he was fine with it."

As she talks, Sarah stands behind Natasha, playing with her hair and rubbing her back; they are obviously good friends. She looks at Erin, who has been standing in the back, listening to the chatter. "Erin has helped me so much," Sarah said. "I'd never done this before." Erin nods briskly. "This [work] will leave you with a chest full of colorful stories to tell when you're eighty years old and sitting on a porch somewhere," she says, and the young women laugh, as if amused by an image that, to them, must seem impossibly remote.

Too soon, it's time to leave for the rally, and Julie and I head downtown in her huge white suv. As we drive by Cooper Square, we can see a cluster of people with pink umbrellas milling around. Julie takes a sharp right and heads to a small corner lot that has cars stacked on top of each other; she seems to know every off-street parking space in Manhattan. Having been a working girl in New York City since the early '80s, Julie never takes public transit if she can help it.

By the time she parks her suv and we hike the two blocks back to Cooper Square, the backpage protest has kicked into full gear. About twenty-five people, including a priest and several nuns, are marching in a circle, pink umbrellas held high. Several women have tape over their mouths; others are holding signs that say, "Village Voice pimps children." The marchers whose mouths aren't taped are chanting, "Village Voice, you have a choice, prostitution has got to go," and "Village Voice, you have a choice, sex trafficking has got to go." They are accompanied by two dashiki-clad men in dreadlocks banging on drums.

Antitrafficking groups such as CATW and Equality Now openly acknowledge that they are opposed to all prostitution, not just sex trafficking. U.S. law defines trafficking as "the recruitment, harboring, transportation, provision or obtaining of a person for labor or services through the use of force, fraud or coercion."[1] In a recent interview, Taina Bien-Aimé, executive director of CATW, argued that very few women are in the sex trade of their own choice; the vast majority of sex workers, she said, are being exploited by a third party. On its website, CATW says that "all prostitution exploits women, regardless of women's consent," and the organization is adamantly opposed to decriminalizing prostitution for that reason. "Do we want the type of society where we foster second-class citizens who have to cater to a man's fantasy?" Bien-Aimé said. "This is gender-based violence."

In Bien-Aimé's view, the corporations that own backpage.com and Craigslist should not engage in any activity that has the potential to be used in trafficking or exploitation. "A lot of pimps advertise very young girls on backpage," she says. "There has to be some corporate responsibility here."

In Cooper Square, a cluster of attractive young women and men stand on the sidewalk near the CATW protesters, handing out literature to passersby. Two of the women are wearing skimpy low-cut dresses. When I identify myself as a journalist, one of the miniskirted women, who has a bleached blond bob and is wearing a nose ring, explains that she is from the local chapter of SWOP. She identifies herself as Sarah.

"We're just here to provide a counter-argument," Sarah says. The protesters, she notes, are conflating prostitution with trafficking. While exploitation does exist, antitrafficking groups don't seem to recognize or care that many men and women do sex work by choice. SWOP, she says, has long considered itself an antitrafficking organization whose members report traffickers and try to help those who are truly being forced into the sex trade against their will.

A plainclothes police officer strides over to us and says, "I have to clear this area. You can't hand out flyers on the sidewalk." The officer identifies himself as Detective Hernandez, and he seems focused on removing the SWOP contingent; he never approaches the original protesters, even though neither group, I find out later, has a permit to gather. Julie Moya and I move away from the officer, and I start talking to a skinny young man wearing two nose rings and a T-shirt that reads, "I love sex workers." He identifies himself as Mitchell and says he is a sex worker and also a researcher with the Urban Institute, a nonprofit public-policy think tank in Manhattan. "We're here to say that the issues involving sex work are a lot more complex," Mitchell says. "Shutting down backpage is not going to end trafficking. It will just put sex workers and trafficking victims into riskier situations."

Mitchell says advertising online on low-cost sites such as backpage. com actually allows sex workers to be more independent from pimps or others who might exploit their labor. As we stand on the sidewalk in Cooper Square trying to talk over the banging drums and chants of the protesters, he wants to know why CATW and other groups that are so up in arms over online sex worker ads are not marching in the streets for better social services for underage sex workers or victims of trafficking. "I don't see them talking about that," Mitchell says.

Mitchell also says backpage.com works with New York police who are investigating specific sex trafficking cases. (In a later interview, Liz McDougall, general counsel for backpage.com, said the website routinely shares information with police around the country to help them identify people who are suspected of placing specific ads for underage sex workers. Backpage.com also regularly sends reports about ads involving possible underage youth to the National Center for Missing and Exploited Children [NCMEC], so police can trace exploited teenagers.)

A young woman wearing a very short, off-shoulder red satin dress and matching bright red lipstick comes up to us. She identifies herself as a former sex worker. "This is an attack on all sex workers," she says. "When you shut down one website, another one will just pop up."

Once again, we are approached by Detective Hernandez. "You have to move off the sidewalk," he says with a broad sweep of his hand. "You have to move over there." He points to a blocked-in portion of Broadway separated from the protesters by a cement barrier, where the SWOP counter-protesters are being herded, like so much cattle. Julie Moya and I decide it's time to leave, and as we walk away, she takes one last look at the protesters, whose mouths are taped shut, and asks, "Just who is being silenced here?"

# The Madonna-Whore Divide

Maggie Hall, a golden-haired twenty-year-old from Ireland, stepped off a ship in New York City in 1873, eager to conquer a new world. Hall was well educated, outgoing, and beautiful, with pretty blue eyes and a contagious laugh. But like many female immigrants without family or friends in New York, she had trouble finding decent employment, so she ended up working as a barmaid in a Manhattan saloon. There, she met a good-looking bounder by the name of William Burdan, the scion of a wealthy family who had never worked a day in his life.[1] Hall married Burdan, who insisted she change her first name to Molly (Maggie was apparently too common a name for him), and they took up married life in Burdan's Manhattan apartment. Within months, however, his father found out about the secret marriage, and furious that his son had married an Irish barmaid, he discontinued Burdan's allowance. The young man refused to find a job—he spent most of his time gambling and drinking with friends—and he wouldn't hear of his wife's going back to work in a saloon. As their finances worsened, they moved from apartment to apartment and finally landed in a cheap walk-up with no money to pay for food or rent. Burdan talked his wife into selling sex to other men, mostly other gentlemen of his milieu. He claimed that it was the only way that they could survive. Molly Burdan was heartbroken but did what her husband asked.[2]

In 1870s New York, the Victorian double standard was firmly entrenched. While there was no dearth of entertainment—striptease shows and brothels flourished alongside saloons, theaters, and expensive restaurants—these venues catered almost exclusively to men, according to Timothy Gilfoyle in *City of Eros*. Both single and married men participated in what Gilfoyle calls "a sporting male culture,"[3] while their wives and girlfriends stayed home. In the Victorian ethos, middle- and upper-class women were not supposed to enjoy sex; they were cast as Madonnas: pure, sexless creatures whom Victorian men could worship on a pedestal. Since this meant that some men's sexual desires could not be satisfied within the confines of marriage, these men turned to a class of women considered the polar opposite of Madonna: the Whore. Yet while it was acceptable for men of that era to frequent brothels, any woman who had sex outside marriage was deemed a whore.

At the same time, almost all the jobs available to women as the Industrial Revolution gathered steam in the nineteenth century were low-paying positions as servants, store clerks, barmaids, or garment-factory workers. Respectable (meaning middle- and upper-class) married women were not supposed to work, but according to Gilfoyle and others, many working-class women, both married and single, supplemented their income by selling sex.

"Many did not view [prostitution] as a full-time occupation," Gilfoyle writes.[4] A groundbreaking study of prostitutes by a well-known physician of the time, Dr. William Sanger, which was released in 1858, revealed that probably 5 to 10 percent of all young women between the ages of fifteen and thirty who were living in New York City prostituted themselves at some point. They cited "destitution" as the primary reason.[5]

Other researchers also found that the careers of many prostitutes in the nineteenth century were short-lived. Many worked largely for economic reasons from their late teens to their early to mid-twenties, and then they got married or otherwise merged back into the communities from which they had come.[6] In fact, according to William Acton, another researcher of this period, the relative affluence of prostitutes "meant that they consistently enjoyed better health than other working women and were no more likely to fall victim to alcoholism, insanity, suicide," or other problems.[7]

During the colonial era, prostitution largely existed on the fringe of society (in taverns by the docks) and was mostly controlled by women working independently. Indeed, Gilfoyle argues that before 1850, "Women had greater control and influence over prostitution than in any other period of American history."[8] By the 1860s, prostitution had grown into a thriving commercial enterprise in New York City, with six hundred brothels scattered around Broadway and Soho. Those who ultimately benefited from this system, Gilfoyle says, were the ward politicians from Tammany Hall and the police, who extracted bribes to look the other way. "Prostitution became a significant revenue source for the local political bosses," he writes.[9]

Gilfoyle and others set this trend squarely in the context of the Victorian era's sharpening gender divide. "Men wanted control over autonomous and sexually independent women," he writes. "Violent gangs allied to the political machine used extortion, force and outright terror to ensure male hegemony over the profits of prostitution."[10]

Indeed, Gilfoyle and others contend, such institutionalized violence is what gave rise for the first time to pimps. The women who ran brothels were forced to hire men for protection against gangs paid by Tammany Hall, and streetwalkers required pimps to protect them against physical assaults from both clients and police.

Even though prostitution offered women the chance to make a better living, it was a dangerous trade. According to the 1858 study by Sanger, approximately 40 percent of the prostitutes he surveyed said they had contracted syphilis or gonorrhea at least once. Many prostitutes also had to contend with violent clients. As Nickie Roberts writes in *Whores in History*: "A violent pimp was often the least of the whore's worries; every prostitute was, on the other hand, afraid of the possibility of being attacked—even murdered—by a client. The whore-stigma ensured that the protection and safety of prostitutes was low on the police agenda, and few prostitute-killers were actually caught."[11]

Underage prostitution was also rampant in 1870s New York. Numerous brothels promoted the availability of nubile young virgins amid a general atmosphere of "youthful carnality."[12]

Even then, Sanger found that less than one-fifth of girls selling sex in

New York said they had been seduced or forced into prostitution. Many came from broken homes, where there were too many mouths to feed and no male breadwinner; others were newly arrived immigrants trying to survive in a cold, hard city.[13]

Against this backdrop, Molly Burdan was growing increasingly tired of the carnal demands her husband and his friends were imposing on her. In 1877, she left William Burdan and traveled west. She spent time in Chicago, Virginia City, Nevada, the Dakota Territory, and San Francisco, becoming a sought-after prostitute everywhere she went. "The price for her favors was high and she had acquired an expensive wardrobe, which included furs and exquisite jewelry," writes Anne Seagraves in *Soiled Doves*.[14] In 1884, when Burdan was thirty, she read about the rich gold strike in Coeur d'Alene, a lake district in northern Idaho. She took the train to Thompson Falls, Montana, and there purchased a horse and joined a pack train on its way to Murray, Idaho. But the pack train of people, some on horseback, some on foot dragging a toboggan with all their worldly goods, was hit by a blizzard. Riding on horseback, Burdan noticed that a woman, who was carrying a small child, had stumbled in the snow and fallen. Burdan got off her horse, put both the woman and the child up on the saddle, and then remounted, according to newspaper accounts. But neither of them was dressed for the blizzard, and Burdan could see they were freezing. So when the pack train came to a battered hut off the side of the path, she dismounted, and they took shelter in the hut, all three huddling in Molly Burdan's furs. The rest of the people in the pack continued onward, never expecting to see the three stragglers again.[15]

The next day the entire town was surprised to see Burdan and her wards galloping down the street. She ordered a cabin and food for the mother and child, saying that she would foot the bill. As for herself, she announced that she wanted "cabin number one." In Murray, and throughout the west, Seagraves writes, "cabin number one was reserved for the madam of the red light district."[16] When an Irishman named Patrick O'Rourke asked the fur-clad lady on her horse what her name was, she replied, "Molly Burdan." But he misunderstood and responded in his heavy Irish brogue, "Well for the life of me, I'd never of thought it. Molly b'Dam." This was the beginning of the legend of Molly b'Dam, who became known throughout the West for her kindness and generosity toward those less fortunate than herself. [17] Burdan's considerable charms are on display in an undated photo of her, draped coquettishly in furs, which hangs in the Spragpole Museum in Murray, Idaho.

A few years before Molly Burdan arrived in Idaho, another young woman, by the name of Veronica Baldwin, ventured west to embark on what she too hoped would be an exciting new chapter in her life. An émigré from Britain, she had no idea that the unforgiving chauvinism of the era would relegate her, just like Molly Burdan before her, to cabin number one. Veronica's wealthy older cousin, Elias J. Baldwin, had invited her to come and work as a schoolteacher on the Santa Anita ranch he owned in the foothills outside Los Angeles. By 1880, "Lucky" Baldwin, who had made his fortune buying and selling gold-mining interests in the West, owned more than 40,000 acres in Los Angeles County, including the Santa Anita ranch, where he bred racehorses.

Veronica Baldwin, a willowy, dark-haired woman with striking hazel eyes, burst into the news on January 4, 1883, when she shot Elias Baldwin through the left arm as he left the private dining room of the Baldwin Hotel (which he owned) in San Francisco. According to the *San Francisco Call* of January 5, 1883, Veronica Baldwin, then twenty-three, said, "He ruined me in body and mind. That is why I shot him." She told reporters that Baldwin had sexually assaulted her and then dismissed her from her job for improper conduct. According to news accounts, she said, "I did not try to kill him. I hit him just where I wanted to, for I am a good shot and never miss anything I aim at."[18]

In the end, Lucky Baldwin declined to testify against his cousin, and she was acquitted. She immediately left for what was then the Washington Territory, according to news reports of the time. Three years later, she reappeared in California, threatening to sue her cousin for the support of a child whom she insisted he had fathered. According to *Lucky Baldwin,* a 1933 book about the multimillionaire, "that threat was also hushed quickly and again the girl vanished, only to reappear in the news a third time when she was found to be violently insane and committed to the state asylum at Napa by Judge Lucien Shaw." Horace Bell, a San Francisco lawyer turned investigative reporter, raged about the case in the *Porcupine,* a muckraking sheet he had founded. "Our hellish statutes protected [Baldwin] and enabled him to send his victim to an insane asylum," Bell wrote.[19]

As Carl Glasscock, the author of *Lucky Baldwin,* notes, Elias Baldwin, who married four times during his long life, almost always to women much younger than himself, was sued by a number of other young women for staining their virtue and breaking promises to marry them. "Lucky Baldwin's reputation as a Lothario was growing even faster than his reputation as a turf-man, a multi-millionaire and a great landed proprietor and promoter," Glasscock writes.[20]

Around the time that Veronica Baldwin was involuntarily dispatched to the state asylum in Napa, Molly b'Dam was pursuing a happier existence in Murray, Idaho. According to newspaper reports, Molly was good to the girls in her brothel and the locals were good to her. She was always feeding hungry families, and those who were down on their luck knew that Molly b'Dam would provide them with warm clothing and shelter. Although she lived in luxury, Molly never hesitated to ride on her horse over treacherous mountain trails to nurse a sick prospector.[21]

## Women: A Rare Commodity

In the mining economies of the West during the latter part of the nineteenth century, women were a rare and precious commodity. In 1860, only 5 percent of the residents of Virginia City, Nevada, were female, according to Barbara Brents, a professor of sociology at the University of Nevada, Las Vegas, and coauthor of *The State of Sex: Tourism, Sex and Sin in the New American Heartland.*[22] Prostitution, gambling, and drinking were mainstays of the local economy, and by 1870, which marked the height of Virginia City's prosperity, prostitution was the most commonly listed occupation for women. Prostitutes worked out of dance halls, saloons, or one-room shacks known as cribs. Many prostitutes, particularly those who were no longer young or pretty enough to work in the high-class brothels or saloons and had fallen to the bottom of the food chain—working out of cribs—lived in squalid quarters. An 1886 newspaper account describes the crib of a Denver, Colorado, prostitute who had killed herself:

> The walls and ceiling were absolutely black with smoke and dirt, excepting where old, stained newspapers had been pasted on them . . . to exclude rain and melting snow. Around the walls were disposed innumerable unwashed and battered tin cooking utensils, shelves, for the most part laden with dust, old clothing, which emitted a powerful effluvium, hung from nails here and there, or tumble down chairs, a table of very rheumatic tendency, on which broken cups, plates and remains of food were scattered all over its surface. An empty whiskey bottle and pewter spoon or two. In one corner and taking up half the space of the den was the bedstead strongly suggestive of a bountiful crop of vermin, and on that flimsy bed lay the corpse of the suicide, clad in dirty ratted apparel, and with as horrid a look on her begrimed, pallid features as the surroundings presented. No one of her neighbors in wretchedness had had the sense to open either of the two little windows in the room to admit pure air, hence the atmosphere was sickeningly impure and almost asphyxiating. "My God," exclaimed Coroner McHatton, used as he is to similar scenes and smells in his official capacity. "Isn't this awful?[23]

While some prostitutes led very difficult lives and suffered greatly, others turned the economics of commercial sex to their advantage. In the smaller mining towns, some single working-class women ran saloons as independent prostitute-proprietors. In Butte, Montana, some prostitutes were the widows of miners, and they worked out of cribs during the day while their children were in school.[24] According to historians, there was a certain respect for the place of prostitutes in mining economies. They were not the same as "good proper wives," but they held a certain status.[25]

Julia "Jule" Bulette, for example, was one of the first unattached white women to arrive in Virginia City, Nevada, after the Comstock Lode silver strike in 1859. Bulette, described in various accounts as beautiful, slim, and full of good humor,[26] had left an abusive husband behind in New Orleans, and she became a favorite of the Comstock miners. She owned her own cottage in Virginia City, and like Molly b'Dam, she became known for feeding the poor and nursing sick and injured men back to health. Because of Bulette's donations to the Virginia City fire department, local firefighters made her an honorary member of the Virginia Engine Number 1, and on July 4, 1861, Bulette rode the fire truck as Queen of the Independence Day Parade.[27] Yet six years later, Bulette, then thirty-five, was murdered, and all her valuables were stolen. A French drifter was arrested and hanged for the crime, although he maintained his innocence to the end.[28]

Molly b'Dam also died young but not by violent means. In 1886, smallpox swept into Murray. Residents of the small mining town barricaded themselves behind closed doors in a futile attempt to keep the scourge at bay, and bodies began piling up everywhere. Molly Burdan took charge, calling a town meeting and berating the town's residents for their cowardice. With the help of her girls and a few other volunteers, she cleared out the hotels and turned them into makeshift hospitals for the sick, and Burdan and her girls became nurses. "It has been said that Molly worked tirelessly. She was everywhere, nursing patients until she could no longer stand. She barely ate and didn't take time to even change her clothes," Seagraves writes. "The town survived—but Molly was never to be the same."[29]

In October 1887, she developed a constant fever and hacking cough, and on January 17, 1888, Molly Burdan died of what was then called consumption and is now known as tuberculosis. On the day of her funeral, more than a thousand people came from the surrounding area to bid farewell to a prostitute whom they admired and loved. Today, in the few remaining saloons of Murray, Idaho, a song written in her honor, *The Legend of Molly b'Dam,* is still sung.[30]

A few years after Molly died, Veronica Baldwin was discharged from the Napa state asylum. In the 1890s, she turned up in Denver, Colorado, with the means to open an upscale brothel on Market Street. "It was said that Lucky Baldwin provided her with the money she needed," writes

Seagraves in *Soiled Doves*. "It was also said that the lady displayed no evidence of insanity."[31]

The years, however, had left their mark on Veronica Baldwin: "Although Veronica was still young, lines were etched upon her comely face, her hair was prematurely gray, and she walked with a slow measured step. She was no longer the same person that California newspapers once described as 'the most beautiful girl on the Pacific Coast.'"[32]

In her upscale Market Street brothel, Veronica Baldwin, dressed in royal purple with a touch of white lace, served her customers imported delicacies (including fresh oysters in season) and fine French wine in crystal glasses. Her clients were wealthy businessmen, mining owners, real estate investors, and politicians, and they came by invitation only.

According to several accounts, Veronica hired only beautiful, educated women who were experienced in matters of sex. One evening in 1898, a pretty young woman turned up on her doorstep in the company of a "notorious procuress," the *Rocky Mountain News* reported. When Veronica Baldwin found out that the girl was a virgin and had no idea what she was getting into, she convinced her to go home to her family and then notified local police, who placed the girl in a "respectable dwelling" for the night, according to the *Rocky Mountain News*. The paper concluded its April 28 story with the news that "[the girl]was sent away to her relatives, the police department bearing the cost of transportation."[33]

What this and other news reports of the time indicate is that Veronica Baldwin, like many successful madams and prostitutes of the nineteenth century, had a close and mutually beneficial relationship with local law enforcement. They paid the police and local politicians handsome bribes to look the other way, and in return, the police protected their establishments from drunken gangs and abolitionists who wanted to eliminate prostitution once and for all.

In the 1870s, William Sanger and other medical professionals (backed up by the American Medical Society), together with law enforcement, had pushed to legalize and regulate prostitution in the United States for public health reasons. As Sanger argued, regulating prostitution would enable the authorities to test and treat prostitutes for venereal

disease and clamp down on child prostitution. But several bills in the
New York legislature failed because of opposition by suffragettes such
as Susan B. Anthony. Anthony and others who were campaigning for
equal rights believed, as some feminists do now, that prostitution victimized all women and that it was a "social evil" that had to be eradicated.
Suffragettes joined forces with Christian social purity reformers, and
in the face of their concerted opposition, only a few cities in the United
States, including New Orleans, San Francisco, and St. Louis, passed
ordinances to legalize and regulate prostitution, limiting it to specific
red-light districts.

By the 1880s, these abolitionist groups began to gain the upper hand.
Religious groups had long promulgated a view of marriage to a "good"
woman as a respected social arrangement (because it was the primary
means through which erotic expression was linked to reproduction).
Sex outside marriage threatened that social order, and sex for money
was shunned because it completely divorced sexual intercourse from the
goal of reproduction.[34] Protestant groups were particularly vocal in their
condemnation of prostitution because their religious tenets urged sexual
satisfaction within the marriage and viewed infidelity more harshly than
did Catholicism. And in fact, it was an alliance of evangelical Protestants
and newly empowered suffragettes who led the campaign to outlaw alcohol and prostitution in the late nineteenth and early twentieth centuries.

These reformist groups wielded a potent weapon: the panic over "white
slavery" that was sweeping the nation, fueled by salacious and largely
erroneous newspaper accounts of the hordes of young white women,
both foreign- and native-born, who were being forced into sexual slavery.
Even the great literature of the day, such as Stephen Crane's 1893 book,
*Maggie: A Girl of the Streets*, portrayed young white women as innocent
victims seduced or forced into prostitution by evil pimps and madams.[35]

The image of the white slave, however, was largely myth. Several
studies at the time showed that most young women selling sex were
doing so to earn better wages than they could in domestic service or
factory work. For example, the sociologist Kathleen Davis's 1912 study
of 671 prostitutes showed that many of them also worked at low-paying

jobs (as store clerks, servants, or factory workers). Many of the women who had chosen to sell sex came from broken or low-income homes and needed the money.[36]

Even so, the hype over white slavery had its intended effect, as far as the reformists were concerned. It led to a series of state and federal laws that made it increasingly difficult for brothels and other forms of prostitution to operate as openly as they had before. In Colorado, gangs encouraged by antiprostitution and prohibition crusaders burned down a number of red-light districts in mining towns such as Colorado City and Cripple Creek in the early years of the twentieth century.[37] In New York, laws pushed through by an alliance of purity reformers, settlement-house workers, and wealthy industrialists imposed fines on owners of apartments and buildings who rented to brothels and prostitutes.[38] In 1910, the federal government passed the White Slave Traffic Act, better known as the Mann Act (named after Congressman James Robert Mann), which prohibited the transport of women from state to state for "immoral purposes."

## A Military Clampdown

As World War I approached, the clampdown intensified. Federal authorities, fearful that American soldiers would be laid low by disease-carrying prostitutes, began pressuring state officials to close down red-light districts throughout the country. By 1915, most red-light districts in the United States, including the famous Barbary Coast in San Francisco, the Levee district in Chicago, and Storyville in New Orleans, had been shuttered. Denver's red-light district was also closed, and Veronica Baldwin's brothel with it. Baldwin moved into one of the city's most fashionable neighborhoods and continued to live a "quiet dignified life," according to news reports of the time.[39]

Prostitution, of course, didn't disappear. It simply moved underground. After decades of visibility in theaters and concert halls and on the streets, prostitution became a clandestine activity. "Call girls" operated out of private apartments, and as prostitutes found themselves more vulnerable to abuse from police and clients, pimps became a permanent fixture, providing women with protection, emotional support, and legal assistance.[40]

Once Prohibition became the law of the land, in 1920, prostitutes also began to operate out of the illegal speakeasies that were popping up in basements and private clubs all over the United States. Prohibition and the speakeasies had the paradoxical effect of breaking down the taboos against men and women drinking and dancing together in public. As Gilfoyle notes, the "sporting male culture" was replaced by more heterosexual forms of entertainment.

At the same time, attitudes toward enjoyment of sex in and outside marriage began to change—sex was increasingly seen as a basic expression of love within marriage—and premarital sex became more common. The increasing availability of birth control contributed to this profound shift in American attitudes. As a result, visits to prostitutes declined. In his seminal 1948 report, *Sexual Behavior in the Human Male*, Albert Kinsey reports that the frequency of American men's sexual intercourse with prostitutes declined by as much as one-half to two-thirds between 1926 and 1948.[41]

The Prohibition-era speakeasies, of course, were largely run by organized-crime groups, which imported bootlegged alcohol and paid cops to look the other way. Organized-crime syndicates also controlled prostitution after World War I. As Nickie Roberts, author of *Whores in History*, puts it, "After the First World War, [organized-crime] syndicates dominated the sex market in US cities, securing their positions in alliances with local elites—the police and politicians who had earlier made fortunes out of the segregated red-light districts. . . . In all of this there was only one major victim: the whore."[42]

This reality is perhaps most vividly illustrated by the story of Polly Adler, a Jewish émigré from Russia who was sent to the United States at the age of thirteen by her tailor-father in 1913. He intended to follow with the rest of the family, but World War I intervened. Once war broke out, her father could no longer get money to America to pay for her upkeep (she had been living with friends of friends in Holyoke, Massachusetts), so she was pulled out of school and put to work in a paper factory at the age of fourteen. After two years of grueling labor, she fled to New York, where she found a job in a corset factory and roomed with a cousin in Brooklyn. By the time the United States entered World War I, in 1917, the corset factory had closed, and Polly Adler was working in a factory that made shirts for soldiers. At the age of seventeen, she was raped by the factory's foreman, who beat and impregnated her. In her memoir, *A House Is Not a Home,* Adler described how she obtained a back-alley abortion and how the experience changed her. "I had lost heart, I no longer had hope," she wrote.[43] The foreman continued to harass her, so Adler was forced to find a job at another factory, where she worked until January 1920. In her memoir, she recalled those months as a time of "unrelieved drabness, of hurry and worry and clawing uncertainty. . . . It was a bitter, hope-quenching, miserable sort of existence for a girl of 19."[44]

By then, like many young working girls of the time, Adler had discovered the dance halls, where she would go every Sunday afternoon and dance her worries away. Through a connection, she was introduced to a beautiful young actress from a wealthy family whom she identifies in her memoir as Joan. Joan offered Adler a place to stay in her family's nine-room apartment on Riverside Drive, and under Joan's wing, Adler began making friends with "celebrities, directors, writers and composers, all smoking opium." But having seen what drugs were doing to Joan, who had become addicted to cocaine and heroin and was sabotaging her acting career, Adler had no inclination to join in. In 1920, Tony, a bootlegger friend of hers who was having an affair with a married woman, asked Adler to take an apartment (he'd pay the rent) so he could meet his mistress on the sly. Still unemployed, Adler agreed. In time, Tony asked her to find him "a new girl," and that was the beginning of Polly Adler's career as one of New York's best-known madams.

In the early years of Adler's business, much of her clientele consisted of gangsters and hoodlums, "most of whom died with their boots on."[45] But in the mid-1920s, she moved her operation to a spacious apartment on Seventh Avenue and began entertaining young men from Harvard, Yale, and other Ivy League schools. In time, she says she was able to restrict her clients to "the upper brackets" of New York's social, financial, literary, and theatrical worlds. In 1927, when her house was raided by police, the customers bailed her and her girls out almost as soon as they were booked, and the case was quickly dismissed. Many of the prostitutes who worked for Adler were struggling actresses, singers or dancers, showgirls between jobs. "Not one of them had any intention of staying in the business," she writes. One of her "smartest" girls got married; another was a student of journalism at Columbia University who left the business when she graduated and became a well-known novelist. One can't help wondering who that well-known novelist was. Adler never tells; in her memoir she writes, "I have kept [her] secret, as I have kept many secrets."[46]

Adler does acknowledge that prostitution was a hard life, in large part because it was illegal, and she could understand why so many sex workers became addicted to alcohol and drugs. In her memoir, she writes, "Whoring is a slow form of self-destruction. . . . By becoming a prostitute, a girl cuts herself off not merely from her family but also from such a great part of life. She is isolated not just by social custom but by working conditions and she has to some extent deprived herself of her rights as a citizen for she has forfeited the protection of the law. It is not syphilis which is the occupational disease of the prostitute, but loneliness."[47]

Adler was speaking from firsthand experience. According to her memoir, she received several marriage offers over the years. The most serious proposal came from the leader of a popular New York swing band in the '20s, with whom she had a long-running affair. Adler says she loved him but had qualms about marrying a guy who liked to hit the bottle too much. She also knew his band's reputation would suffer if he married a madam. In the end, she turned him down and remained single the rest of her life.

In 1929, like many other Americans, Adler lost all her savings in the stock market crash. But paradoxically, her business was better than ever. "Men wanted to go out and forget their troubles," she writes. "The atmosphere, at times, was more like an insane asylum than a bordello."[48]

The good times, however, were short-lived. In 1930, then Governor Franklin Roosevelt asked the New York courts to investigate corruption by judges, court magistrates, and local police and named Judge Samuel Seabury to head the inquiry. The Seabury Commission soon uncovered massive bribing of New York's vice squads, court officers, and judges to ignore the city's flourishing gambling, bootlegging, and prostitution activities. At one point, Adler was warned that she was about to be served with a subpoena because she had "paid thousands of dollars in bribes to keep my house running smoothly and my girls and myself out of jail."[49] She fled town, ending up in Miami for an extended vacation.

Adler eventually returned to New York, got back into the business, and almost immediately came under the thumb of Dutch Schultz, a notorious Jewish gangster of the time. Against her will, she says, Schultz made her establishment his headquarters. She describes Schultz (whose real name was Arthur Flegenheimer) as "businesslike, cold and incisive, colorless and deadly," and says she never lost her fear of him.[50] In 1935, she tried to leave the "whorehouse business" and invest in a legitimate concern, such as a factory or restaurant, but her notoriety got in the way. "I exhausted all my contacts, but every door was closed to me, sometimes with a tactful lie, sometimes with the blunt announcement that people couldn't afford to be associated with me," she writes.[51]

In the 1930s, the Great Depression swelled the numbers of women who turned to prostitution, but the dangers of being harassed, arrested, and prosecuted for prostitution grew in the years before World War II. Congress passed a law forbidding prostitution in designated areas where there were troops, and the military pressured local authorities to clamp down in an effort to once again combat venereal disease among soldiers.

Ironically, research published in the early 1940s showed that the vast majority of venereal disease cases among soldiers came from casual sex between soldiers and girls they had picked up, not from sex with prostitutes.[52] A 1944 study for the U.S. Army, which traced the individual contacts of infected soldiers, found that 32 percent of sexually transmitted infections among white soldiers came from "friends," 62 percent from "pickups," and only 6 percent from prostitutes.[53] Even so, the military's actions resulted in the arrest and detention of thousands of women for prostitution-related offenses.[54]

As prostitution became more dangerous, more women engaged in "treating"—a practice in which a man took a woman out or helped her financially (paid her rent, for instance) in return for sexual favors. Treating still involved the exchange of sex for money, but it was not as explicit, says Elizabeth Clement in *Love for Sale*.[55]

Polly Adler saw the writing on the wall. In 1943, her house was raided yet again. (She was arrested sixteen times in all but pled guilty only once and spent thirty days in jail.) The latest raid occurred when Adler was sick in bed with pleurisy, and she ended up in Bellevue Hospital. This case, like most of the others brought against her, was dismissed, but her heart was no longer in it. "Everything was an effort, the ringing of the business phone was like a dentist's drill on an exposed nerve, and though I would try to be gay and amusing, I usually ended the evening locked in my room crying into my pillow," she writes.[56]

In 1944, Adler got out of the business for good and moved to Los Angeles, where she enrolled in the Los Angeles Valley College to pursue a lifelong dream: an education. In 1945, she began writing her autobiography, *A House Is Not a Home*. It was published in 1953 and became an unexpected best seller, selling more than two million copies in two years.[57]

Even then, controversy dogged Adler; there were reports that immigration officials were looking into her prostitution-related activities in the years before her naturalization as an American citizen in 1929. Adler handled the news with her usual aplomb. "I know nothing about it except what newspapermen have told me," she said to one reporter. He looked around her sunlit cottage in Burbank, which was filled with ceramic dancing girls and lovebirds, and asked: "What about this place, Miss Adler? Is this house a home?" Polly Adler replied, "It certainly is."

# The ✒Modern ✒Sex ✒Workers'
# Rights ✒Movement

After living quietly for almost two decades in her modest Burbank cottage with carefully trimmed hedges, Polly Adler died of breast cancer at the age of sixty-two. Her death merited a flurry of obituaries, one of which described her as a "notorious madam of the 20s" who ran a "swank establishment" in New York City.[1] Her clientele included police officers, well-known politicians, and industrial magnates, the obit noted, adding: "Her choice of clientele probably was responsible for the fact that, although arrested numerous times, she only spent 30 days in jail."

In her best-selling memoir *A House Is Not a Home*, Adler herself railed against the corruption of New York's finest, detailing how she was forced to make regular payoffs to cops to keep her and her girls from getting arrested. When police did raid her brothel, she would "cup a C-note in her palm" and go around shaking hands with each cop. "Sometimes law enforcement gave me more trouble than my rowdiest clients," she wrote.[2] Adler was particularly upset when she was forced to give fifteen cops a free and very costly (for her) party at her brothel so they wouldn't arrest her, at least not on that particular occasion. During the party, one drunken cop named Johnny explained that he fully intended to bust Adler at some point so he could get himself a promotion. "'The thing is you're newspaper copy, sister . . .'" he told her. "'And my boss goes for headlines, and he goes to bat for the boys that grab 'em off for him.'"[3] Johnny and the other cops proceeded to consume Adler's liquor supply and trash her apartment, "trampling cigarette ends and cigar butts into the carpet, burning, marring and staining what they did not smash." She concludes:

> Almost everybody, I guess, would find it easy to understand why I loathed pimps and drug peddlers, but the average law-abiding citizen would hardly go along with me in my detestation of cops unless he too, at some point or another, had locked horns with a crooked bull. I didn't resent the honest cop, and I was able to stay in business because of the dishonest variety. But the members of gendarmerie who really started my adrenalin flowing like wine were the boys who believed in playing it both ways, and who wouldn't have turned a hair if their own mother happened to be the one caught in the middle.[4]

Had she lived longer, Adler might have found a kindred spirit in Margo St. James, a cocktail waitress who was arrested for prostitution in San Francisco only six months after New York's most notorious madam died in June 1962. It was the dawning of the Age of Aquarius, and St. James, a fun-loving freethinker who grew marijuana plants in her back-yard, had become an indispensable part of the love-in. Her parties attracted local musicians, artists, poets, and writers. The comedian Lenny Bruce and author Ken Kesey (*One Flew over the Cuckoo's Nest*) were regulars at St. James's place, as were some of the undercover narcotics agents who drank at Pierre's bar, where she was a cocktail waitress. As the novelist Herb Gold told *San Francisco* magazine for a cover story about Margo St. James, "She was jolly. It was fun to visit her. She was like an organizer on the scene, the sexual side to the beat revolution."[5]

While St. James was a huge flirt, she prided herself on the fact that she was a party girl, not a prostitute. So when a stranger called and wanted to hang out, saying a friend had given him her name, St. James invited him over, thinking he was some horny football player from out of town who had gotten her name from one of the San Francisco 49ers. "He was not my type, rather scrawny and homely, but being a friendly country girl, I tried to put him at ease," she recalls in an afterword she wrote for the 1980 book *Prostitutes, Our Life*. After hanging out for a while, the man offered St. James money for sex. She refused and told him to leave. At that point, "He flashed his badge, said he was a cop, and told me I was under arrest for *soliciting him!*" she writes. "Several other cops broke in the back door and hauled me off to jail, charging me with running a 'disorderly house.'"[6]

At her trial, St. James, then twenty-five, insisted that she did not sell sex. While it was true that some of her roommates were prostitutes and that she herself enjoyed partying with guests, she told the judge she had never turned a trick in her life. But the judge convicted her of prostitution anyway, saying, "Anyone who uses that language is obviously a professional."[7]

St. James was kept in jail until she agreed to be tested for venereal disease and get a penicillin shot. In those days, police routinely kept women accused of prostitution in jail until they had agreed to a penicillin shot even if they didn't have venereal disease. (This practice, known as quarantining, has since been outlawed in most states as a violation of women's rights; men arrested as johns were never quarantined or tested.) St. James was bailed out the next day, but as a convicted prostitute, she could no longer work in any club in town. The police saw to that. "They would come into the club and say, 'You can't hire her here; she's a whore,'" St. James recalls. "And then I'd go to work at another club and they'd do the same thing."

This was not the first time that Margo St. James had found herself in a tough spot. She had grown up on a farm outside Bellingham, Washington, the oldest of three children. When she was eight, her parents divorced. She was sent to live with her father and his much younger new wife, who was only ten years older than St. James. St. James worked on the family farm, milking cows and learning how to drive a tractor by the age of ten. But she hated living with her father; as she noted in a later interview, "My father believed that if you spared the rod, you spoiled the child, so I got a lot of whippings. My teachers even spoke to my father about it because they could see the marks on my legs in gym class."[8] At age fourteen, she went to live with her mother in Bellingham, but as she acknowledges, "My mom was single and dating. I was running around and not too supervised."[9] As a freshman at Bellingham High, she lost her virginity and spent a lot of time having sex with high school boys behind the football bleachers. When St. James was seventeen, she got pregnant, and she and her boyfriend, the high school baseball star, drove all night to Coeur d'Alene, Idaho, where marriage licenses were issued with a minimum of questions asked. But the marriage didn't take. "I didn't want to get married, I didn't want kids, but my mother's doctor refused to give me an abortion since I wasn't eighteen," St. James says. "My husband never wanted to leave home. We argued a lot."

St. James left her husband and three-year-old son in 1958 to move to Seattle, where she worked at the Seattle Colony Club as a hatcheck girl, janitor, bartender, and de facto manager. But the club was on its last legs, and what she really wanted to do was go to art school in San Francisco. "I got a ticket and my trunk and took the train," she recalls. "And I met a nice cab driver who took me to this cheap hotel in Oakland where musicians and artists lived. I love music and there was a jazz club right across the street."

In San Francisco, with no money or connections, St. James started working as a B-girl in the after-hours clubs. She was an attractive brunette with a slim, athletic build and a megawatt smile. As she recalls, "I only drank phony drinks with men for money and led them on but delivered no sex. I was very proud of the fact that I was not a hooker. . . . By day and early evenings (the clubs didn't open until the bars closed at 2 a.m.), I was a latter-day beatnik and good-time girl in the Italian neighborhood of North Beach."[10]

In 1961, St James landed a bona fide job as a cocktail waitress at Pierre's on Broadway and made enough money on tips to move out of her $30-a-month hotel room into a larger apartment on Grant Avenue and Green Street, which soon became known as the St. James Infirmary (a prescient nod to the medicinal qualities of pot). "I was having a good time," St. James says. "My ass was my own, as Flo Kennedy [the late African American lawyer, civil rights advocate, and feminist] always used to say."

But after her arrest for prostitution, she couldn't find a job at any of San Francisco's night spots. So to pay off her bail, she went to work (for free) for the bondsman who had bailed her out. She also began her own process-serving business with the lawyers she met while working for the bondsman. But she remained furious at the judge who had convicted her. (She later helped defeat the judge when he ran for re-election.) In the course of her work, she met "some of the best legal minds in the city," including the dean of the Golden Gate University Law School, who told her that if she passed a college equivalency test, she would be accepted into his law school. She passed the test and started taking law courses at night in 1963. A few months later, she filed an appeal of her conviction. After her first year, though, she flunked what she calls the "baby bar," the test that all first-year students at the night school had to take. Later that summer, she won the appeal, and her conviction for prostitution was overturned. Shortly afterward, she quit law school.

In her afterword for *Prostitutes, Our Life,* St. James says she quit law school because she "couldn't stand the hypocrisy it supported."[11] In a more recent interview, she says she didn't really want to practice law; she still had dreams of going to art school. To support herself, she began saying yes to the lawyers and judges who were constantly soliciting her for sex. "I wasn't making a ton of money, just enough to pay the bills," she says. "I wanted the fun more than anything."

Some of her clients at this time were narcotics agents and men from the Alcohol and Beverage Commission whom she had met at Pierre's. Others were businessmen. "That's when they still had two-hour lunches," she says with a husky laugh. For a few months one year, a local cosmetics company paid the rent on her roomy new apartment on Alpine Terrace. "These businesses wanted a whorehouse they could go to and take their customers to," she recalls. "I always had a couple of roommates who weren't averse to working."

In 1967, when St. James was thirty, she fell in love with Roger Somers, an architect and musician, and moved out to the woods of Marin County with him. They lived in a community known as Druid Heights where neighbors shared in the gardening and cooking. Alan Watts, the famous British-born author who wrote many books about the value of integrating Eastern philosophy into Western life, was the philosopher in residence there. To augment her income, St. James began cleaning houses, and Watts soon became one of her most reliable clients.

By the late 1960s, the sexual revolution was in full flower across the United States, and the women's movement was gathering steam. Millions of young women across the country were discovering their sexual independence, and commentators of the time predicted that the new era of sexual freedom would finally put the kibosh on prostitution. After all, if men could freely have sex with women outside marriage, what was the point of paying for sex? But if anything, the freeing of sexual mores actually gave rise to a consumer ethic that put sexuality on display in a way that had never been permitted before. Sex became a product, and as Roberts notes in *Whores in History*, the advertising media began selling sex as "the archetypal form of entertainment with which the glamor of consumer goods was (and is) associated."[12] This new permissiveness extended toward commercial sex, and by the 1970s, the United States was seeing a proliferation of strip clubs, massage parlors, and pornography. Explicitly pornographic magazines such as *Screw* and *Hustler* emerged to give *Playboy* and *Penthouse* competition for the American male's eyeballs.

Although the sexual revolution did cut into the trade with some young men, who discovered they no longer had to pay for sex, many middle-class married men continued to patronize prostitutes, researchers found.[13] It seemed safer to pay for an encounter with a discreet and accommodating hooker than embark on an unpredictable affair that might threaten one's marriage and standing in the community. But while male clients, or johns, as they were known, were rarely arrested, the prostitutes who serviced them were routinely harassed by police. Streetwalkers took the brunt of it. Police used prostitution busts to enhance their arrest statistics and earn money for the state in fines, and the ease of arresting streetwalkers meant that cops spent a disproportionate time patrolling tenderloin districts. Some critics at the time even publicly questioned whether such patrols left other neighborhoods open to more violent crimes.[14]

In San Francisco, African American streetwalkers strolling outside the downtown hotels were constantly being picked up by police—one streetwalker might get arrested as many as sixty times a year, St. James says. "They'd book them, and the bail bondsmen would make a lot of money bailing them out." At the same time, police looked the other way when white call girls worked inside the hotels. Indeed, St. James says, some officers had nighttime jobs at the hotels, and like their compatriots in cities throughout the United States, they received payoffs or free sex from the prostitutes. "They pretty much got to choose who was working at which hotels," she says.

Living just outside the city, cleaning the houses of wealthy single men and couples where many wives felt trapped at home, Margo St. James had a front-row seat to the prevailing double standard, and she loathed it. Watts, who had become a close friend and spiritual adviser, encouraged her to view the political and sexual hypocrisy she saw around her in activist terms. At a party around this time, St. James says, she also had a conversation with Richard Hongisto, the newly elected San Francisco County sheriff, about what the National Organization for Women (NOW) was doing for the rights of hookers. Hongisto replied, "'Nothing, Margo. Someone from the victim class has to speak out.'"[15]

That got her thinking. Initially, she formed a group she called Whores, Housewives and Others. "I thought the housewives need a little politicizing, so I decided to get the hookers, housewives, and other intellectuals together and think about what they have in common," St. James recalls. "We had our first meeting on Alan [Watts's] houseboat in Sausalito. One of the housewives even traded places for one night with one of the hookers, who was a high-priced call girl and had some regular customers who were older businessmen." Both women enjoyed themselves, as did the housewife's husband, who was in on the switch, St. James says.

One day, while she was cleaning Watts's house, St. James came across the galleys of Tom Robbins's first book, *Another Roadside Attraction*. She loved the book and wrote Robbins a fan letter. So when Robbins came to Berkeley in 1971, the same year his book was published, he visited St. James, and several women to whom she had given Robbins's book came over and danced for him. Robbins, who was high on mushrooms, thought he was in the middle of the Arabian nights, St. James says. "The next morning, I'm fixing him the chanterelles and eggs for breakfast and he looks at me and says, 'I know who you are,'" St. James recalls. "And I said, 'Who?' 'cause I'm looking for identity, you know. He says, 'You're the coyote trickster.'"[16]

That conversation gave St. James a name for her burgeoning political movement, and in 1972, a songwriter friend of hers came up with the words that spelled out the acronym: Call Off Your Old Tired Ethics (COYOTE). With that attention-grabbing moniker, the modern sex workers' rights movement was born.

The same year, a precocious teenage runaway by the name of Julie Hahn began working as an exotic dancer in Larry Flynt's Hustler Club on Walnut Street in Cincinnati, Ohio. Julie may have been only fifteen, but she had the body of a woman, full breasts, slim waist, and long blonde hair. With her flashing green eyes and youthful energy, Julie was an immediate hit with the club's patrons. For the first time in her life, she had her own money and apartment upstairs from the club, where Flynt (who would launch *Hustler* magazine in 1974) lived with his wife, also an erotic dancer at the club.

It was a heady time for Julie. She had run away from a difficult home life, where her stepfather refused to acknowledge her and her mother was too busy raising five younger children to pay much attention to her oldest daughter, who had been born out of wedlock and never knew her biological father. It was hardly a surprise that thirteen-year-old Julie gave herself to the first young man who said he loved her, and when nineteen-year-old Jack impregnated her, they got married and moved in with her family. But Jack soon cleared out. "He couldn't take all the craziness," Julie recalled years later. "He left when we were married about four months. It was a very lonely, depressing time."

When she was fourteen, Julie gave birth to a little girl with a serious heart defect. "When we came home to my mom's house, [the baby] was blue and struggling to breathe," Julie recalls. Little more than a child herself, Julie felt overwhelmed by guilt and remorse and a feeling that she had to get out of there. So she ran away and lived on the streets, going home with other people she met, sleeping on couches or with guys who were kind to her. After a few rough months, she ended up at the Talbert House, then a place for troubled teens run by the University of Cincinnati. She lived there for nine or ten months, until a girl she had met brought her down to the Hustler Club.

"I loved dancing—it was fun and I was so starved for attention," Julie recalls. "Working in the Hustler Club was like being a movie star."

At first, Julie didn't like being touched by the customers or having to hustle them to buy expensive drinks. But after a time, she learned to distance herself from all that and became friends with the men who ran the club. "The guys would say, 'Jill (that was the name I went by), Are you of age yet?'" Julie recalls. "And I'd say, 'No, not yet.' I was there for years before I came of age, and nobody cared. Larry Flynt knew; everyone knew. A lot of us were underage."

When she was sixteen, Julie says she had her first paid sexual encounter, with Larry Flynt's lawyer. She describes her foray into prostitution matter-of-factly one hot summer evening in July 2011, while we are having dinner at an unpretentious family-style bistro in Tribeca, the lower Manhattan neighborhood a few blocks from Ground Zero. Julie is dressed casually in a low-cut black tee and black jeans, her silky blond hair cut at shoulder length. When she rushes into Edwards Restaurant, fifteen minutes late, she apologizes profusely. "I was dealing with a situation with my grandson," she says as we settle around the corner table I have staked out in the back of the bistro. Julie explains that her five-year-old grandson was recently removed from their home because his father, Julie's younger son, Jerry, was letting the boy touch his girlfriend's breasts. "I noticed a change in his behavior; he was screaming at night and going around, grabbing breasts," Julie says. "My son has been around [working] girls a lot. But this isn't right. My grandson is only five."

The boy's mother, a sex worker, disappeared shortly after he was born, Julie says, and she had become his maternal caregiver; Jerry and her grandson lived with her. But now that the child had been placed in foster care and New York's child services department was considering pressing abuse charges against his father, Julie had temporarily moved out to Long Island to be closer to where her grandson was living. Several years ago, she had brought Jerry, now twenty-six, into the business with her, hoping to eventually pass it on to him when she retired. But furious at her son for endangering her grandson's welfare, she said she was trying to separate the business into two brothels, one run by her and the other by Jerry.

"We have two places now, with regular customers," she says. "Everything is very . . . ." She pauses and intertwines her long slender hands to show how enmeshed the business has become. And then she sighs. "I made a lot of mistakes when I was young. I wasn't a great mother. I'm trying to do better with my grandson."

Midway through dinner, Julie, who is picking at a Tribeca Cobb salad, resumes the story of how she crossed the line from topless dancing to selling sex. "I did something with a lawyer for Larry Flynt and he paid me. The lawyer was in his sixties and I was sixteen," she recalls. "I didn't like that at all. Yuck. I was repulsed by it. I didn't have my armor on."

Julie did, however, like the economic independence that selling sex provided. So a year or two later—she is coy about her exact age at the time—she began turning tricks on a regular basis. "I liked the money," she says. "I always wanted to please people. I liked to give presents to my family. It made me happy." By then, she had reconciled with her family and regularly visited her daughter, who was being raised by her mother.

By the time Julie was nineteen, she had begun working as a prostitute for a gambling friend of Flynt's by the name of Marshall Clay Riddle, who ran a prostitution ring. Julie would later testify that she entertained clients in an apartment she had on Lehman Road in Cincinnati, in the same building in which Riddle lived, according to news reports and court transcripts.[17] She was driven to nightclubs in Cincinnati and northern Kentucky, where she gave her phone number to potential clients, some of whom would then arrange to visit her at her apartment on Lehman Road. On one occasion, she said, she and another prostitute made $600 for a weekend in Huntington, West Virginia, with a coal mine owner and one of his workers.[18] At other times, she and another woman who worked for Riddle would knock on doors at area motels in Ohio and

Kentucky in search of tricks. In January 1977, Riddle transported Julie and several other women to Florida to service clients there.[19]

When she came back to Cincinnati a few weeks later, Julie, who was still dancing at several strip clubs and turning tricks on the side, says she was told to hand out cards at the clubs for a truck-stop brothel in Tennessee in an effort to recruit women who might be interested in working there. The brothel was known as a lockdown because the prostitutes had to work sixteen hours at a time and couldn't leave for weeks at a time, Julie says. Unbeknownst to Julie, local police had begun investigating the Tennessee lockdown and some other places of prostitution operated by Riddle and his cohorts. Because she was handing out the lockdown's cards, local police arrested Julie for promoting prostitution in late February. She was carted off to jail, and her bail was set at $5,000. "The guys who owned the lockdown put up my bail," she recalls.

A day or two after being bailed out, Julie overheard Riddle and another pimp discussing how they were going to have to either get rid of her or put her in a lockdown because the police were putting too much pressure on her. "I got afraid," she later testified. "I ran upstairs and got a couple of my things and left."[20]

With the help of a sympathetic police officer, her mother arranged to smuggle her out of town. "He gave me the birth certificate of a girl who had died in a car accident, and he knew another officer in San Bernardino, California, who met me at the airport," Julie recalls. "She was really nice, and she showed me where it was safe to work" as a dancer and sex worker.

Acutely homesick after a few months, Julie drove back to Cincinnati to see her family. But she had a car accident when she got home, and the police ran her fingerprints and realized she was wanted for skipping bail. After she was booked and released in the summer of 1977, she fled town again.

"I ran off to Florida and was dancing in this club in Orlando," she says. But she and the other girls had been ordered to dance nude, and they got arrested for indecent exposure. Police in Orlando discovered that Julie was wanted in Cincinnati and extradited her back to Hamilton County in the fall of 1977.

By this time, the FBI had joined local police in investigating Riddle and other pimps for running a multistate prostitution ring that transported women across state lines to work as prostitutes in Ohio, Tennessee, Kentucky, West Virginia, North Carolina, Pennsylvania, New Jersey, and Florida in violation of the federal Mann Act. Some of the workers may also have been underage, according to Julie and the U.S. attorney who prosecuted the case. Julie, who knew something about the prostitution ring and was sitting in the Hamilton County jail awaiting trial for skipping bail, feared for her life. "When I was in jail, a correctional officer who knew Riddle came into my cell in the middle of the night and told me to keep my mouth shut," she says. "All of a sudden, the FBI came in and boom, took me out of there. They knew my life was in danger."

Julie agreed to testify against Riddle and the other pimps she knew, and the FBI put her into the witness protection program. They gave her a new name, Ingrid Hudson, and moved her to Minneapolis. In the spring of 1978, federal authorities arrested Marshall Riddle along with twelve other men and women allegedly involved in the multistate ring, according to news reports at the time.[21]

By the time Julie was whisked into hiding, Margo St. James's movement to improve the lot of working girls was well on its way. With a $5,000 grant from the *Whole Earth Catalog*'s Point Foundation, COYOTE held its first convention in 1973 to raise awareness about the archaic state laws that criminalized prostitution and forced prostitutes into the hands of exploitative pimps and corrupt police officers. Organizations such as the American Civil Liberties Union (ACLU) signed on to help overturn California's codes against prostitution, as did some young women who were attending the University of California at Berkeley and paying for their tuition by working as call girls. "They worked in our office for free," St. James recalls.

Jennifer James, St. James's friend and an anthropology professor in Seattle, convinced NOW to make the decriminalization of prostitution part of the plank at its 1973 convention. The landmark resolution calling for decriminalization highlighted the double standard in society's views toward the sexual activities of men and women and the fact that police almost always arrested the prostitute but not her customer. The NOW resolution also noted that because of laws criminalizing prostitution, sex workers could not seek the protection of police and were thus forced to ally themselves with pimps for protection and legal support.

The same year, Margo St. James and COYOTE members protested in front of the San Francisco hotels where police were busting black street-walkers while permitting white sex workers to operate inside as long as they paid off the off-duty officers. In the fall of 1974, St. James and her friends hosted the first Hookers Ball on Fisherman's Wharf in San Francisco.

"The firefighters helped us hang decorations," she recalls. "They were happy as a clam that we were coming down [to the wharf]." The poet and children's book author Shel Silverstein wrote a song for the occasion entitled *Everyone Needs a Hooker Once in a While*, and Dr. Hook and the Medicine Show played at the event in the Longshoreman's Hall.[22]

The money from the Hookers Ball provided the group with enough funds to publish a newsletter, *COYOTE Howls*, and the ball became a San Francisco institution, a rowdy Halloween costume party that at-tracted local artists, musicians, celebrities, and, of course, hookers. In 1978, nearly 20,000 people attended the biggest Hookers Ball of all at the San Francisco Cow Palace, a raucous affair featuring a very drunk George Carlin and Margo St. James dressed up as a prim and proper Dianne Feinstein (then mayor of San Francisco) and riding in on an ele-phant. "The crowd went crazy, the fun began, much dancing, dangling, drinking, and a hazy cloud of smoke enveloped the arena," one of the organizers later wrote. "No one felt any pain."[23]

With the help of sympathetic lawyers and doctors, St. James and COYOTE were able to convince San Francisco officials to eliminate the practice of quarantining prostitutes in the city's jails. COYOTE also worked to curb police harassment of streetwalkers working downtown San Fran-cisco and other nearby towns. In 1975, a superior court judge in Alameda

County (which includes Berkeley, Oakland, Fremont, and other municipalities across the bay from San Francisco) ruled that Oakland police
were discriminating against women in their enforcement of prostitution
laws. According to the lawsuit filed by the ACLU, the Oakland police
had arrested and charged more than 800 women with prostitution the
previous year, while only 36 men were given citations for participating.[24]
In response to the judge's order, Oakland police temporarily stepped up
their arrests of male johns, using undercover female cops as decoys, but
St. James says the stepped-up enforcement with respect to male clients
didn't last long. Police did, however, reduce their arrests of streetwalkers
throughout the greater San Francisco area. "Because of our lobbying,
they left the streetwalkers alone. And women moved off the streets as
much as they could," St. James recalls.

The publicity from this legal victory and the Hookers Balls made
COYOTE a national name and enabled it to establish the National Task
Force on Prostitution.[25] In 1978, Carol Leigh, a member of COYOTE and
a sex worker, poet, and writer whose pen name was Scarlot the Harlot,
coined the term "sex work." As she explained, catering to a client's sexual
needs was work and should be treated as such. The phrase suggests that
sex work is no better or worse than other forms of service work.[26] It has
since been widely adopted by researchers, advocates, and policy makers
throughout the United States and abroad.

But COYOTE had less luck changing municipal or state laws that make
it illegal to sell sex. And while the group had some success in curbing
the excesses of law enforcement in the San Francisco area, the abuse of
sex workers at the hands of the police remained a problem in other U.S.
cities. According to a study by sociologist Bernard Cohen, published
in 1980, New York City's vice squad actually procured prostitutes to
service judges and politicians. One woman, whom Cohen interviewed,
acknowledged having sex with a state legislator to avoid arrest. She told
Cohen, "I didn't charge. That was public relations."[27]

Violence against sex workers also worsened during this period. The
number of sex workers who were reported murdered increased tenfold
from 1974 to 1980, according to a national study of prostitution-related

homicides published in the *Journal of Forensic Sciences* in 2006.[28] In her afterword for *Prostitutes, Our Life,* St. James argued that "the prohibition of prostitution contributes to the escalation of violence, and the mix of prohibition and *defacto* [*sic*] legalizing provides pimps and police with undue power over women's mobility and private activity, a power which is widely abused."[29]

There is ample evidence that during this period law enforcement in the United States treated violence against sex workers with indifference, often not even bothering to investigate the rape and murder of prostitutes. As just one example, a young woman named Karen who was working as a street prostitute in Fresno, California, in the early 1980s was raped by a client wielding an ice pick. "He kept me for about three hours and then was walking me to a park, not far away, where he said he was going to kill me," Karen relates in *Sex Work,* a collection of essays by sex workers and researchers first published in 1987. Luckily, a friend of hers spotted them and managed to get Karen away from the man. When they reported the rape to the police, one of the officers said that "it was impossible because I was a prostitute and could not be raped." The police picked up the suspect and recovered the ice pick, but even though Karen said she wanted to press charges, the Fresno police would not file a report. "They just took him to jail for being drunk in public" and released him after three hours.[30] One can't help but wonder how many more women this predator ended up raping and possibly killing.

When Julie Moya first started doing sex work, she would occasionally walk the streets, and she remembers one violent incident in which she feared for her life. She was twenty and on the lam in California, standing outside the Stardust Hotel in Los Angeles. A man drove by and picked her up. "He took me to a room in this remote hotel," she recalls. "We had sex and then he put a knife to my throat and robbed me. He scared the hell out of me."

Working for a pimp could be just as dangerous. Julie recalls that when she and another prostitute were working in Florida for Marshall Riddle in early 1977, he became furious because they didn't make as much money as he expected while on the stroll in Miami Beach. As Julie later testified, Riddle told her that if she didn't start making better money, he would "disembowel" her. The three of them had taken a room at the Sheraton Hotel, and according to the court transcript, Riddle pushed Julie and then took her shoes and beat the other sex worker in the head with them. "Her head went through part of the window in the hotel [room]," Julie testified.[31] Neither woman sought medical attention, and the three fled the hotel before the hotel staff could investigate.

According to a former federal prosecutor, what drew the FBI into the Riddle case were reports that teenage girls and women were being transported across state lines in violation of the federal Mann Act. "There may have been some involvement of underage girls," says Cleveland Gambill, one of the former assistant U.S. attorneys who prosecuted the case. "The FBI worked that case very hard. I know they put a lot of resources into it."

The trial of Riddle and the other pimps named in the indictment began in the summer of 1978 in the federal courthouse in Covington, Kentucky (two miles south of the Ohio border from Cincinnati). Julie remembers being flown back and forth from Minneapolis by the FBI several times to testify. Whenever she came to town, the FBI would put her and other witnesses up at a local hotel. "I remember how hot it was and swimming in the hotel pool with the feds and the other witnesses," she says. "It was almost like a party."

Julie, whom nature had endowed with silky blond hair, dyed her hair black for the trial to disguise herself as much as possible. "The newspaper referred to me as that raven-haired girl," she says with a wry laugh.

Shortly before the trial, Julie's daughter, then six and living with Julie's mother, underwent what was supposed to be a simple procedure to repair her heart defect. But the surgery triggered a series of strokes, and Julie's daughter lapsed into a coma. News accounts of the trial describe Julie's breaking into sobs whenever her daughter was mentioned.[32] "The [state prosecutors] were getting aggravated with me," Julie recalls. "And then they did rebuttal. It was horrible."

Even so, on the strength of the testimony from Julie and the other witnesses, nine of the defendants pleaded guilty to lesser offenses,[33] and four of them were convicted of conspiracy to promote prostitution and transport sex workers across state lines. They received sentences ranging from one year, for Riddle's common-law wife, who had worked as a prostitute and procurer, to eight to ten years, for the three men charged with running the ring. Riddle received the longest sentence: ten years in prison.[34]

For her part, Julie Hahn (alias Ingrid Hudson) remained in the witness protection program in Minneapolis, where she worked in the shoe section of the Dayton Hudson department store. But the straight life couldn't hold her for long. "I was kind of bored so I started dancing again and then ended up doing sex work," she says. At the strip club, she met a petroleum coke refinery worker named Marty, and they fell in love. When Julie became pregnant, Marty proposed to her and they became engaged. But she made the mistake of telling him she had been a working girl. "He was real angry. He was saying he didn't know if it was his child," Julie recalls. Marty ended the engagement. "It really broke my heart," she says.

Julie gave birth to her older son, Tommy, in Minneapolis in 1980. Now a single mother, she went back to sex work and serviced clients in her Minneapolis home to support herself and her son. She also began traveling to New York City to work as a call girl, leaving Tommy in the care of her aunt in Ohio. "I could make so much more money in New York," she says. "I loved New York. I used to get very lonely and I liked having people around me all the time. There was always somebody up and awake, and I felt safe just looking out the window and seeing all the traffic and people going by outside."

Julie moved to New York permanently in 1982, living in a penthouse apartment and working as a high-end call girl. She reclaimed her given name, figuring that with Riddle and the other pimps behind bars, she would be safe in a city that prized anonymity. When I met her for the first time, in January 2011, she had brought with her several yellowed clippings of articles about her life in the 1980s. One of the clips featured her on the cover of a now-defunct magazine called *NYC Adult Today*. In that grainy black-and-white cover shot, a much younger Julie is grinning, her ample cleavage spilling out over a low-cut dress. She is hoisting a glass of bubbly and is clearly delighted to be part of the Big Apple party scene. There is little hint in her smiling countenance that she has any idea that one day she will assume the mantle that Polly Adler once wore—as one of New York City's most notorious madams, a favorite target for law enforcement and the media alike.

# Sex Work Goes Online and Indoors

When Julie Moya opened her first brothel in Manhattan, in 1993, she advertised for clients in print magazines such as *Screw* or *Action*—like everyone else in the industry. But some months later, a satisfied client set up a website and registered her brothel on this newfangled thing called the Internet. That's when her business really took off. "We started to get a really nice clientele, and it just boomed," Julie recalls. "We were one of the first on the Internet. It changed our business in a day."

Julie had embarked on her career as a madam on the advice of a prosecutor. In the early 1980s, she had met an Argentinian drug dealer named Eduardo Moya who lived in the same building in Manhattan as she did. At the time, she was living with the pimp who brought her to New York in 1982. But he was arrested for bringing prostitutes across state lines, and some months after she gave birth to his son, Jerry, he was sent to prison. She and Eduardo soon moved in together. She married Eduardo in 1985 and five years later moved to Argentina with him, when he decided to retire and live off his illegally acquired gains in a gated community in Mendoza, eleven hours west of Buenos Aires, near the border with Chile. But Julie hated Mendoza.

"The men didn't treat the women there well at all. It was like being a pack horse," she says. So she moved back to New York in 1991 and began earning money transporting drugs. In February 1992, she was arrested for moving three kilos of cocaine for Columbia drug runners, and the Manhattan district attorney prosecuting the case advised her to get back into the sex industry. "He told me to become a madam, that that was a victimless crime," she recalls.

So while Julie was still on probation for the drug conviction (it was a first-time offense), that's exactly what she did. "I was thirty-eight, and I thought, I can't work as a hooker much longer," she says. "So I got an apartment and brought in a few girls."

Julie soon stopped working herself; she let her girls party with the men, and she ran the place. Thanks to the Internet, by the mid-1990s, she had twenty-five to thirty women working out of two apartments. She grouped them into three categories—Julie's classics: "Those were regular girls, maybe not beautiful but pretty and they always gave good service," she says; Julie's private stock: "These girls were really pretty and higher-priced"; and finally, Julie's elite: "These girls were models; they had perfect bodies, no tattoos. They were $600 an hour girls."

Julie's elite attracted professional sports athletes, wealthy tourists, and Wall Street hedge-fund managers willing to pay top dollar. Her sex workers also drew businessmen, lawyers, judges, writers, and a lot of cops, Julie says. "We used to have cops all the time as customers," she says. "I never paid bribes to cops, just [gave] free sessions."

Having worked for other escort services, Julie wanted to do something different, something better. "Other places treated men really badly," she says. "I wanted to make my place different, and I did. My place was cited as 'Best GFE [Girlfriend Experience]' on this website where men exchange notes about their experience."

Twenty years later, Julie still relies on the Internet to attract clients to her midtown brothels. These days, she advertises on websites such as eros.com, backpage.com, and Craigslist. And she is no longer alone; almost everyone who works in the sex business advertises online, whether they are independent sex workers or pimps, madams, escort services, or gentlemen's clubs. Indeed, the Internet has transformed the sex industry, making it much easier for sex workers to control where and when they meet clients and who those clients are. While streetwalking had been the dominant model of sex work since the 1920s, that began to change in the '60s and '70s. Socioeconomic trends, including the gentrification of major cities and relentless police patrolling of areas where streetwalkers hung out, pushed most sex workers indoors. Sex workers' rights activists have estimated that by the 1980s, streetwalkers accounted for only 20 percent of all prostitutes in urban areas. The transformative power of the Internet and the intensifying gentrification of cities such as New York and San Francisco accelerated this trend. By 2001, only about 2 percent of American sex workers were streetwalkers, according to one researcher.[1] While streetwalkers can be a surprisingly diverse population, including sex workers who sit and read books while they wait for clients outside grocery stores, many still on the stroll today are drug addicts desperate to make money for their next fix or runaway teens selling sex for survival.

Even as most sex workers have moved indoors, the Internet, together with other technological advances, has fed a growing demand for their services. With business increasingly conducted on a global scale, the ensuing rise in business travel and tourism has spurred a demand by heterosexual and gay men for commercial sex.[2]

The booming trade in live sex shows via web cams is a perfect example of this. Voyeurs from around the world can tune into live sex shows being performed by women or men stripping and masturbating with sex toys in their homes in places as far-flung as New Mexico and Australia. Elle St. Claire, a sex worker in Massachusetts, has been performing live sex shows on the web for the past five years. She charges by blocks of time (ten, fifteen, thirty, or sixty minutes or "by the minute," with charges ranging from $1 to $5 per minute, depending upon what is being shown. She juggles the web-cam shows with phone sex and in-person transactions with clients who visit her in the apartment upstairs from her living quarters. Elle St. Claire (her stage name) also offers Virtual Reality, a computer-mediated sexual interaction between two people using vibrators and other sex toys that can be attached to the computer. "I can be sitting around and working on the phone and cam, while I wait for the next call," says Elle. "I find that enticing people online in a Virtual Reality often leads to a cam show or phone sex."

Similarly, the Internet allows men in Germany or Japan to correspond via email with a sex worker at one of Nevada's legal brothels and arrange to visit her the next time they fly in for business. And of course, the Internet, together with ubiquitous cell-phone service, allows sex workers to attract and screen potential customers without stepping outside, giving them greater autonomy than ever before. Such autonomy, however, comes with risks, as the murders of five women whose bodies were discovered in shallow graves on Long Island in 2010 and 2011 attest to. All five women were escorts who had advertised online; they disappeared after arranging assignations on Long Island with a still unknown predator.[3]

Because of such risks, Julie Moya says she doesn't have any problem finding young women over the age of twenty-one who want to work in one of her midtown brothels. In fact, she says, she has to turn away many more women than she accepts. Despite the autonomy the Internet provides, many young women, particularly those just getting into the trade, prefer to work in a place where clients are screened for them and there is security on hand, should someone get out of line.

At the same time that new technologies have made it much easier to provide and obtain sexual services, sociologists point to another trend that is spurring the demand for commercial sex: the growing number of men who view sexual pleasure as a recreational activity that takes place outside a monogamous relationship. Over the last two decades, an increasing number of men have been visiting prostitutes while traveling on business, and they view paid sex not as compensation for something that is lacking in their marriages but as a venue that gives them access to multiple sexual partners. Sociologist Elizabeth Bernstein refers to this trend as "an unfettered consumeristic 'playboy philosophy'"—an indulgence that many men feel they are entitled to.[4]

This playboy philosophy goes hand in hand with a postindustrial information economy that requires extensive travel and 24/7 work schedules. Bernstein and others contend that such work demands make monogamous relationships difficult. The decline in marriage rates, the doubling of divorce rates, and a 60 percent increase in the number of single-person households in recent decades are all profound shifts in family composition that have contributed to a redrawing of what intimacy means.[5] As

Bernstein argues, "Whether in the public sphere of work, in the private sphere of the family, or in the embodied sphere of desire, the postmodern individual tends toward ever-increasing autonomy and mobility, unfettered by any form of binding or permanent social ties."[6] This sense of disconnect from community and traditional moral values is precisely what the late cultural critic Neil Postman warned about in his book *Technopoly: The Surrender of Culture to Technology*. His book was published on the cusp of the Internet revolution, in 1992, but it has turned out to be eerily prescient. Postman argues that a world dominated by technology casts aside traditional values in favor of "technical expertise and the ecstasy of consumption."[7]

Indeed, many consumers of commercial sex today are high-tech executives and traveling businessmen who prefer the "clear and bounded nature" of a commercial sexual encounter to the messy realities of an actual relationship.[8] Take, for example, David, a clean-cut Asian man in his early forties who is a regular at Julie Moya's brothel in midtown Manhattan. David is an entrepreneur who made his first million with a high-tech start-up. Even though he is married, he comes to Julie's place for sexual variety, to experience pleasure without getting emotionally involved.

Or consider Steve, a married thirty-five-year-old insurance manager who lives in a California suburb and has turned to prostitutes because sex with his wife has become infrequent since the birth of their child. For Steve, the "market-mediated sexual encounter is morally and emotionally preferable to the 'nonprofessional affair' because of the clarifying effect of payment," Bernstein writes. Steve believes that seducing someone into an affair is inherently more dishonest than the "clean cash-for-sex market transactions" that he participates in.[9]

Neil Postman would not have been surprised to hear that many men today turn to the Internet to find sexual partners who fulfill their longing for intimacy and adventure. According to Bernstein and other sociologists, such men are seeking a real and reciprocal erotic connection but one with no strings attached. They want a girlfriend experience for an hour, a few hours, even overnight, but in the end they are not interested in traditional attachments. Yet many of these men, who call themselves "hobbyists," exchange notes in online chat rooms, discussing how authentic the sexual partners they paid for were, how well they approximated the girlfriend experience, even to the point of kissing and not asking for money up front. Some clients even boast of their ability to give their paid partners authentic pleasure. In a 2012 survey of clients who posted comments on the Erotic Review website, 70 percent of the men, when asked to list the most attractive characteristic of the sex workers they frequented, chose "they act like girlfriends and not like prostitutes at all."[10]

Indeed, while some men who post on this website are very clear that their relationship with a sex worker is fantasy and not based on any real or genuine connection, a majority of the men whose comments were catalogued in the 2012 study felt that their relationships with certain sex workers involved genuine expressions of intimacy, however limited by the paid transaction. As the study coauthors Christine Milrod and Ronald Weitzer note, these men feel "they are in a paid relationship—albeit part-time and remunerative—rather than simply paying for sex."[11] Here is what one such client posted about his relationship with a sex worker: "She's been very open about her life and husband, as I've been about mine and my wife. We give each other emotional and intellectual support. When I think of her, I do not think so much about the particular sexual things we do (which are certainly fine) but about who she is . . . what she's going through this week, etc. Yes, it's a paid friendship —but it's still a friendship. After all, a wife is in a real economic sense often essentially paid too (Bostongreg)."[12]

Bernstein argues that it is "precisely the flexibility, transience and flux of postmodernity" that create clients' yearnings for what she calls "bounded authenticity." The act of sexual purchase, she says, "serves as a temporary salve to clients' contradictory desires for both transience and stability, for fungible intimacy as well as durable connection."[13]

Needless to say, such contradictory impulses can cause emotional upheaval. According to the comments on the Erotic Review website, some men end up falling in love with the women they call their "providers" and that creates problems, particularly when the sex worker doesn't reciprocate those feelings or makes it clear she wants to maintain intimacy only within the context of a paid relationship. A few men commented that they were particularly confused when a sex worker said she loved them; they didn't know whether this was part of the fantasy they had created together or a more genuine emotion. A number of the hobbyists commenting on the Erotic Review website cautioned others about the emotional risks involved in long-term associations with a particular sex worker and talked about how to avoid getting hurt. As illustrated by comments posted on the website, for some clients, long-term relations with a sex worker can wreak emotional havoc (just as noncommercial sexual relationships can). At the same time, Milrod and Weitzer note, "For the majority of clients in our sample, the phenomenon of "bounded authenticity" is recognized and accepted. They cherish what they believe are genuine feelings but also realize that they are paying for intimacy during a set amount of time."[14]

Indeed, paid sex in postmodern America is increasingly exchanged like any other service, such as domestic labor, take-out cuisine, or child care. There is, however, one major difference between sex work and other services — it pays much more. And that is the primary reason why a growing number of young working- and middle-class women in the United States are turning to sex work. Even for many college-educated women in our postindustrial economy, there is quite simply a dearth of good-paying jobs. Bernstein again: "Compared to men with similar educational backgrounds and middle-class origins, women in postindustrial economies are much more likely to find themselves working in the lowest paid quarters of the temporary help industry, in the service and hospitality sectors, or in other poorly remunerated part-time jobs."[15]

There are any number of reasons for this disparity, chief among them the fact that women constitute only 28 percent of employees in the IT industry. They are also less likely to go into well-paid fields such as engineering, finance, and oil and gas exploration. So for some young women, with or without college degrees, sex work, whether it is strip dancing, performing in web-cam shows, or selling sex, is an economically attractive alternative to the poorly paid service jobs that proliferate in the United States today.

Consider Jillian (her work name), who became a sex worker just shy of her twenty-first birthday. A raven-haired, blue-eyed young woman from an Orthodox Jewish background, Jillian dropped out of college and moved to Northampton, Massachusetts, to be near friends. She soon discovered that the only work she could find was minimum-wage retail employment in a clothing store or café.

"I realized that with these jobs I wouldn't be able to do what I wanted to do with activism," says Jillian, who sees herself as a latter-day Emma Goldman working on the behalf of disenfranchised people to create a more egalitarian society. "It would be forty hours of unskilled labor, and I'd be too tired to do anything afterwards."

A few weeks after she arrived in Northampton, in 2001, Jillian spotted some ads for erotic services in the *Valley Advocate*, the local alternative weekly, On a whim, she called one of the services, which turned out to be run by two women who worked as independent sex workers and were interested in taking a younger woman into their business. After meeting Jillian and liking what they saw, the women took her to the Salvation Army and outfitted her in what she calls "instaho clothing"—a tight skirt and frilly blouse—which Jillian, who usually wears a T-shirt and cargo jeans, had never worn before. "It was kind of like dressing in drag for me, and it felt very powerful and beautiful," she says.

The first time Jillian turned a trick, it seemed like magic. "It was an older man who wanted a 10-minute hand job, and I came out with $150," she recalls. "Patty Smith's song "Free Money" was blaring in my brain as I galloped back to the car."

Jillian has always felt like an outlier, a rebel. The first time I meet her, at the Yellow Sofa café on Main Street in Northampton, she arrives wearing a long black skirt and a black leather jacket adorned with a button that says "Activist." She has a bracelet tattooed on her left wrist and wears a real silver bracelet on her right. Her long hair is jet-black, and she has a full figure and freckles across her nose. Jillian orders a latte, which I pay for, and as we talk, she sips her latte and fiddles with an unlit Liggett Select cigarette.

Jillian grew up in Framingham, Massachusetts, the oldest child of Russian Jews who immigrated to the United States in the 1980s. She herself was born in Rome while her parents awaited a visa to enter the United States. Jillian's father soon found a good job as a computer scientist, but her mother, who had been a librarian in Moscow, felt out of a place in an American suburb where she struggled to learn English. She turned to the Lubavitch, a branch of the Hasidic movement, for comfort and enrolled her precocious ten-year-old daughter in Maimonides, an Orthodox Jewish day school in Brookline, Massachusetts. But Jillian hated the strict dress code and many other aspects of the school. "The class tension [at Maimonides] was incredible. They looked down on recent Russian emigrants," she says. Also, "It was a really misogynist environment. There was that feeling that you couldn't understand the Talmud as well as a man. And they were into making sure you were chaste and modest. Shirts up to your elbows and skirts below your knees. At the same time, it was intellectually stimulating, for someone who was really into textual analysis, as I was."

Jillian remembers being called down to the school office and berated for her questioning of Orthodox Jewish beliefs. "That was one aspect of the pressure on me," she says, waving her cigarette. "There were also a lot of parental pressures—scholastic achievement is incredibly important to Russian Jewish intelligentsia."

In tenth grade, Jillian swallowed some pills in a half-hearted attempt to kill herself. Her parents had her committed to a private mental health hospital, where doctors put her on a cocktail of Zyprexa, an atypical antipsychotic, and Prozac, an antidepressant. Her doctors soon added Depakote, another antipsychotic, to the mix, and Jillian spent the next two years in a drug-induced haze. In 1999, after working with an insightful therapist who weaned her off some of the drugs, Jillian finally got her high school diploma from Framingham State College. She was accepted at Bryn Mawr, a select women's college in Pennsylvania, but during her freshman year there, her parents divorced. At the same time, Jillian stopped taking all her medications cold turkey.

"I didn't know these drugs had withdrawal problems, and I was having horrible emotional and physical withdrawal symptoms," she says. "I couldn't sit still. I felt horrible, restless, nervous."

To calm her jitters, Jillian started smoking "an incredible amount of weed. That didn't help my academic career at all," she says. "I could never finish assignments because I had pothead attention deficit disorder." She dropped out of Bryn Mawr in the spring of her freshman year.

About twenty minutes into the interview, Jillian asks if we can go outside so she can smoke. Before she finishes one cigarette, she has already pulled another one from the pack. At one point, she says, "I'm really off my game," and when I reassure her that she sounds quite articulate, she waves me off, saying, "You don't have to keep reassuring me. I have a lot of self-confidence."

Before she became a sex worker, Jillian read many books about the profession. "When I was seventeen, I read about the second-wave feminist view that not all prostitution is exploitation," she says. "It's a matter of choice. It's my choice what I do with my body."

Jillian still works as an escort in western Massachusetts about ten hours a week. She spends the rest of her time agitating for change. As a member of Arise for Social Justice, a nonprofit that works for the rights of poor and low-income people, Jillian was involved in the fight to keep alive the needle exchange program for drug users in Holyoke, Massachusetts.

A few years ago, Jillian and other local activists managed to defeat a proposed ordinance that would have outlawed panhandling in Northampton. City officials had initiated the ban in response to store owners whose customers complained of being harassed by homeless panhandlers. Jillian and her friends mobilized against it, leading street protests up and down Main Street, handing out literature, and arguing at public hearings that the ban was an attempt to "gentrify" Northampton. Jillian, who is a talented writer, dashed off press releases and was interviewed by reporters from local TV affiliates as well as the *Springfield Republican* and the *Daily*

*Hampshire Gazette.* In February 2009, the Northampton City Council tabled the ordinance indefinitely.[16]

Jillian currently advertises as an escort on backpage.com and cityvibe. com. In one recent ad, she called herself "a snow white look alike waiting to be kissed awake." Jillian charges $250 for an hour (a no-frills visit) and $150 for a half-hour. She is very picky about whom she will party with. She recently got a query from someone who said he was an agent for the NFL who wanted to pick her up in a car and take her to an undisclosed rendezvous with, as she describes it on her blog, "some possibly steroid raging footballer." She passed up the offer, telling the agent, "I'm just a small-town escort who sees mundane middle-class guys. This is totally outside my range of experience."

Jillian likes to keep things simple. She doesn't have her own website and is decidedly more low-tech than other escorts. As I was soon to learn, a classy website with alluring photos and skillfully written ads can make a huge difference in an escort's earnings, enabling her to attract a more affluent, educated clientele. But it also puts her on the police radar screen.

Madeleine Colette and Michelle Christy are two of the web-savvy escorts whom I met at the 2013 annual meeting of the Desiree Alliance, which bills itself as a coalition of health professionals, social scientists, educators, and sex professionals working together to improve public understanding of the sex industry. Both Madeleine, twenty-five at the time, and Michelle, forty-four, do sex work in Washington, D.C. They have come to the July conference in Las Vegas to improve their business and be part of a community of sex workers who aren't ashamed of what they do.

Madeleine Colette, whose work name is a homage to the legendary French novelist and performer Sidonie-Gabrielle Colette, has a professionally designed website that shows nothing more graphic than a Victoria's Secret catalogue might. Her website manages to be classy and come hither at the same time. In person, Madeleine, who goes by "Maddy," is very pretty and fresh looking, with blonde hair (twisted in a braid), an upturned nose, and laughing hazel eyes. She looks every inch the offspring of "the southern Mayflower country club family" that she says she hails from. But she is as much a rebel as Jillian. Maddy, who began doing escort work while living abroad in Spain a few years ago, came home to North Carolina to continue her schooling and became engaged to a young man she met at school. She found out she was pregnant after she had broken up with him. But she refused to have an abortion, despite her parents' entreaties. Her daughter is now sixteen months old. "She is such a loved child," Maddy says. "My parents have come around."

Now in her midtwenties, Maddy does all her advertising online with a prepaid card phone number that clients can use to reach her. She has incorporated her business and runs it through a limited liability company (LLC). She even has a day job as a translator as a cover for her frequent visits to the D.C. area to meet with clients. Her family has no idea how she truly earns her living, and while Maddy sits in the ballroom of a Las Vegas hotel daintily consuming a box lunch with four other sex workers and a journalist, her family has been led to believe that she is at a continuing education interpreting conference.

"I hate the lie, but I feel like I'm living my life with integrity," Maddy says. "The problem is that society cannot accept the way I live my life. I am in school and I am a single mother and I have a day job and I do this."

To Maddy, sex work is simply a well-paying job, a way to support herself and her child. "Sometimes it's fun, and sometimes it's just real hard work," she says. Two other sex workers at the same table giggle knowingly, and Maddy vamps, "Oh, honey, it feels so good," sparking more laughter around the table, including her own.

Maddy charges $1,200 for two hours of her time. "One hour is too short," she says, "It doesn't give me enough stability. I don't like rushing anything. It's about the companionship, not about the sex. If someone just wants sex, I'm not for them."

She sometimes travels overnight to vacation homes and resort destinations with affluent clients. "I've been to Taos [New Mexico], a weekend in New York City, to [a client's] mountain home or their boat," she says. She has a simple rule for these overnight assignations: she never travels with new clients. "These are clients I've seen before," she says. Like many high-end escorts, Maddy puts new clients through a rigorous screening process. She makes sure to ask where they work, and she always checks up on them.

"Google is a friend," she says. "Since most of my clients are CEOs and top government officials, they have a profile page, so I know who they are. I also share provider references with other sex workers." She giggles. "We're all so careful; it's kind of hard for men to break into our community." And if the client won't reveal where he works, Maddy has a simple response. "I tell him, 'I'm not for you,'" she says.

Like Maddy, Michelle Christy (her work name) commands top dollar. Michelle says she currently makes between $2,500 and $3,500 a week, usually seeing only four clients. Her clients are often married corporate executives who want more than sex; they want someone to be an interesting, nonjudgmental companion for a few hours.

"Sex is the least of what they want. I've got the CEO of a major NASDAQ company who comes to see me twice a month," she says. "His second wife hates his first wife, and he needs a place where he can go and unwind. He's thrilled to give me $1,000 to sit and talk."

Michelle has agreed to meet me in the air-conditioned lobby of the Alexis Park Hotel, a resort-style lodging with three pools and a conference center a few blocks from Las Vegas's famously gaudy strip. Sitting on a plush sofa, her long legs primly crossed, Michelle looks like the corporate executive she once was. She is a tall, well-endowed brunette whose parents emigrated from the Soviet Union to the United States before Michelle was born. (It's pure coincidence that two of the more articulate escorts I encountered for this book hail from a Russian-Jewish background.) Michelle says she received a good education, earned a master's degree at American University, and for many years worked as a sales executive for a large health care company. But she had too little time for her family and grew to hate her work.

"I have two teenage daughters, and I found I was working seventy-five to eighty hours a week," she says. "I was beaten up on a daily basis to meet quotas, and I was working for a company that I found highly unethical. So I left for freedom. I call my own shots now."

Michelle says that for every ad that she places on eros.com, she gets between one hundred and four hundred responses. "My ad says I'm an educated professional who chooses to do this work. I'm interested in exploring who I am and my body, and I'm interested in men who are interested in exploring who they are," she says.

Michelle looks me in the eye. "The men who come to see me are not necessarily interested in my blow job, although it's pretty damn good." She points to her head with two well-manicured fingers. "They're interested in what's going on up here," she says.

Like other high-end escorts, Michelle says she can tell a lot about potential clients from the email exchanges. "Is there a respectful tone, are they requesting naked pictures or sending me naked pictures?" she says. "I don't see anybody like that."

Instead, Michelle might respond to an email that says, "'Michelle, your ad really spoke to me,' or 'I'm a fifty-two-year-old man and my wife has MS [multiple sclerosis] and I have needs,'" she says. "As long as you come to me honestly, that's what matters."

Like Julie Moya, Michelle has developed her own system for screening out abusive customers or undercover cops. "One of the things I do to guard against violence is make sure there's evidence of impulse control," she says. "If they can't wait to see me until next week, then I don't want to see them. As a rule, I don't see anyone under thirty-five. Kids don't understand discretion. Rule number one in this business: never be with anyone who has less to lose than you do. I only deal with men who have something to lose."

If a potential client emails her that he wants to meet her in Virginia, she may respond that she's in Maryland. "Cops don't generally cross state lines," she explains.

Michelle usually meets her clients in midpriced hotels in Washington, D.C. (Security at high-priced hotels can be too intrusive, and the kind of clients Michelle seeks won't come to low-priced venues.) She will only do "outcalls" (visiting with a client at a destination of his choosing) if she has met him before. "If they say come to my yacht, I'm not impressed and I don't go," she says. (The murdered sex workers whose remains were found on Long Island had all arranged to do outcalls with a stranger or strangers who answered their ads online.)

Michelle's two daughters (from her previous marriage) don't know what she does. Like Maddy, she has a "cover" job. "I tell my kids I'm a ghostwriter," she says. "I used to write a sex blog, and my kids would read it, so they won't be shocked when I do tell them what I do. But right now I don't think it's an appropriate time."

Michelle, who is divorced and has recently remarried, says she was initially open about her line of work with her second husband, a fifty-eight-year-old criminal defense attorney. "He was supportive, but he couldn't handle it; he ended up in the hospital with a heart attack," she says. "So after that I lied and said I was only going to do foot fetishes. And I do have some clients who have foot fetishes." These are men who become extremely aroused at the sight of an attractive woman's foot and like to lick, suck, and sniff her feet.

Michelle also has clients she refers to as adult babies. "They wear diapers and regress back to an infant when they're with me," she says. "I feed them, burp them, and they play with their toys, and then they go home to their wives."

Michelle will satisfy other fetishes as long as there is no pain or humiliation involved. "When I'm with someone, I get pleasure out of seeing them get pleasure," she says. Her work, she says, doesn't get in the way of intimate relations with her husband. "The sex is a much deeper, real experience," she says. "If anything, my job has enhanced my relationship. It reminds me of the importance of listening."

That evening, I find Michelle, along with a group of other sex workers, splashing in one of the hotel's pools. (The July sun in Las Vegas is too hot to even sunbathe near a pool during daylight hours.) Michelle is talking to Donia Christine, who owns a consulting company in New York and works with men and women in the sex industry to help them improve their business.

"Eros.com's days are numbered," Christine is saying as I wade over. Michelle, who is wearing a one-piece black bathing suit with a plunging neckline, is dangling her legs in the warm pool water. "They are charging sex workers too much and attracting third-party players who bring phishing software [used to con browsers of the site into giving away personal information] to the site." Christine, who has submerged much of her body in the pool, talks up Slixa as a good website on which to advertise for adult sex.

"Backpage is a good site too, particularly for high-end escorts, because there are so many low-end prostitutes advertising there," she says. (In 2013, the company that owns backpage.com sold all its print publications, including the *Village Voice*, to another publishing entity, Voice Media Group. But it retained the lucrative online website, which competes with Craigslist in posting all kinds of ads, including ads for paid sex.)

Michelle listens intently, and by the end of the evening, she has agreed to pay Christine $8,000 to do a website for her with better search engine optimization, including new photos and a more upscale look. "I'm willing to pay that much if it allows me to clear between $4,000 and $6,000 a week," Michelle later tells me.

Michelle is confident that mastering the art of online branding will boost her business. And she is not alone. The next day at the conference, a late-afternoon panel session titled "Hooker-nomics: The Business of Sex or Your Pleasure Is My Business" attracts an overflow crowd of sex workers who are eager to learn the tricks of the trade. All the seats in the conference room have been taken, and people are sitting in the aisle or standing against the back wall. While there are three or four young men scattered around the room, most of the attendees are women, ranging in age from their twenties to their forties and fifties. Everyone is dressed for the heat (the air conditioning isn't working too well), some in shorts and sleeveless T-shirts, others in cool flowing skirts and low-cut blouses. I spot Michelle and Maddy in the back of the room. Donia Christine is on the panel, as are three female sex workers and a male escort who calls himself Legendary Dave.

Dave, who strolled into the room barefoot and bare-chested, in cut-off shorts, with close-cropped graying hair and gray chest hairs to match, tells the crowd he has been working as a gay escort in Washington, D.C., for nine years. "I really enjoy it," he says. "It's been a challenge, since I'm a parent and I wasn't comfortable doing incalls, having people to my home. So I have a separate incall apartment ten minutes from my house."

In response to a question, Dave explains that he requires a 50 percent deposit on all his appointments because that weeds out people who are not serious about meeting with him. "I try to stay away from credit cards and PayPal," he says. "PayPal froze my account and kept a couple thousand dollars for a year. So I don't use PayPal anymore."

Dave says he usually only accepts cash deposits, and he asks clients to FedEx them to him. "It's not kosher to send cash through FedEx," he says. "But in my case, I live a little outside of rules. I recently had $6,000 sent to me via FedEx. I have a P.O. box where it is sent to."

Other sex workers mention a number of vendors, such as MoneyPak, Green Dot, and Intuit, through which they have had deposits sent to them anonymously. Donia Christine chimes in: "If you have a bank account through Chase, they have a prepay account, and you can use completely anonymous email that doesn't indicate your name. Amazon gift card is another good idea. They will send it to any email you give them."

One sex worker asks how to go about branding herself. Christine suggests that the brand can be whatever her expertise or specialty is. "I don't think people give enough thought to this when they put themselves out there, so they get lost in a sea of adult sex workers," she says. "It's about identifying the thing that you're the expert at. You have to build on what you're most authentic at."

One of the other panelists, a pretty, light-skinned woman whose black hair is tinged with green highlights, agrees. "You have to ask two questions first: who do I want to be while I'm doing this, and what kind of clients do I want to have," says the panelist, who had introduced herself earlier as Sophie Laurent. "You want a brand that will attract the clients you want."

Heads nod, and around the room people scribble furiously on notepads or tablets. Someone strolling by might think they had stumbled onto a typical corporate conference, and in one very real sense, they would be right. The women and men in this room are serious about their work and intent on building successful careers. They are the new generation of sex workers, whose lives have been shaped and transformed by the Internet, for better or for worse. If Julie Moya had been in the room that day, she would have felt right at home.

# Why Women and Men Do Sex Work

## VARIATIONS ON A THEME

In one sense, Julie Moya fits the stereotype that many Americans have of why and how women become prostitutes. She ran away from a difficult home life in her teens and began selling sex to survive. She was also repeatedly molested by a relative at the age of ten. The perpetrator was an uncle (by marriage) who gave Julie the attention she craved as a child. "I would sit on his lap, and he would feel me up and want me to touch his, you know . . . " she recalls. "It was just hands. It happened for months. But I liked it—the attention and stuff."

Antiprostitution activists claim that almost all sex workers were molested as children. They use this "oppression paradigm" as an argument for trying to abolish prostitution.[1] But research provides a much more nuanced reality. Teenage runaways, like Julie, who resort to selling sex for survival or are coerced into prostitution by pimps, are indeed more likely to have been abused than those who choose to become sex workers at a later age. In fact, abuse at home is often why they ran away in the first place. A 1985 analysis of the research literature on adolescent prostitution found that between 31 and 67 percent of juvenile prostitutes reported being sexually abused as children.[2] A 1987 Canadian study found that even though juvenile prostitutes were twice as likely as respondents to the country's National Population survey to have been victims of unwanted sexual acts as children, victims of sexual abuse constituted a minority of the sex workers surveyed. Sixty percent of the female respondents in the juvenile prostitution survey and 78 percent of the males did *not* report experiencing "unwanted sexual acts" while they were under the age of eighteen.[3]

In a 2010 study of youth engaged in the sex trade in New York City, 33 percent of the 226 young people interviewed described being sexually abused or exploited by adults in their lives. The John Jay College of Criminal Justice researchers, however, did not specifically ask about past sexual abuse; the abuse narratives came up when the youth were queried about how they got into sex work.[4] For example, one eighteen-year-old white youth from Yonkers said he was initiated into the sex trade by his uncle at the age of twelve: "My uncle . . . he used to molest me, and he used to do stuff to me. And basically—in my town, he knew people, and they were a bunch of perverts—and he pretty much got money for me to do stuff with them."[5]

There is no question that sex work is traumatizing for teenagers who have been molested as children. In the John Jay College study, one fifteen-year-old black girl from Brooklyn, who had started selling sex at age twelve, hated what she was doing because it "makes me feel dirty." She was scared that someone was going to rape her again, but she felt she had no choice. "Like, I'm doing this for money, but this is the only way I know how to make a living," she said.[6]

Indeed, most of the youth interviewed in the John Jay College study said they had started selling sex out of economic desperation. Financial reasons are in fact why most sex workers get into the trade. According to a 2005 study by the Urban Justice Center in New York City, which surveyed 52 adult sex workers who work for brothels, escort agencies, or private clubs or who worked on their own, 67 percent of those surveyed said they got involved with sex work because they were unable to find other work that paid a living wage.

Similarly, the teenagers in the John Jay College study said they didn't have families who were willing or able to support them, and they felt they needed to sell sex to survive. One eighteen-year-old Hispanic girl said she started in the trade at age seventeen to help her aunt, with whom she was living, pay bills and avoid being evicted from their apartment.[7] An eighteen-year-old white girl said she started selling sex at the age of fifteen after running away from the foster home where she had been molested. "My mother died and I was placed in foster homes. My foster father would touch me and I ran away. I ended up coming to New York and I was on the streets," she told the John Jay College researchers.[8]

Pimps prey on such vulnerable runaways. Andrea Powell, the executive director of FAIR (Free, Aware, Inspired, and Restored) Girls, a nonprofit organization in Washington, D.C., that helps sexually exploited girls, tells the story of one fourteen-year-old who ran away from an abusive situation at home. When she was approached at a mall by a man who offered her a place to stay for the night, she felt he was her savior. But over the next few months, she was forced to have sex with men at truck stops and hotels up and down the East Coast, including Maryland, Virginia, and the District of Columbia. One day, fearing for her life, she ran to a church in Washington, D.C., and a church member called FAIR Girls. The organization helped her find a job and a place to live and provided legal counsel and even assistance in applying for college. The girl now has her own apartment and a full-time job, Powell says.

Sometimes, traffickers (the term Powell prefers to pimps) use more sophisticated tricks to entrap vulnerable teens. One aspiring eighteen-year-old rap singer from Texas saw an advertisement online for a rap contest in Washington, D.C. She was trying to escape an untenable home life and had no one whom she could really turn to for advice. Her mother had died when she was twelve and her father had killed himself, so she had gone to live with a relative who turned out to be abusive. The rap contest, with its offer of prize money, sounded like the answer to her prayers. But when she arrived at the posh D.C. hotel where the contest was supposed to be taking place, she realized she had been duped. She was assaulted by several men and forced to engage in commercial sex. Seeing no way out, she pretended she was into it and eventually convinced the pimps to give her a cell phone so she could make her own appointments. Then, when her captors got drunk and stoned on the Fourth of July, she called the police. They arrested the men and called FAIR Girls to help the girl. Powell herself answered the summons. (Her organization has a staff of seventeen, but on holidays, including the Fourth of July, she is on call.) In order to keep exploited girls out of harm's way until FAIR Girls can find them more permanent housing or get them back in touch with family, someone from the nonprofit usually stays with the girl overnight at a safe location, such as a hotel or rented apartment. "All the hotels were booked on the Fourth of July, and the only hotel I could find with a room was really expensive," Powell recalls. "I begged and pleaded and got a really good rate. She was starving, so we had to find her food. It gets pretty crazy on these emergency responses."

Police were not able to build a case against the eighteen-year-old's traffickers (there was no evidence, no photos of her posted on adult websites), so after a few days in jail, they were released. However, Powell says FAIR Girls was able to help the girl find a better place to live. "She is now in college in Texas, but it's hard," she says. "She doesn't have any family."

Powell says that most of the clients her organization works with began doing sex work while they were underage. "The majority of girls who are trafficked today are not chained to their beds or kidnapped," Powell says. "They're lured by someone who is offering them a false sense of love and security. But when it goes south and becomes violent and abusive, they have no one else to turn to."

Since all underage prostitution in the United States is defined by federal law as trafficking, it will be discussed in greater depth in the next chapter, which focuses on human trafficking. But let me say here that underage prostitution is an unacceptable problem, which demands our urgent attention and best minds to solve.

While underage prostitution remains an intractable problem here and abroad, the reality is that a majority of sex workers in developed countries begin working in the profession when they are eighteen or older. A 2010 study of 557 street and indoor prostitutes working in three Dutch cities found that the median age of entry was twenty-seven for non-drug-using workers, twenty-five for drug users, and twenty-four for transgender workers.[9]

Similarly, while research indicates that streetwalkers are more likely to begin selling sex when they are underage, many of the women who do indoor sex work in North America begin working in the trade when they are eighteen or older. One survey of thirty-nine off-street prostitutes in British Columbia, conducted in 2006, found that the average age of entry for these women was twenty-two; the majority had started working between the ages of nineteen and twenty-four.[10]

Jillian, the Jewish activist from western Massachusetts, is one of many escorts who began working when she was of legal age. And she defies the conventional stereotype in other ways as well. She was not sexually molested or physically abused as a child, and she began doing sex work by choice just shy of her twenty-first birthday. She says she likes sex work for several reasons: it gives her the economic independence she needs to pursue community activism, it allows her to set her own hours, and it makes her feel powerful and in control. As she writes in her online journal, "I love being the most beautiful woman in the world for that one hour. I love the performance art. I love the anonymity. I love the world beginning again in the confines of that room populated by only two strangers."[11]

On a hot August afternoon, Jillian arrives at the Yellow Sofa café in Northampton for our second meeting, sweaty and red in the face. She has walked a half-mile from her house, dressed all in black: black pants, low-cut short-sleeved black shirt, and a big black hat. Her witch-black hair is plastered to her forehead. She apologizes for being late and orders an iced latte. As we settle in at a table near the back of the café and begin to talk, Jillian keeps putting on her oversized black glasses and taking them off. But she settles down as the conversation turns to her work and why she does it. She says that by the time she decided to do sex work, she had already slept with a "fair number of people"—both female and male—and realized she was bisexual.

"I'm not ashamed of my sexuality," she says. "I've found that it's easier for me to let go in my personal sex life because of [what I do]." With her clients, Jillian slips on a wild, sensual, anything goes persona—for an hour, a half-hour, or however long she is with them. She tells her clients, mostly married middle-class men, that she won't laugh at anything they desire, that "we're going to play with it, we're going to have fun with it; in this room, it's going to be fulfilled." And for that allotted period of time, Jillian is sex incarnate, the most beautiful woman in the world, as she herself once wrote, "a Mata Hari" of the twenty-first century.

Indoor sex workers like Jillian are much less likely than street workers to have experienced sexual or physical abuse as children.[12] This is particularly true in countries where prostitution has been legalized. A survey of 127 street and indoor prostitutes in the Netherlands, where adult consensual prostitution has been legal in certain venues since 2000, found that only 16 percent had experienced sexual abuse prior to the age of sixteen.[13]

Even more surprising, a Dutch researcher who conducted an in-depth study of 187 prostitutes in the Netherlands in the early 1990s found striking variations in well-being among the women she surveyed. (To determine well-being, the researcher, Ine Vanwesenbeeck, considered psychosomatic complaints, work-related physical complaints, and problems with depression, anxiety, and social insecurity, as well as job satisfaction.) The survivors of childhood sexual abuse who worked as prostitutes did much worse physically and emotionally than other women on these measures. Thus, about one quarter of Vanwesenbeeck's total sample (which included the victims of child molestation) fared worse than a control sample of non-prostitute women. However, approximately half of the prostitutes surveyed were doing better than expected, Vanwesenbeeck found, "only slightly less well than the average non-prostitute." And in a poke to conventional wisdom, more than one quarter fared "quite well" or "even better than the average non-prostitute."[14]

Vanwesenbeeck's study is not the only research that reveals huge variations in how sex workers feel about themselves and their work. A 2001 study of twenty-nine prostitutes in New Zealand (twenty-seven worked as call girls or escorts or in massage parlors and two worked the streets) found no differences in physical health, self-esteem or mental health, as compared with an age-matched sample of non-prostitute women.[15]

The difference in how sex workers fare seems to depend on several factors: their childhood experiences, working conditions, whether they are drug users or not, and how choosy they can be with clients. Vanwesenbeeck, for example, found that because streetwalkers and window prostitutes in the Netherlands usually work in isolation, they are particularly vulnerable to physical and sexual assault and harassment. Not surprisingly, streetwalkers are also more likely to have been abused as children. A 1984 study found a 60 percent rate of child sexual abuse among street workers in San Francisco.[16]

Such childhood trauma, coupled with difficult working conditions, is predictably associated with depression, anxiety, and lower job satisfaction. Studies in other countries have found similar disparities in the experiences of indoor sex workers as compared with those who work the street. A British study comparing 115 streetwalkers with 125 women who worked in saunas or as call girls found that the street workers were more likely than the indoor workers to be robbed (37 vs. 10 percent); beaten (27 vs. 1 percent); punched, slapped, or kicked (47 vs. 14 percent); and raped (22 vs. 2 percent).[17]

The problem of violence for street workers is intertwined with the fact that they are much more likely than indoor workers to use drugs.[18] In a New Zealand study, done by researchers at the University of Otago, Christchurch School of Medicine, three-quarters of streetwalkers reported using drugs while working as compared with one-third of indoor workers.[19] In many cases, drug use preceded their involvement in commercial sex. For these streetwalkers, prostitution is a means of securing the funds needed to feed an already established drug addiction. Desperate to score their next fix, addicted workers are often not as careful to screen out dangerous clients or practice safe sex.[20]

That was the case with Kisha, a transsexual sex worker whom I met at the drop-in center of Helping Individual Prostitutes Survive (HIPS), a nonprofit organization that does outreach to streetwalkers in Washington, D.C. HIPS sends out several mobile vans three nights a week, and workers in those vans travel fifty miles per night within city limits, handing out free condoms, coffee, and hot chocolate and arranging free HIV testing, counseling, and referrals for other health-care services to streetwalkers. Funded by the District of Columbia Department of

Health and numerous private donors, HIPS dispenses 750,000 condoms a year and, since its inception in 1993, has helped hundreds of streetwalkers get off drugs and off the streets.

Kisha, a name she uses professionally, is one of those sex workers. Now in her thirties, Kisha is an articulate African American male-to-female transsexual with a feminine body and a pretty face. A native of Washington, D.C., she says that she began doing sex work after getting hooked on crack. "I started sex work to feed my habit," says Kisha in an interview at the HIPS drop-in center on Rhode Island Avenue in northeast Washington. But as a childhood victim of sexual abuse, she adds, "I was really doing sex work at ten, for a shoe, a few dollars. It was a way to survive." Kisha is now clean and off the streets; she still does sex work—on her own terms, she says—and she also works for HIPS, reaching out to men and women who are still on the streets.

Other studies have found that some sex workers turn to drug and alcohol as a way to cope with the work they do.[21] Tasha, for example, started using drugs to numb her emotions while doing sex work. A handsome African American transsexual, Tasha (her professional name) left home when she was sixteen, knowing that her family would not accept who she was—a woman trapped inside a man's body. Young and on her own, she became intrigued by the lifestyle.

"Once I saw the strip [malls] and the girls strolling and the makeup and the clothes, I knew that's where I wanted to be," she says. Now thirty-four, Tasha is wearing a frilly off-white blouse pulled tight across her breasts and a black leather jacket. She has a long, carefully groomed black wig and a scar under her nose. Her liquid black eyes seem haunted. "I didn't have any money, so I went to Macy's and took a wig off the mannequins," she recalls. "And it worked. I felt so good, and the men just pulled up and the money came in."

At first, Tasha says, her life was one big party. She was living in an apartment with six other "girls," and they would sleep all day and get gussied up at night and go out on the stroll. Tasha, who has known she was different from a young age, wanted desperately to fit in, and so she started doing what her new friends were doing: smoking weed. "Everything was moving so fast," she says. But then she began using harder drugs to numb her emotions while on the stroll. "I had to get high on something, you don't know who you're going to touch, it was man after man," she says. "I had to do something because I couldn't do it [sober]."

Tasha started smoking crack, and that, she says, is when "I really got stuck." Desperate to pay for her next fix, Tasha became careless about whom she would "date" and what she told the johns about herself. She says she was raped on numerous occasions, and once she was stabbed six times while giving a man a blow job.

"I was on drugs, on New Jersey Avenue, and there were two guys, a man and a boy. And I'm on my knees doing the job, and the boy comes and stabbed me six times. I'm walking and the blood and I'm screaming, and I was walking down the street to the fire station and holding the wound in," she says, pressing on the side of her stomach to demonstrate how she tried to keep from bleeding out. She survived that attack, only to be shot twice by another client, who she thinks went berserk when he discovered she wasn't a woman. "I was saying, 'Here, come here,' in a high voice, and then I went back to my regular voice once I got him in the web. He figured it out, and before I knew it, he had shot me in my thigh and I was lying on the ground, and then he shot me in my chest," she says. "The bullet is still in my back."

In 2009, Tasha was arrested for robbing another john while high on drugs. She did three years in jail for armed robbery, and when released on probation, she went back onto the streets. But then she discovered HIPS and, with the help of its outreach workers, began to, as she puts it, "get stable." "They were there [on the street] with condoms and hot chocolate," she says. "And they had a bad-date list [of johns known to be violent], so I knew these were people who actually cared."

Until she came off the streets, Tasha says, drugs and sex work were her whole life. And indeed, researchers have found that street workers, because of their circumstances, are less able than indoor workers to separate their private lives from their sex work.[22] While some psychologists argue that such separation of self is inherently damaging, others see consensual sex work as not that different from the kind of role play or acting done by other service workers who work with demanding customers (for example, nurses, waitresses, flight attendants, even Walmart clerks). Such researchers argue that a separation of one's core self from the role one is playing is a necessary strategy for managing emotions while working.[23]

Even more surprising, a number of studies have found that escorts and brothel workers often develop higher self-esteem after they begin doing sex work. The 25 percent of prostitutes who fared even better than the average woman in Ine Vanwesenbeeck's study were self-employed and able to determine their own working conditions. They served fewer customers because they were able to charge more per customer. A 1986 study by sociologist Diana Prince found that 97 percent of call girls (another term for escorts) reported an increase in self-esteem after they began working in commercial sex, as compared with 50 percent of brothel workers and only 8 percent of streetwalkers. According to Prince, call girls expressed positive views of their work, and brothel workers were generally satisfied with their lot.[24] Similarly, a 1979 study of indoor prostitutes, most of whom worked in bars in a midwestern city in the United States, found that three-quarters of them felt that their life had improved after entering prostitution. None said it was worse than before.[25]

In the Netherlands, three-quarters of indoor workers report that they enjoy their work, according to a 2004 study.[26] And an Australian study the same year found that half of call girls and brothel workers felt that their work was a "major source of satisfaction in their lives," while seven out of ten of those surveyed said they would "definitely choose" this work if they had to do it over again.[27] (Prostitution was decriminalized in several regions of Australia in the 1990s.)

Male sex workers (who typically serve gay customers) report even higher levels of satisfaction. A significant segment of the male prostitute population surveyed in a 2007 study reported enhanced self-esteem. And another study found that for transgender sex workers in Brazil, prostitution was the only sphere of life that enhanced their self-image. Being sex workers, they said, gave them a sense of personal worth and self-confidence.[28]

While many sex workers, whether working on the street or indoors, do not perceive themselves as victims, they are acutely aware of the stigma involved in doing sex work. The perception by the general public that sex work is immoral, dirty, or tainted and that no self-respecting woman or man would do such work explains why even high-priced escorts do not tell family members, sometimes even their partners or close friends, what they do. Many sex workers, both those who walk the streets and those who work indoors, say the stigma involved in what they do, and the secrecy required, is the most demoralizing aspect of their jobs. "The hardest and most frustrating aspect of this work is that I can't be honest with people I care about," says Maddy Colette, the high-end escort from North Carolina whom I met at the Desiree Alliance conference. "Living a double life is hard."

Kimora, a twenty-eight-year-old African American transsexual (male to female) who used to walk the streets in Washington, D.C., agrees. "Society is really judgmental," she says in an interview at HIPS. "You say to someone, 'I used to be a sex worker,' and they look at you with judgment, without letting you explain this is what you were going through at the time in your life."

Western cultures view prostitutes through a particularly harsh lens, in large part because the Judeo-Christian religious ethic has long sanctified marriage and vilified prostitution. The late sociologist Kingsley Davis provided a more socioeconomic explanation for this centuries-old stigma in his landmark 1933 paper "The Sociology of Prostitution." Davis noted that "the basic element of what we call prostitution—the employment of sex for non-sexual ends . . ." applies to all institutions in which sex is involved, including courtship and marriage. "Prostitution therefore resembles, from one point of view, behavior found in our most respectable institutions," he noted. The stark difference in the way these institutions are viewed lies in the social functions they serve. Since the most important function, from the point of view of a civilized society, is reproduction (producing the next generation), Davis argued that marriage is held in the highest esteem because "it is the chief cultural arrangement through

which erotic expression" is linked to reproduction. But when sex is exchanged for money, the buyer clearly has pleasure and not reproduction
in mind. "To tie intercourse to sheer physical pleasure is to divorce it
both from reproduction and from the sentimental primary type of relation which it symbolizes," Davis notes.[29] In other words, the paid sexual
relationship is inimical to our most sacred institutions (marriage and
reproduction) and thus must be condemned as a social evil.[30]

What Davis neglected to mention is the patriarchal or chauvinist
frame through which this condemnation takes place. In patriarchal so-
cieties, women who behave sexually outside the norm of marriage are
marked as deviant, while men who are equally promiscuous avoid blame.
Sex workers are thus considered the most deviant of all (more on this in
Chapter 10).

While some feminists believe that women should be able to choose
how they express their sexuality (even to the point of selling sex), other
contemporary feminists have reframed prostitution as an inherent evil
because they believe it objectifies and oppresses women. Donna Hughes,
a women's studies professor at the University of Rhode Island whose
online profile identifies her as a leading researcher on human trafficking,
writes, "Men who purchase sex acts do not respect women, nor do they
want to respect women."[31]

Andrea Dworkin, the late feminist, argued that when men turn to
prostitutes, they are expressing a "pure hatred" for women. "It is a con-
tempt so deep, so deep, that a whole human life is reduced to a few sexual
orifices, and he can do anything he wants," she wrote in *Life and Death*, a
2002 collection of her essays and speeches.[32] (In the 1980s, Dworkin and
Catherine MacKinnon, a law professor at the University of Michigan,
employed similar rhetoric in their battle against pornography.)

Melissa Farley, a clinical psychologist in San Francisco who founded
the nonprofit organization, Prostitution Research & Education, also
argues that prostitution "dehumanizes, commodifies and fetishizes
women."[33] In a 2013 article Farley published comparing prostitution to
slavery, she writes, "In prostitution, johns and pimps transform certain
women and girls into objects for sexual use. . . . Women who have sur-

vived prostitution say that the experience is profoundly degrading and that it is as if one becomes 'something for him to empty himself into, acting as a kind of human toilet.'"[34]

In an interview, Taina Bien-Aimé, the executive director of the Coalition against Trafficking in Women (CATW), used much the same language to explain why her organization is opposed to all kinds of prostitution, not just trafficking. "How can a government allow an industry that exploits women like this?" she asked. "[The client] can spit on you, defecate on you, use any orifice of your body."

For some sex workers, particularly those forced into prostitution as teenagers, prostitution is indeed degrading and profoundly damaging, as the John Jay College study and other studies have shown. But what antiprostitution feminists fail to acknowledge is that some sex workers, both those who work as escorts and those who walk the streets, actually view their work as liberating.

In an interview with sociologist Elizabeth Bernstein, Eve Pendleton, a former street worker in San Francisco, argued that prostitution was empowering to women because, unlike conventional relationships, it at least compensated them for their submission. "I have more independence than the women who have to do for their husbands and make their dinner," she said.[35]

Kimora, one of the transsexual sex workers I met at HIPS, also spoke of how proud she is of being financially independent and not being a burden to her mother, who has eleven other children, plus four stepchildren. Sitting across a seminar table from me in a conference room at HIPS, Kimora is garbed in a tight-fitting purple dress cut low to reveal her ample breasts. She wears dangling silver earrings and a black sailor's cap set jauntily over a cascade of silky black hair, and when she waves a hand in the air, her beautifully manicured French nails (painted purple to match her dress) sparkle in the fluorescent lights. It is not at all obvious that biologically Kimora is a man.

When she was younger, Kimora says she was molested by her stepfather, a former Marine. When she came out as a transsexual in her teens, her stepfather would belittle her. "He would call me a clown and make fun of me in front of my siblings," she says. Even so, Kimora finished high school and began taking college courses. That's when she started doing sex work, she says, because she needed money for books, for clothing, for everyday living. "I wanted to show my mom my independence."

Kimora says she started out streetwalking and then began posting ads on Craigslist because it was so much safer than walking the streets. Now twenty-eight and in law school at Howard University, she says she still posts online ads "every now and then if I need a quick coin for a bill."

At first, she says, her mother had a hard time with her daughter's sexuality and how she makes ends meet. But just last year, her mother, who is no longer married to the Marine, told Kimora how proud she was of her. As she relates this anecdote, Kimora starts to cry, and Tasha, who is sitting next to her, rubs her arm with genuine concern. Kimora smiles gratefully through her tears. "[My mother] said, 'You are my heroine for being able to live your life the way you want to,'" Kimora says. "That made me feel so good."

Just as sex work can be an avenue for some women to take control in a situation where they had none, some sex workers and psychologists see it as a way to triumph over tragedy. That's certainly how Maddy Colette, the high-end escort from North Carolina, frames it.

When Maddy was seventeen and on a vacation trip to Costa Rica with her mother, she was violently raped and left for dead. "My Mom had to call hospitals to find me," she says. She recovered physically but turned to drugs to escape from the trauma and ended up being expelled from school in North Carolina. At the age of eighteen, Maddy went to live in Spain, and that's where she began working as an escort.

"My Spanish clients were paying me thousands of euros and it was very empowering," she says. They gave me extravagant gifts, took me out to the opera. That feeling of being in control helped me heal." She acknowledges, however, that her rape experience plays into how she views sexual relationships. "That event helped me separate the physical from the emotional," she says. "In my personal life, I can have tremendous emotional intimacy."

Maddy says she first started thinking about sex work at the age of thirteen after reading a science fiction book by Jacqueline Carey about a fantasy world in which being a courtesan was a highly respected profession. "I started reading it before it was confiscated by my mother, who gave me a stern lecture about my book preferences," she says, grinning wickedly. "That was my first realization that I saw relationships differently than other people do. I'm open to a serious relationship, but I will never be monogamous."

A year after Maddy moved to Spain, she met another American woman on the Metro who was an escort. The older woman introduced her to a high-end escort service that catered to men in the upper echelons of society. "This is an acceptable aspect of society there," she says. "It's acceptable for men to bring escorts to cotillion dances, opera, art events, and social gatherings. So it ends up being more about companionship than sex."

Being a sex worker is not illegal in Spain, although it's a crime to sell someone else. As a result, there's less exploitation of women than there is in the United States. Spanish escort agencies are very careful not to dominate or exploit anyone; they just take care of the bookings, Maddy says.

Maddy doesn't see herself as a victim. She says she remains in charge of every interaction and has never experienced violence from a client. "You have to re-educate some clients," she says. "Because of the things they see or hear, they do things they shouldn't—like spitting on a woman. It's really common in pornography, and it's disgusting."

The few times that clients have spit on her, Maddy stopped what she was doing and pulled away. "I said, 'I'm going to go clean up now. This doesn't work for me,'" she says. "I have very strong boundaries. My risk of HIV is lower than a woman in a monogamous relationship because I insist on condoms for every sexual encounter."

Julie Moya has a similar view. "I see prostitution as a way of getting back control over your body," she says. "Some women who've been molested become totally against sex, but other women like [sex work] because it gives them control over sex." In the course of a sexual transaction, Julie says, "We're the powerful ones."

That's precisely what some sexuality researchers have found. The late John Money, a psychologist at Johns Hopkins University who studied sex offenders, developed a theory to explain individuals' divergent and sometimes deviant sexual fantasies and practices. Money coined the term "lovemaps" to describe the mental template of sexual desires that is stamped on all of us in childhood. In his 1986 book, *Lovemaps*, Money described how adults can "vandalize" children's sexual development by punishing them for innocent childhood play or by abusing them. He argued that when a vandalized lovemap tries to heal itself, it sometimes becomes skewed and distorted. For example, when young boys are humiliated or excessively punished for early sexual behavior (including cross-dressing), their mortification is transported into erotic arousal as a way of "triumphing over tragedy," Money says. And that can produce fetishes such as the desire to cross-dress or be tied up and spanked. Harsh sexual abuse in childhood can produce more dangerously distorted lovemaps or paraphilias, such as the desire to kill women and have sex with their dead bodies. According to Money, this theory also explains why some boys who have been sexually abused as children grow up to be men who become aroused when they sexually abuse young boys or girls.

Boys are more vulnerable to what he calls "developmental lovemap disabilities" than girls are, Money says, perhaps because boys are more dependent on visual imagery for arousal. Since lovemaps are shaped by input from the social environment, he hypothesizes, boys' greater dependence on visual input may explain why they experience a greater variety of what he calls "paraphilic disruptions."[36] Money also notes that just as boys are more likely than girls to experience developmental delays and reading disabilities, so too are they more likely to develop distorted lovemaps.[37] Females, however, are not immune. Money notes that the vandalism of lovemaps in girls can lead to either a lifetime of frigidity (not enjoying sex) or, in some cases, to a desire or compulsion to have sex with multiple partners.[38]

Money argues that when a society endorses (instead of punishing) early erotic play in children, normal lovemaps predominate and paraphilias are rare. Rather than criminalize commercial sex or condemn pornography, he says, one way to minimize deviant sexual behaviors would be to teach children about sex and discuss its positive moral benefits in appropriate relationships. Ironically, he uses the example of how the Catholic Church, which has fostered such a distorted view of sexual intimacy over the centuries, teaches young children about death and crucifixion: "Millions of children learn in explicit detail, with vividly realistic models and pictures, how to perform a crucifixion. They learn also the moral principle involved, and they do not play crucifixion games with their dolls and playmates."[39]

Some health professionals argue that commercial sex provides an important outlet in a society where distorted lovemaps and fetishes exist but often cannot be acted out in the marital bed. And indeed, many sex workers feel they are providing a valuable service to clients who have unhealthy or unusual sexual impulses. "Sex work can be really preventative of child sexual abuse—clients can indulge their fantasies with us rather than with their children," says Maddy Colette during lunch at the Desiree Alliance conference.

Commercial sex can also provide an outlet for men who might not get laid otherwise. Jillian had one such client, a mentally challenged man in his forties who worked in a candle factory in western Massachusetts. He was "sweet, consistent, and predictable, despite his odd, close-smelling room and his standard of hygiene," she recalls. "I feel as if I'm performing a service when I have sex with him."

Many sex workers describe what they do in much the same terms. Elle St. Claire, the escort who does live web-cam shows in Massachusetts, compares herself to a therapist, even an educator. "A true professional fills the gaps of every other professional out there," she says. "Even a sex therapist has certain guidelines they can't cross. I have a lot of clients who ask me a lot of questions and I answer them openly. It's my job to make sure people have a safe and healthy erotic experience."

Elle and Jillian belong to an informal network of sex workers in western Massachusetts who share a bad-client list, and Elle contacted me after Jillian spread the word on a private listserv that I was interested in talking to sex workers. After we spoke on the phone, Elle emailed me the link to her website, which featured photos of her posing seductively in various states of undress. But when I met Elle St. Claire (her stage name) for the first time at a restaurant near where she lives, I was shocked to discover that, anatomically, she is a man.

On that warm September evening, Elle is wearing high heels and a short, tight-fitting black leather dress with spaghetti straps that reveal broad shoulders and long, toned legs. A bracelet tattoo circles one of her muscled upper arms, and Elle's hair is long and dyed red, dark roots visible at the part. She has arrived with Jessica, whom she introduces as her fiancée, a much shorter, curvier woman with an angelic-looking face framed by blond curly ringlets. Jessica is wearing a very short ruffled skirt and a short-sleeved blouse with a plunging neckline that shows off her ample breasts to advantage.

When the maître d' escorts us up the stairs to the dining room, he attempts to seat us at a separate table near the bar, just underneath a noisy television screen. I ask for a booth, and he darts a quick look at the three of us but in the end obliges. As we seat ourselves, I notice that the people in the booth behind us are staring. A group of four people who are seated at the table next to us a little later also can't seem to stop ogling. When Jessica gets up to have a smoke, she walks right by their table and says loudly, "We're married, you know."

When I tell Elle I thought she was a woman, she giggles—a high-pitched, oddly discordant rasp that contrasts with her deeper speaking voice. "I make that clear on my website," she says. "I also put it in the ad [on Craigslist]. Sometimes people show up and they say they didn't know, even though it's in the ad. If they're not comfortable with that, I make light of it and I say I'm not offended. I say, 'If you're interested in a woman, you can see Jessica.'"

Jessica is a former erotic dancer who has performed in several slasher movies—"I'm very good at screaming," she says at one point. She also does sex work.

Both Elle and Jessica say they were never molested as children. Elle (whose name at birth was Richard) had a fairly typical working-class childhood. His father, a first-generation Irish American who served in the Korean War, was an alcoholic, and Richard's parents divorced when he was eight. His mother eventually remarried, and Richard became captain of the football team and class president at a private all-boys Catholic school in Massachusetts. He was also a gifted dancer and musician (he played the saxophone), and in his senior year, he was accepted at the Berklee College of Music in Boston. But he couldn't afford the tuition, and his stepfather refused to sign a waiver so that Richard could obtain financial aid. So after winning a coveted slot with the popular singing and dancing troupe, Up with People, he decided to tour with them instead. It was while he was on a world tour with Up the People that Richard got an inkling of his true identity.

"We were walking around the red-light district in Amsterdam and knocked on some doors, and the shade went up and I went in," Elle recalls. "And it was like, wow. The penis was flopping around and the tits were flapping. When I saw my first transsexual in Amsterdam, my first reaction was that it is so hot, and then I realized I'm not sexually attracted to this person, I am this person."

Richard decided to come out as a transsexual in 1994, even though he was married by then and the father of two young boys. His wife kicked him out of the house and told everyone she knew that her husband was a transsexual, ruining his career in real estate. "Within twelve hours, I found that the life I had built was gone," Elle says. She changed her name legally to a woman's name (she asked that her legal name not be identified) and began driving a cab. Nine months later she received custody of the boys after their mother had a breakdown, was confined to a psychiatric hospital, and was ruled an unfit parent.

In 1996, Elle decided to physically change her body to match how she felt inside. "I'm non-op [meaning no surgery]," she says. "I chose hormones. I like to be natural."

Elle is dressed more casually the second time we get together, at the white-shingled duplex she and Jessica are renting in Holyoke, a former mill town in western Massachusetts. Surrounded by an ugly chain-link fence, the three-story house sits on a side street in a down-at-the-heels neighborhood a few blocks from downtown. Elle and Jessica live on the ground floor, record their live web-cam performances on the second floor, and meet with clients on the third floor. Elle, who is thirty-nine, greets me at the door in black pants and a green ribbed sweater that sets off her striking green eyes. Her dark roots are even more obvious this afternoon, but her long nails are beautifully manicured with purple polish and white stars on the tips.

When I ask how she became a sex worker, Elle explains that she started out in the industry as an entertainer, producing and starring in pornographic films about bondage, dominance, and submission. Her film production work eventually led her into sex work in the late 1990s.

"After a film was released, I would begin getting emails," she says. "They would say, 'Are you the Elle St. Claire I saw in this film?' And I'd say, 'Yes,' and they'd say, 'Well, I'm going to be traveling through your area, I'd like to spend a little time with you.'"

Elle chain-smokes Marlboro cigarettes as we talk. She says she smokes a pack a day, and she lights up within a few minutes of my arrival. Our conversation eventually circles back to her philosophy about the importance of sex work. "There's a need in society for educated providers. [Sex work] is a healthy release for people who don't feel comfortable getting help any other way," she says. "This is why you have sexual predators and stalkers. Unhealthy sexuality manifests itself in all of those crimes."

Echoing many other sex workers, Elle says that people don't hire a prostitute just for the sex. "They share their deepest secrets, their deepest fantasies with me," she says. "They ask for advice. People contact me for 101 reasons, and one of them is information about their own sexual identities."

Elle says she makes referrals to counselors when she sees clients with serious psychological issues. "Maybe they were raped as a child and they have a lot of emotional issues, so my next question is, 'It sounds like you haven't dealt with that issue. You're trying to deal with that issue by covering it up with sex, which is not healthy.' So then I ask them—I know some really good counselors—'Do you want a referral so you can work on those issues?'"

Most of Elle's clients, of course, are not deviants; they simply want some variation or excitement in their sex lives. For many of the reasons outlined by John Money in *Lovemaps*, sex is not always about romance or straightforward love. As Alain de Botton observed in his 2012 book, *How to Think More about Sex*, "[Sex] is not fundamentally democratic or kind; it is bound up with cruelty, transgression and the desire for subjugation and humiliation. It refuses to sit neatly on top of love, as it should."[40]

As a longtime sex worker, Elle understands that better than most people. "Some people like spanking, but they won't come out and tell anybody they like spanking," she says, holding her cigarette neatly between two long manicured fingers. "They couldn't begin to address that with their wife, so they hire a provider."

This afternoon, Elle explains that she has a 1:30 p.m. appointment with a regular client, a doctor in his midforties who Elle says is happily married with a family. For this man, spending time with a transsexual is a way of relaxing and disappearing from his responsibilities, his public persona. "He works in a crisis center, and a lot of the patients are children. It can be heart wrenching, and he needs to escape," Elle explains. "He gives me a call and hires me for an hour or so and really just breathes."

While Elle is talking, Jessica wanders in and out of the room. She is wearing a black silk blouse unbuttoned almost to her navel and a very short, frilly black skirt riding low on her hips. Like Elle, she has a French manicure, her nails painted deep blue with white at the tips, and she is sporting a huge rock on her left ring finger, which Jessica assures me is a real diamond.

Elle and Jessica's cell phones sit on the table in front of them. At one point, Jessica's cell phone starts jangling, and Elle says calmly, "We're going to have to pause here. Clients don't like to hear voices in the background." Jessica gets up and walks into the kitchen, and I hear her say, "I'm sorry, I'm booked for the day." And then she hangs up and walks back to the table. "I didn't like his attitude," she says. "He didn't address me like a lady. He said, 'Hey, you available?' That's not acceptable. I'm picky about who I'll meet with."

Both Elle and Jessica say they routinely turn down clients who they don't think meet certain "basic standards of etiquette" or who refuse to give them their phone numbers so that the sex workers can verify that the clients are who they say they are. After an appointment is booked, both women run the client's phone number through the online bad-client database they share with other sex workers in the area. "I don't accept blocked calls because I have no way to put this person through the bad-clients list," Jessica says. "You go on the list if you're a jerk, you're uneducated, you're rude, or you have no respect for the girls in the industry and you blow them off."

Elle says she and Jessica get phone calls almost every week from police checking their online ads. But because they always check the phone numbers and verify the callers' identities, she says they have never been arrested for sex work. "Once I was arrested for a bounced check," Elle says. "But that's it." (A check of her criminal record at the courthouse confirms this.)

Indeed, just like Margo St. James and many other sex workers, Elle says she has had clients who are in the FBI, the CIA, and local law enforcement. She and Jessica consider themselves "good citizens," and on the rare occasion when they do have to deal with a stalker, they say they can rely on the police for help. "If someone is parked outside and staring at the house or driving by too much, we'll call the police and ask if maybe an officer could drive by," Elle says. "And as soon as a police cruiser drives down the street, off they go."

The local police, Elle says, know her and Jessica as "porn stars," and since pornography is not illegal, the police respond to her complaints as they would to those of any other ordinary citizen. The two women, of course, don't call the police when they are having a problem with a john. They handle those problems themselves. Their house is rigged with a number of security cameras as well as an intercom system.

"We listen to each other, so if something happens [during a session], I'm up the stairs with a claw hammer in my hand," Jessica says. "If anyone doesn't pay up front, he will get hurt."

Elle admonishes her mildly. "I don't like to talk about violence," she says, adding that there are other ways to ensure compliance. One time a client of hers took off down the stairs without paying her. Jessica, who had been monitoring the conversation via intercom, raced out and snapped his picture from the front porch. "I told him it would be on the Internet tomorrow if he didn't pay up," Jessica says. "He ended up coming back and giving Elle what he owed."

Elle goes into the bedroom and comes out dressed in a short, black, belted silk robe, her long legs bare. Jessica looks at her and says, "Girl, you better cover it up." She stands up and walks away, and Elle sits back down at the table and takes out another cigarette. We resume our conversation, but a few minutes later, her doctor-client calls and she tells him to go right on up. "If you'll excuse me," she says, just like the lady she is, and disappears up the back stairs to meet him.

# The Truth about Sex Trafficking

I n the winter of 1997, one of Julie Moya's working girls, a dark-haired Russian émigré who went by the name of Natasha, said she knew of several other Russian women who might be interested in working at Julie's place. Julie was intrigued — if these women were as good-looking and popular with her clients as Natasha was, they would be good for business. A few days later, Natasha introduced Julie to a couple in their thirties, a Russian American husband and wife who spoke both Russian and English. "I remember the woman's name was Lisa," Julie recalls. "They said they knew some girls who were interested in working for me."

But when Lisa brought two Russian women over to one of Julie's brothels — at that time, an apartment on 74th Street between York and First Avenues — Julie discovered that they didn't speak a word of English. They were, as advertised, beautiful. One young woman, whose name was Alana, was very pretty and slender, with blue eyes and long blond tresses; her compatriot, Marina, had long dark-brown hair, porcelain skin, and a fine figure. Both said they were in their twenties. But almost immediately, Julie sensed that something was not right. Both girls seemed afraid of the Russian couple, who delivered them to her place and picked them up when their shifts were over. And unlike her other girls, who were always running out to buy cigarettes or other essentials whenever they had a break, Alana and Marina never left the apartment except when accompanied by Lisa or her husband. It didn't take long for Julie to discover that neither of them had ever sold sex before.

The first time Marina went into a private room with a client, a regular by the name of Brian, he soon called Julie into the room. "This girl doesn't know what she's doing," Brian said. "She doesn't know how to use a condom." At first, Julie thought Brian was kidding. The Russian-speaking couple had said that both girls had done sex work before. So Brian's assertion confused Julie, and at that moment, she didn't have time to deal with it. She had to get over to her other brothel, where she and her girls there were hosting a private party for some Wall Street high fliers. "Well, can you show her how to use a condom," she replied and left.

But the next time Brian came in, he took Julie aside. "You know that girl, Marina?" he whispered. "She was a virgin." Julie stared at him and finally said, "You're joking." Brian shook his head and walked away, and Julie tried to put the episode out of her mind. But then she saw Alana crying in the lounge one evening, and a few days later, when Marina came to the apartment, she had bruises on her arms and legs. Something was very wrong, but Julie couldn't figure out how to communicate with the two women, who didn't speak much English. How could she find out what was going on? She didn't trust Natasha enough to ask her. She knew that Natasha and Lisa went to the same Russian Orthodox Church in Brooklyn. Whatever she said to Natasha would find its way back to Lisa, of that Julie was sure.

The next morning, Julie was absently watching her twelve-year-old son, Jerry, draw something for a school project when the idea struck her. That evening, she took Alana aside, gave her a piece of paper and a pen, and indicated that she should draw something. What Alana drew made Julie's stomach turn over. First, Alana drew crude stick figures of herself with her younger brother and mother, smiling. Then she drew a picture of her mother and brother, tears in their eyes, being pounded by another, bigger stick figure. Finally, she drew a stick picture of herself, big loopy tears falling from her eyes. The truth hit Julie with the force of a sledgehammer—these women were being trafficked, held against their will and forced into sex work. Why had she not seen this before? She realized that she had been in denial; the truth had been staring her in the face from the first day Alana and Marina were brought to her place, but she had been unwilling to face up to it. She had wondered why Lisa or her husband always turned up at the end of the night (or more accurately, at 1:00 or 2:00 in the morning), when Julie and her managers toted up the day's earnings and doled out cash to the girls working that day. Even though Alana and Marina were paid directly, their money always ended up in Lisa's hands.

So now the question was, what could Julie do? She could, of course, refuse to let Alana and Marina continue to work for her, but she knew that their traffickers would simply beat them bloody and force them to work somewhere else.

Julie spent a sleepless night wrestling with the dilemma, and by morning, she knew what she had to do. She picked up the phone and called a longtime friend of hers, Vincent DeFilippis, a high-ranking probation official with the New York Division of Parole. She had met him during her own run-in with the law, and he had treated her with dignity and respect. DeFilippis said he would send over an immigration official who spoke Russian. Could she somehow arrange for this official to meet one of the Russian women outside the apartment? Julie promised to see what she could do, and the next time Lisa dropped off Alana and Marina, she took Lisa aside and explained that there was a client who really wanted to take Alana out for a few hours on the town, go to dinner and maybe a hotel — an outcall, as it was known in the trade. Lisa said she had no problem with an outcall. A day or two later, the immigration officer, disguised as a client, arrived and whisked Alana away.

A few weeks later, Lisa dropped by Julie's place and said she needed to talk to her in private. Julie's stomach lurched; had Lisa found out about what she had done? But Lisa only wanted to confide in her. She and her husband also ran a brothel out of an apartment in Manhattan; Alana, Marina, and several other Russian women were forced to work there as well. "Lisa told me that she was being followed by the feds," Julie recalls. "She didn't know that I had turned her in."

A month or two later (Julie doesn't recall the exact time frame), DeFilippis called her. Federal immigration officials had swooped in on

Lisa's brothel and taken a number of Russian women, including Alana and Marina, into custody. They also grabbed Lisa, but her husband, who was not on the premises at the time, was still at large.

It was months before Julie learned the full story. "Apparently, these women thought they were coming here to be nannies, but they were thrown into prostitution, and their families were threatened and their visas were taken away," she says. "They were being trafficked."

Alana and Marina were sent back to their families in Russia, and Lisa was eventually convicted of trafficking, although she spent only a year in prison. Natasha disappeared, and Julie later heard she had gotten into drugs and died of an overdose. "It was such a shame," Julie says. "They were really sweet girls."

Julie was not the only madam dealing with this issue. By the late 1990s, trafficking had become a growing problem in the United States and Europe. After the collapse of the Soviet Union, the number of women being trafficked into Western Europe and the United States from Eastern Europe had multiplied. Globalization and the growing divide between the haves and the have-nots had spurred a broader rise in the trafficking of women and men (for all kinds of labor) from poor to wealthy countries.

Some feminists soon seized on trafficking as a new weapon in their fight against a trade they considered inherently harmful to all women. In 2000, Donna Hughes, a women's studies researcher at the University of Rhode Island, published a seminal paper titled, "The Natasha Trade," in which she detailed the trafficking of women from the former Soviet bloc countries.[1] Hughes talked about how the trafficking of women had become a highly profitable market for organized-crime networks and labeled trafficking a "modern-day slave trade."[2]

Later the same year, Congress passed the Trafficking Victims Protection Act of 2000, which separated sex trafficking from other forms of labor trafficking and defined human trafficking as a commercial act induced by "force, fraud or coercion." And then came 9/11, which spawned a dramatic escalation in the U.S. government's efforts to monitor and keep out potential terrorists, along with illegal immigrants trying to gain access to the wealthiest nation in the world.

At first, Julie Moya didn't notice the chill. In the immediate aftermath of 9/11, her girls gave free sessions to firefighters and others volunteering at Ground Zero. She even turned over one of her apartments in lower Manhattan to volunteers who needed a place to bunk. It was a time, she recalls, of great warmth. New Yorkers drew together, united against a common enemy. But that feeling of camaraderie didn't last long. As the country geared up for war and Congress passed the Patriot Act and other laws aimed at helping the United States fight terrorism, the mood of New Yorkers seemed to change. "Before 9/11, the clients all wanted to hang out and stuff," Julie says. "But afterwards, they just wanted to be serviced and leave. I would be driving home to Long Island, and I'd go through the midtown tunnel and see soldiers with guns and all the military vehicles, and you could see the whole city becoming kind of paranoid."

A similar mood shift was occurring nationwide. The State Department's escalating war on illegal immigrants dovetailed nicely with the Bush administration's morality-based attack on the sex industry. Conservative groups, allied with feminist scholars such as Hughes, argued that all prostitution was trafficking, that women were never in the trade by choice. All sex workers, they insisted, were victims of exploitation by some third-party person. By 2005, the official U.S. position had locked onto this conflation, with federal officials stating in one position paper "that prostitution is inherently harmful for men, women and children, and that it contributes to the phenomenon of trafficking in persons."[3]

Even today, the State Department and other federal and state agencies conflate voluntary prostitution by adults with trafficking cases, according to criminal justice experts. "There is an underlying conceptual problem distinguishing between consensual prostitution and human trafficking," says Jay Albanese, a professor of criminology in the Wilder School of Government and Public Affairs at Virginia Commonwealth University, who has studied trafficking and worked with law enforcement on this problem. "These terms are mixed together on the State Department website."

Albanese and other researchers say the statistics bandied about by federal officials and antitrafficking activists on the number of people trafficked in the United States and globally are inaccurate and highly inflated. In 2003, for example, the U.S. State Department estimated that 600,000 to 800,000 people were being trafficked across international borders each year. But as Albanese notes, that estimate was not based on an actual count of trafficked persons, and a few years later, a federal oversight agency, the Government Accounting Office (GAO), concluded that such estimates were flawed. "The accuracy of such estimates is in doubt because of methodological weaknesses, gaps in data and numerical discrepancies," the 2006 GAO report concluded.[4]

According to a report on trafficking from the United Nations Office on Drugs and Crime, the total number of victims identified in a sample of seventy-one countries (which had the best data) was 14,900 in 2006.[5] Another reputable source of information, the International Organization for Migration, reported assisting 7,771 victims of trafficking between 1999 and 2005.[6]

Yet these more realistic estimates haven't prevented sensationalistic accounts. Antitrafficking activists continue to argue that millions of people are being trafficked globally and that hundreds of thousands of women and children are trafficked into and around the United States every year. A recent U.S. Department of Justice report, however, could identify only 389 confirmed trafficking cases (which led to 144 arrests) and 527 victims between 2008 and 2010.[7] Another comprehensive study, involving 1,515 municipal police agencies around the country, found that of 2,397 cases investigated for trafficking between 2000 and 2006, only 876, or 37 percent, resulted in an arrest. And of those arrests, only 43 percent (or 377 cases) resulted in a conviction for trafficking.[8] These numbers, of course, represent only trafficking cases that came to the attention of municipal law enforcement.

As many researchers note with chagrin, there has yet to be a trustworthy count of victims trafficked to the United States or globally. "When it comes to this crime, never has there been so much written based on such little data," Albanese says. "There is no good count. A worthy estimate is based on an underlying actual count and there has been no such count done for human trafficking." The 2000 Trafficking Victims Protection Act brought all juvenile prostitutes, even those who were ostensibly in the trade by choice, under the trafficking umbrella. It stipulated that anyone under the age of eighteen who was caught selling sex should be legally considered a victim of trafficking. While this part of the law was well intentioned—no reasonable person would consider child prostitution permissible—many experts say that the provisions of the law and the way in which it reframes underage prostitution have contributed to a growing misunderstanding of why and how most minors end up on the street selling sex.

"Trafficking conveys this notion that most of these kids are being taken around from jurisdiction to jurisdiction, if not imported into this country, and that is not true," says David Finkelhor, a professor of sociology and director of the Crimes against Children Research Center at the University of New Hampshire. "Our research suggests that most of these kids are operating in their home cities and towns." Other research reveals the same pattern. A 2008 study of 226 youth who began selling sex as minors on the streets of New York City found that 92 percent of them were born in the United States and 56 percent were New York City natives.[9]

Finkelhor, a slender, genial man in his midsixties with two Harvard degrees (one in social relations, the other in sociology), has been studying the problem of child victimization for over thirty-six years. He began examining the issue of child sexual abuse for his dissertation and received his first National Institute of Mental Health grant to study familial sexual abuse in 1978, the same year he was awarded his Ph.D. in sociology. These days, Finkelhor finds himself both irked and astonished at the level of misleading information spread about underage prostitution.

In recent years, for example, antitrafficking activists have repeatedly claimed that between 100,000 and 300,000 children are trafficked in the United States every year. And once again, the mainstream media have picked up the cry without bothering to check the veracity of these figures. The *New York Times, USA Today,* CNN, and the *Boston Globe* have all breathlessly reported that between 100,000 and 300,000 American-born children are sold for sex each year.

Respected researchers such as Albanese and Finkelhor have debunked those figures in their own studies. Even the authors of the original 1999 study that gave rise to those inflated numbers acknowledged that "100,000 to 300,000" came from an estimate of the total number of children "at risk" of physical or sexual exploitation because of problems at home and the conditions in which they live. To reach that "at risk" estimate, the authors even included all transgender kids, female gang members, and children who live near the Mexican or Canadian borders and have their own transportation.[10]

So what are the actual numbers on child prostitution? A study by Finkelfor and colleagues at the University of New Hampshire found that police nationwide arrested or detained 1,450 juveniles for prostitution in 2005.[11] That number closely corresponds to an earlier study, which analyzed data from the FBI's Uniform Crime Report, and found that 1,400 juveniles were arrested nationally for prostitution and commercialized vice in 2003.[12] Of course, as Finkelhor notes, that is not the right number either. "That's just juvenile prostitutes known to law enforcement," he says. "People who have statistics on it are blowing smoke. Nobody really knows how many cases [of juvenile prostitution] there are."

Unfortunately, that hasn't stopped activists from continuing to spew false information. In a December 2013 interview, Taina Bien-Aimé, the executive director of CATW (the Coalition against Trafficking in Women), informed me that between 250,000 and 500,000 children in the United States are sold into prostitution every year.

## A New Name for Pimps

Besides spreading false statistics, antitrafficking proponents have deliberately changed the language for a problem that has existed for decades. Pimps, mostly men who target vulnerable runaways from dysfunctional homes and promise them affection and security, are now called sex traffickers, according to Finkelhor and those who work directly with sexually exploited youth.

"The traffickers used to be called abusive pimps," says Andrea Powell, the executive director of FAIR Girls, the nonprofit organization in Washington, D.C., that provides services to sexually trafficked girls. Powell says that more than 90 percent of the girls her organization serves are American citizens and the majority are girls who were in the foster care system or have run away from violent or abusive situations at home. "Boyfriend is beating the mom or the girls themselves have been sexually molested by a family member," she says. "The traffickers know who to target. We're talking about American girls who are being exploited in their own communities."

Powell says the new nomenclature is more effective in arousing public concern. "When you say 'pimp,' it doesn't have the magnitude of saying 'sex trafficking,'" she points out. When I mention that the term "trafficking" connotes movement across borders and might confuse people, Powell shrugs. "It's your job as a journalist to explain it," she says.

This new narrative, however, cuts deeper than mere semantics. While it may be effective in raising money for advocacy groups such as CATW and FAIR Girls, it obscures the real reasons youngsters are out on the street selling sex. And that, in turn, impedes efforts to truly help these youth. While there is no question that some teenage runaways who have left home because of abusive situations are being entrapped and exploited by ruthless pimps, there are also many kids, both boys and girls, who are selling sex as a way to survive on their own, Finkelhor says.

For example, the John Jay College study of teenage sex workers in New York City found that most of these youth were not recruited by or under the control of pimps. While pimps or so-called boyfriends were clearly a route into the market for some girls (14 percent of this sample), only one boy and no transgender youth reported being recruited or controlled by pimps. Of the 226 youths in the John Jay College survey, only 10 percent said they currently had pimps, the researchers found. By contrast, about 45 percent were recruited into the "business" through friends. The John Jay College researchers said that they had made a special effort to recruit pimped girls and concluded that while "it seems likely that [pimped youth] were more difficult to recruit than youth that did not have pimps, there is little reason to believe that the proportion of pimped girls was much higher than reported here."[13]

A 2014 study of sex workers in Atlantic City found much the same thing: pimps played a small role in the initiation and operation of street-based prostitution in that resort city. Most of the street workers surveyed did not know a pimp at the time of their interview, and those who said they had a pimp typically described the relationship as "more mutual and easier to leave than the stereotypes suggest," the researchers found. They concluded that "the conventional narrative of deception, force, or the captive slave—recruited and tied to a pimp through love, debt, addiction, authority, or coercion" did not apply to the majority of streetwalkers they studied.[14]

While pimps are not major actors in the commercial sex market in New York or Atlantic City, they clearly control those teenagers who work for them, according to the John Jay College study. Most of the girls who worked for pimps had negative things to say about them. Some of them described being beaten and emotionally abused, and many said they didn't like not being allowed to spend the money they earned on themselves. A seventeen-year-old Puerto Rican girl told the researchers that her pimp takes whatever money he wants and "doesn't protect me."[15] An eighteen-year-old black woman from Queens, who said that she had started selling sex when she was fifteen, witnessed horrific abuse against the other girls who worked under her pimp:

> We all shared a room. Two of the girls in our house . . . one does coke and the other one is a heroin-crack user. Like, a lotta her dates she goes on, she gets beat because . . . she's like ten, twenty dollars for this, so that she could get that next high. He beat on the 15 year old . . . he hit her like she was a man. She's short and small—so it's like when he hit her, it dropped her the first time. But he didn't stop hittin' her, he just constantly was beatin' her. She was like, "Daddy, I don't wanna go . . . on the stroll, I don't wanna be on the stroll. I wanna be in a club—with the rest of the girls—I can't be out there because I keep getting' arrested. Police keep

stoppin' me." He was like, "You gonna go wherever the fuck I tell you to go." And he hit her. My first reaction was to stop him. But I knew if I interfered with that, it was just gonna make the situation worse for me . . . I'm like, "I gotta get outta here." So I left with what I had on my back.[16]

Others, however, spoke somewhat fondly of their pimps and portrayed them as protectors or father figures. An eighteen-year-old woman of Haitian ancestry who had grown up in the Bronx said that her forty-one-year-old Jamaican pimp contacted clients for her. "Sometimes, when I don't wanna do some kinda things, he understands and just gimme the money," she told the John Jay College researchers. "So, it's like a father to me, just in a different kind of way."[17]

Regardless of whether underage sex workers are pimped or selling sex on their own, no one I've interviewed for this book considers underage prostitution acceptable. "This is a very serious problem and it's something that does merit some mobilization," Finkelhor says. "But we need more science and knowledge for that mobilization." For example, studies show that successful strategies for helping children who run away from dysfunctional families and end up selling sex for survival involve treatment for trauma from childhood abuse, job training, safe housing, and specialized educational services.

"Putting a focus on the prostitution end of things makes people think that the solution is getting them out of prostitution," Finkelhor says. "My sense is this is not the way these kids see themselves or their problems either. If you're defining a problem differently from the target population you're trying to help, that's often a recipe for failure."

The study by the John Jay College researchers found, for example, a higher number of underage boys than underage girls selling sex on the streets of New York City.[18] While that doesn't mean there are more boys than girls working in the city's sex trade—more underage females may be performing this work indoors as opposed to walking the streets—the study does indicate a large population of underage prostitutes (gay and straight boys) that is often overlooked by the conventional antitrafficking narrative. "There are a considerable number of gay boys involved who are dealing with the fact that they haven't been helped to transition into managing a gay identity and have had to run away," Finkelhor says. "The clear prevention approach to this particular subgroup is to have supportive people in every community who can help gay youth get adjusted to that particular world. But that aspect of the problem has been completely ignored."

The same complexity, researchers say, holds true for adult prostitutes. According to Albanese, there are several populations involved in prostitution in the United States: first, people who are doing sex work by choice and running what might be considered small business enterprises; second, sex workers addicted to drug and alcohol who are desperate for money to feed their addictions and are often under the sway of pimps; third, migrants who have been smuggled into the country voluntarily and sell sex in order to make a better living than they could otherwise; and fourth, those who are truly being forced into the sex trade against their will. A 2005 study of indoor sex workers in New York City, conducted by the Urban Justice Center, found that only 8 percent of the study's respondents were trafficked into the country for prostitution. The majority (67 percent) of the indoor workers (who worked independently or for brothels, escort agencies, or private clubs) said they got involved with sex work because they were unable to find other work that provided a living wage.[19] While some adult sex workers are definitely being exploited by pimps, for others, the men in their lives whom law enforcement would label as pimps are actually lovers, bodyguards, or drivers who share in their earnings. These men, many sex workers insist, don't control them; they work together, so-called partners in crime. "I think the general debate never separates out these different groups," Albanese says.

The irony is that even studies by antitrafficking groups indicate that more people are trafficked into untenable labor situations in the agricultural, domestic service, hotel, and construction sectors than in the sex industry. Surveys by the Coalition to Abolish Slavery and Trafficking (CAST) showed that of the trafficked victims that CAST helped in the Los Angeles area in 2013, 40 percent were victims of sex trafficking and 60 percent were victims of trafficking in other industries, such as agriculture, domestic service, hotels, and construction. In 2012, the trafficked victims CAST surveyed included 32 percent in sex trafficking and 68 percent in other sectors.[20] But media attention remains fixated on sex trafficking because, as Albanese says, "it sells a lot more newspapers. It's not that big news to find a lot of people being exploited on a farm somewhere."

As a result, federal and state authorities routinely put more money and resources into fighting sex trafficking than into combating the more ubiquitous types of labor trafficking. And they continue to pursue what many researchers and even some law enforcement officials consider a misconceived approach. Ken Lanning, a retired FBI officer who specializes in crimes against children, says there may indeed be too much focus on the law enforcement aspect of trafficking and not enough attention paid to eradicating the causes of underage prostitution.

"Part of the solution has to be dealing with the root causes—parents who may be physically or sexually abusing their children and abusing drugs and alcohol," Lanning says. "But all of that is complex, difficult, and expensive to address. Americans like problems we can solve. So even though kidnapping by strangers is the least common problem, it's the one we talk about the most because it's the simplest to understand."

## How Trafficking Laws Harm Victims

In recent years, Congress has reauthorized the Trafficking Victims Protection Act several times, setting up multiagency task forces to expand the powers of law enforcement in investigating trafficking cases and spending more than $64 million to support those task forces and local police training in the United States.[21] At the same time, forty-three states have passed antitrafficking legislation.

Yet research indicates that, in some cases, the proliferation of state and federal laws has ended up hurting the very people these laws were designed to protect. For example, since the original Trafficking Victims Protection Act was passed in 2000, the total number of arrests of underage prostitutes has actually increased by almost 9 percent.[22] Even though juveniles are supposed to be treated as victims, many end up being processed through the criminal justice system. In some cases, police arrest underage prostitutes in an effort to ensure that these kids get the services they need. "Some cops say the only way we can separate them from their pimps or get them off the streets is to arrest them," Finkelhor says.

Police make a similar case for arresting adult sex workers. Melvin Scott, who heads up the Narcotics and Special Investigations Division of the Metropolitan Police Department in Washington, D.C., says that during a May 2014 raid on a brothel in the city, police found a young Mexican woman who said that she had been forced into prostitution when she was a minor and had been transported to brothels all over the United States for the past nine years. The young woman was not charged with prostitution; instead she was deported to Mexico.

Scott argues that without laws criminalizing prostitution, police would not be able to build cases against traffickers or pimps who exploit sex workers. "A lot of this information comes in after we arrest [prostitutes], and we have people saying, 'Thank you for bringing me in, let me tell you what's going on,'" he says.

However, researchers and legal advocates say that criminal laws actually create an atmosphere of mistrust and adversarial discord between police and sex workers, whether they're underage or adults. "Why do you have to use the criminal law with punishment and the deliberate infliction of pain [on victims] in order to catch traffickers?" asks John Lowman, a sociologist at Simon Fraser University in British Columbia who has studied the sex industry in Canada for decades. "Sex workers are much more likely to come forward if you just talk to them than if you arrest them."

In fact, exposure to the criminal justice system can end up making the situation worse for trafficked victims. Some of the youngsters arrested for prostitution are sent to juvenile criminal facilities or foster homes where they are molested and traumatized all over again. And in the John Jay College study, some underage prostitutes said they were sexually assaulted by police or forced to provide sexual services for free.[23]

Underage sex workers are not the only ones harmed by antitrafficking laws. The researchers conducting the 2010 study of 1,515 municipal police departments around the country discovered that immigrants who were being trafficked were more likely to be deported than to be designated as victims deserving of a special visa and support services.[24] This finding may explain why some victims who are truly trafficked remain reluctant to seek the help of law enforcement officials.

In eleven jurisdictions in New York State, including Brooklyn and Queens, sex workers who are arrested for prostitution are assumed to be victims of human trafficking and can choose to attend five or six sessions in a diversion program instead of being charged as criminals. However, the prostitution charges are kept on their (publicly available) records for six months before the records are sealed, thus limiting the sex workers' ability to find employment outside the sex trade. As a columnist for the *Nation* noted, New York's Human Trafficking Intervention Courts (as they are officially known) also lump trafficking victims and other sex workers together, thereby inflating trafficking statistics and violating the rights of women to decide on their own if, when, and how they want to leave sex work.[25]

Many states continue to disproportionately arrest individual sex workers even when state officials agree that the focus should be on traffickers, exploitative pimps, and those who patronize prostitutes. For example, although the state of Illinois recently passed legislation designed to stiffen penalties against traffickers and patrons or clients, prostitution-related felony charges continue to be brought almost exclusively against sex workers. According to an analysis of data from the Cook County State's Attorney's Office, performed by the *Chicago Reporter*, sex workers accounted for 97 percent of the 1,266 prostitution-related felony convictions in that county between 2008 and 2012. The *Chicago Reporter* article concluded that such data exposed an "unbalanced system that came down hard on people in prostitution but rarely held their patrons accountable."[26]

The same pattern can be found in other states. In Alaska, for instance, the state's trafficking law (passed in 2012) has been used primarily against sex workers who are not involved in trafficking, according to Terra

Burns, a researcher at the University of Alaska at Fairbanks. In 2013, Karen Carpenter, the owner of an Anchorage massage parlor (where she worked with two other women) was charged with sex trafficking in the third degree (inducing an adult into prostitution), managing a place of prostitution, and inducing a person under twenty into prostitution. She was found guilty of sex trafficking in the third degree (a felony) as well as the misdemeanor prostitution offense, according to the *Alaska Native News*.[27] An independent adult escort in Fairbanks was also charged with sex trafficking in 2013, even though (as the public defender argued), Alaska's laws make it clear that the offense should apply to people who are trafficking others for the purpose of prostitution.[28] While that case was later dismissed, the original trafficking charges against this woman can easily be found in public court records, making it difficult for her to rent an apartment or find more legitimate employment. "In Alaska, landlords and employers regularly search CourtView [a website] before renting or hiring, and you can see how even suspicion of sex trafficking could make it difficult to obtain housing and employment," Burns says.

Furthermore, some police departments are using the increased federal funding they receive for the purpose of fighting trafficking to expand their efforts to arrest adults engaged in consensual prostitution. Sex workers' rights advocates say this is happening in Las Vegas, San Francisco, Rhode Island, Ohio, and Alaska. In a 2012 interview published on Indybay, an online news collective for the San Francisco Bay area, Alexandra Lutnick, a researcher with RTI International, an independent nonprofit research organization, said the San Francisco police department had recently used federal trafficking funds to do a sweep of adult streetwalkers on Polk Street. "Money that is supposed to be used to prevent the trafficking of young people is being used to arrest adults," Lutnick said.[29]

Alaska's Special Crime Investigations Unit recently set up a sting to find sex workers advertising on Craigslist and used an undercover officer to arrest a twenty-six-year-old white woman who was clearly not being trafficked by anyone. According to the April 2014 police affidavit, the woman was a drug addict with a seven-year-old son and a boyfriend serving time in jail for selling drugs.

In May 2014, California police raided a number of Asian massage parlors in Alameda County, which includes Oakland and other cities on the East Bay of the San Francisco area, and arrested nineteen people as part of an investigation into human trafficking.[30] Yet none of the sex workers swept up in the raids were actual trafficking victims, according to Maxine Doogan, founder of the Erotic Service Provider Legal, Educational and Research Project, a nonprofit group that provides services for San Francisco Bay area sex workers.

Nancy O'Malley, the district attorney for Alameda County, which conducted the raids, disputes that contention. "Some were trafficking victims, some weren't," she says. "Some would not admit that's what it was." O'Malley says that none of the fifty sex workers picked up in the raids are being prosecuted or deported. "Anybody who was here without documentation, we worked with them to get them linked into services so they could get T visas," O'Malley says. "We view them as victims." (Some illegal immigrants are granted T visas if they can prove they have been trafficked.)

The same month (May 2014), Rhode Island police raided an apartment in a run-down triple-decker in Providence and arrested two men and an undocumented Mexican woman who told police she had come to the United States of her own accord. After six years of cleaning jobs in New York, she decided to work as a prostitute to make more money. Police charged one of the men with trafficking and the other man (the customer) with a misdemeanor prostitution charge. The woman, who had been sending money home to her family, was taken to a shelter. By the next morning, she had vanished.[31]


THE ZEAL TO CURB trafficking (even when it isn't happening) may also have been the motivation behind the joint FBI–New York Police Department raid that led to Julie Moya's arrest in 2005. As Julie recalls, that frigid January day began like any other work day for her. The temperature outside was in the single digits, and her Honduran maid, Denora, brought her breakfast in bed, bustling in with a cup of Julie's favorite Hawaiian Kona coffee and a bowl of hot cream of rice cereal arranged on a tray. As Julie sipped her coffee and contemplated the day ahead, she thought about how much she had to be thankful for. She owned her four-bedroom house in Freeport, Long Island, overlooking the canal. From her living room windows, she could almost see the marina where her thirty-two-foot Family Cruiser was docked. Zulu and Natalie, her two African grey parrots, jabbered away down the hall, and Pamela, her brightly plumed cockatoo, cooed softly in her cage nearby.

Julie Moya had worked hard for all of this, and at forty-six, she was still working more than twelve hours a day, six days a week. It wasn't easy running a top-of-the-line escort business, which she liked to describe as "the nicest, friendliest brothel in New York City." Her day often started at 11 a.m., when the phones began ringing at the office downtown, men booking lunch appointments with one or another of the girls. While Lucas, her trusted office manager, answered the phones and made appointments, Julie was always on call if a problem arose—one of the girls calling in sick at the last moment or a client insisting on a woman who wasn't available that day and refusing to take no for an answer. Julie herself was usually on site by 4 or 5 p.m. as the evening rush started, and she often found herself settling squabbles among the women. A new girl might try the dirty hustle when a customer came in and was introduced around, running up to him and kissing him or bending down to show him her cleavage, and that would set off the other girls. Julie's day would continue until well past 1 a.m., when the last clients left and all the girls would troop over to the office on 46th Street to get paid, order in Chinese food, and share war stories over laughter and occasional tears.

While Julie was starting to think about retiring and turning things over to Lucas and her son Jerry, she knew retirement was still a few years off. She had a taste for expensive cars, and her hobby—rescuing abandoned or neglected pets and getting them the care they needed until they could be resettled in loving homes—didn't come cheap. In addition, Julie was sending money to her now-grown daughter, who had been born with a heart defect and remained in fragile health. Julie's mother and daughter lived together in Cincinnati, in the same house that Julie had run away from at the age of fourteen. When she could, she also helped out her older son, Tommy, who lived in Cincinnati with his wife and four children and worked for an oil company. With all these expenses, Julie knew she hadn't saved nearly as much as she needed to retire—not yet anyway. But she had time. This was the year of the rooster, according to the Chinese zodiac, her year, Julie thought, as she set aside the tray and swung out of bed.

Two hours later, showered and dressed, Julie and her son climbed into her black Cadillac Escalade. Before they headed into Manhattan, they had to drop off Earl Grey at the vet—the old tomcat had feline AIDS and needed surgery—and run a few other errands. So it wasn't until around 3 p.m. that they drove into midtown and picked up Julie's long-time assistant, Patrina, at one of the 49th Street brothels. Patrina was a hard-working single mother from Guyana, whom Julie was training to help out in the office. She had worked as a maid at Julie's brothels for years, and even though customers occasionally asked for her—she had fine features and a curvaceous body herself—she always said no.

They parked in their usual spot at the 51st Street garage and started walking down the street to Julie's favorite Thai restaurant for a late lunch. But at the last moment, she felt a craving for shrimp mofongo, so they turned around and walked up Ninth Avenue to El San Juan, a Puerto Rican eatery. Only later would Julie realize how serendipitous her change of heart had been. The police, she later discovered, had been waiting for her at the Thai restaurant, and they would have arrested her right then and there.

When her shrimp mofongo came, Julie ate quickly, anxious to check in and see how things were going at work. But when she called the office on her cell phone, there was no answer. She looked at her watch; Lucas should have picked up. "That's weird," she said. Julie hadn't installed a landline at the 49th Street apartments for security reasons; she didn't want police tapping the phones. Instead, she punched in the number for Beverly, who lived at the 46th Street brothel and looked after that location, but there was no answer there either. Julie's heart began racing. This was beyond strange. Beverly was almost always around in the afternoon. She tried the 46th Street number again. No answer. Finally, she called home, waiting for Denora to pick up. But the phone kept ringing and ringing.

Julie threw some cash on the table and pulled on her parka. "Let's see what's going on," she said and hurried out of the restaurant, Patrina right behind her. (Jerry had left the restaurant before she started calling; he said he was going to buy a CD and would meet them at the office.) They turned down 49th Street, and the Mexican guy who owned Spoiled Brats, a tiny shop that sold stuffed animals, poked his head out the door and said casually, "There's a party going on up the street. You might want to go back." Julie could see dozens of men clustered outside the entrance to the two buildings where her apartments were.

"If we turn around now, they'll notice," Patrina whispered. "Put your hood up and keep walking." So Julie threw her hood over her head and continued walking as if she owned the street, as if what was going down at 336 and 326 49th Street was no concern of hers. As they passed by, she could see the FBI and New York Police Department logos splashed across the back of the men's jackets, and she was sure they could hear her heart thundering in her chest. But none of them even glanced her way. She and Patrina kept walking until they reached the end of the block, and then they turned the corner. Julie collapsed against a wall, breathing heavily. It looked as though the Feds and New York's finest had teamed up to raid her business. They had, no doubt, already busted into the 46th Street office and her home on Long Island, maybe even the brothel on 35th Street.

As Julie was later to discover, the New York police had not forgotten the time she had asked their help in getting the two Russian sex workers away from traffickers. Indeed, when news of the raid on Julie's brothels hit the local papers, there was speculation from police sources that she was involved with trafficking Russian virgins. The *Daily News* reported that "authorities are investigating possible links to kidnapping and human smuggling in which children were brought to Julie for the specific purpose of taking their virginity. . . . A source familiar with the case said the girls were of Russian descent."[32]

Julie Moya was never charged with trafficking, but that didn't stop the media circus. That afternoon, all she could think about was that the moment she had long dreaded had finally, irrevocably, arrived. After calling Jerry and warning him off, Julie threw her cell phone away (she knew the FBI could track her by its GPS), grabbed a cab to her bank, where she withdrew $10,000 in cash, and bought a prepaid phone. She then hid out for a few days, meeting with her lawyer and sending her mother to collect clothing and other items, whatever was left after the raid on her Long Island home. She also parceled out some of her beloved pets to friends and relatives. Her older son, Tommy, took the two aging pit bulls she had rescued from animal shelters. Julie's younger brother took Gucci, her yellow-naped Amazon parrot, and she gave the two African grey parrots to a friend of hers who had a big aviary on Long Island and sold exotic birds. There was nothing she could do about Earl Grey, who was recovering from surgery, except to hope that the vet would take care of the old tomcat.

On January 31, four days after the raid, Julie Moya walked into the 7th Precinct on the Lower East Side, her lawyer by her side, to give herself up. As she later wrote on her blog, "It was a terrible time and it only got worse. . . ."

# From Bad Laws to Bad Cops and Violence against Women

L ike Julie Moya, Elle St. Claire remembers the months before 9/11 as the calm before the storm—but for very different reasons. By the summer of 2001, Elle was living openly in Worcester, Massachusetts, as a transgender single parent, raising two sons and making a name for herself in the local community. She volunteered with a parenting group at the school her sons attended and was active in a local antipoverty organization known as the Worcester Community Connections Coalition. The Worcester County District Attorney's Office had asked her to serve on an antigay bullying committee it had set up. A few folks had even suggested that she run for a position on the Worcester City Council. While some knew that she worked in the adult entertainment industry, modeling and doing films, she didn't advertise the fact that she was an escort.

Better yet, Elle was in love. She had recently become engaged to Carmen Rudy, a young woman who, like herself, was single and raising two children. Carmen carried an outsized zest for life within her deceptively petite 5'2" frame. One of nine children born to a French Canadian mother and a Puerto Rican father, she was an attractive woman with billowy black hair—"the wild child" of the family, according to her older sister, Jackie Rudy. "Carmen was a force of nature; she was the one who would try new things out," says Jackie, who lives with her five children on the second floor of a dilapidated three-story row house in Worcester. "When she was a teenager, she started hanging out with the wrong friends, and they introduced her to heroin."

Carmen married young (at age seventeen) but became addicted to heroin after losing her brother and best friend in separate car accidents. In time, the addiction destroyed her marriage and resulted in temporary loss of custody of her son and daughter to the state. But by the time she met Elle, in the spring of 2000, Carmen, then twenty-seven, had kicked her habit and regained custody of her children.

Carmen and Elle had recently moved their blended household into Elle's cramped two-bedroom apartment on Eastern Avenue, and Elle was working hard to expand her film business so that they could afford to move into a larger place—either that or find Carmen and her children some subsidized housing nearby. "Our kids weren't getting along well and I wanted to get them separated," Elle recalls. "My apartment was a very small area and there was lots of clutter."

In September 2001, Elle attended a meeting of the Worcester Community Connections Coalition and noticed that a top official with the city's Department of Social Services (DSS) was there. She decided to ask the woman about the possibility of subsidized housing for her fiancée. The bureaucrat's response filled Elle with foreboding. "When I mentioned Carmen's name, she smirked and said [Carmen] wouldn't be needing any housing," Elle recalls. When asked why, the DSS official told Elle that Carmen was going to lose custody of her children. Elle was shocked. "For what?" she asked. "I know she's had issues in the past, but she's doing great now. She's clean and going to a methadone clinic, and she's in counseling." The woman responded, "Oh, she has a long history." She paused and then said, "Trust me, you're going to lose your kids too."

The DSS official was right. In January 2002, state officials accompanied by police picked up Carmen's ten- and twelve-year-old children at Belmont Elementary School and took them into state custody. Carmen and Elle began fighting to get them back, but three months later, while Elle was on a business trip to Los Angeles, trying to find investors for her film production business, her own two sons, then nine and eleven, were taken away the same way. DSS officials levied a string of accusations against Elle—all of them unsubstantiated and later dropped. During the protracted battle over custody, Elle's sons were bounced back and forth between their maternal and paternal grandparents and a series of foster homes. After a five-year battle, the state dropped all charges against Elle and opened the path for her to regain custody. But by then, the boys had embarked on new lives and chose to stay with their grandparents.

Elle's sons are now grown and have a close relationship with her, especially the older son, T.J., who moved back in with Elle for a time when he was eighteen. (When I met T.J. in 2010, he said he had no problems with Elle's transgender identity or her sex work, although he still refers to her as his father. "I think my dad is a wonderful parent. He's nice and easy to talk to. I can go to him about problems. If I need help with school, he helps me," T.J. said. "My dad is there for me.")

To this day, Elle believes the state's action against her and Carmen was motivated by politics and gender. "I was becoming a strong political figure in Worcester, and I believe that was the reason I was targeted," she says.

For Carmen, the loss of her children proved devastating. As both Elle and Jackie Rudy recall, Carmen slipped back into using drugs, and by August of 2002, Elle had had enough. She has a rare blood platelet disorder that causes her blood to clot and that, if left untreated, can be deadly. After being diagnosed with the condition while hospitalized the previous October, Elle had been prescribed medication to thin her blood, which she initially self-injected using hypodermic needles.

"I caught [Carmen] stealing my shots, emptying them out, and selling them to drug addicts as needles so she could raise money on the sly to get drugs herself," Elle says. "I didn't need the meds anymore; I was keeping them on hand and taking pills. The thing is that every hypothermic needle is marked and tagged, so that's how I discovered my needles were ending up on the street."

Elle confronted Carmen and ended up throwing her out. "I had tried everything I could to get her clean again, but nothing was working," she says. "It broke my heart, but I had to do it." Carmen went to live with friends, but Elle says they were in touch almost every day. Then in late September 2002, Carmen Rudy suddenly disappeared. She was twenty-nine years old. Elle knew immediately that something was wrong.

"She disappeared on a Monday, and she was supposed to give me a call that day. She didn't, and I called the house where she was staying with roommates and they said she would call me when she got back," Elle says. "Tuesday was the first day I had visitation with my children after they had been removed, and she was supposed to meet up with me in downtown Worcester and be with me and my kids. She never showed up. We had a court date on Wednesday [on the custody issue], and she never showed. I knew without a shadow of a doubt that something had happened to her."

The next day, Elle went to the police station to report Carmen as a missing person, but the police refused to take her statement or allow her to file a report. They told her that only relatives could file a missing person report. So Elle called Jackie Rudy, who had remained close to Carmen. According to Jackie, Elle drove her to the police station, where she filed a missing person report. Jackie too sensed something was wrong. Carmen, she says, never went four days without talking to her. "I gave the police a picture of Carmen, but they didn't question me about her disappearance," Rudy says. "They didn't question anyone. They didn't care."

Frustrated with the police's seeming indifference to Carmen's fate, Elle embarked on her own search for her. She knocked on doors, went to shelters and hospitals around the city, and talked to people who knew Carmen. That's when she learned that her former fiancée had been on the stroll—to earn money to feed her drug habit. Elle even put up flyers asking people to contact her if they had seen Carmen before September 25, 2002, the day she disappeared.

"I tracked her to her last movements, right when she got into a vehicle," Elle recalls. "That's when my trail went cold."

IT'S THE WEEK BEFORE Thanksgiving, and we're sitting at Elle's dining room table, which is dressed up with a green and red Christmas tablecloth and matching napkins. Elle is wearing a snug-fitting gray-flannel shirt and jeans. She's carefully made up with lipstick and eye makeup that accentuates her gray-green eyes. She sips beer from a tall Coors can and seems lost in her memories. In the weeks after Carmen went missing, she says, "I was so angry and filled with rage, I blocked out a lot."

In September 2003, a year after her disappearance, Carmen Rudy's skeletal remains were found buried in the woods behind a private boys' school in Marlboro, Massachusetts, about twenty miles northeast of Worcester. Five days later, the remains of another young woman, Betzaida Montalvo, also twenty-nine, were found a hundred yards from Carmen Rudy's grave. A reporter for the *Metro News*, which covers Marlboro and surrounding towns, interviewed John Kelly, a forensic specialist, who speculated that a serial killer might be at work. As Kelly noted, both Rudy and Montalvo fit a specific profile: they were young, single Hispanic mothers who had taken to selling sex on the streets of Worcester to feed drug habits. Despite the press coverage, however, police were reluctant to acknowledge the existence of a serial killer. In 2004, the bodies of two more young women from Worcester were discovered, one of which had been taken across the border and dumped in a trash can in York, Maine. That brought the FBI into the case, and local law enforcement finally said the S-word.

"You have to understand, if the police come out and utter these words, 'serial killer,' here comes the press, and when the press comes in, there is pressure to solve the case," says Kelly, a forensic social worker and the president of System to Apprehend Lethal Killers, or STALK, a nonprofit New Jersey–based organization that profiles suspected serial killers. "A lot of law enforcement agencies aren't interested in having that kind of pressure put on them."

Kelly and others say that many police agencies in the United States simply don't put a lot of resources into solving the murders of sex workers. "The way a lot of local law enforcement [officials] look at it, [the women] are living a high-risk lifestyle. They're out there doing drugs and selling themselves, so [violence] is all part of that game," Kelly says. "There's a double standard here. If four hookers are found dead down the street, they are not going to get the same attention as a lily-white housewife who has disappeared in suburbia. If that happens, [the police] are going to have helicopters up and dogs beating the bushes."

Sex workers have long been viewed as disposable not only by law enforcement but also by society as a whole, which often turns its back on prostitutes, particularly streetwalkers. Such official indifference may explain why prostitutes are more likely to be killed than any other set of women ever studied, according to a 2006 report published in the *Journal of Forensic Sciences*. The researchers found that sex workers were killed primarily by clients. Equally chilling, these researchers found that serial killers accounted for up to 35 percent of all prostitute homicides.[1]

A 2004 study, which tracked homicides from 1981 to 1990 and was published in the *American Journal of Epidemiology*, found that, on average, 124 sex workers were murdered each year in the United States.[2] This study concluded that the homicide rate for prostitutes in the United States is fifty-one times higher than that for the next most dangerous occupation — working in a liquor store.[3]

Conservative groups argue that prostitution itself is what causes this level of violence, but research shows that the profession is not inherently violent. A number of studies show that indoor sex workers are much less likely than streetwalkers to be targets of violence. Indeed, a 2007 British study of 135 indoor prostitutes found that 78 percent of them *never* experienced violence.[4] When a Canadian researcher surveyed thirty-nine indoor sex workers who had never worked the street, she found that the majority of women (63 percent) had not experienced any violence while working in the sex industry.[5] Similarly, in a study of 772 sex workers in New Zealand, conducted after prostitution was decriminalized in that country in 2003, the risk of violence was not perceived to be an issue among indoor sex workers, "as most had never experienced violence."[6]

Most serial killers do not target women in general; they focus on street prostitutes. Gary Ridgway, for example, was the notorious Green River killer, who admitted to killing forty-eight women (most of them streetwalkers) in Washington State and may have killed dozens more. In his statement of guilt in 2003, he said, "I picked prostitutes as victims because they were easy to pick up without being noticed. I knew they would not be reported missing right away and might never be reported missing. I picked prostitutes because I thought I could kill as many of them as I wanted without getting caught."

The sad irony is that some Seattle-area prostitutes, as well as their boyfriends and pimps, knew for years that Ridgway was the Green River killer, says Annie Sprinkle, a former prostitute and porn star who went on to earn a Ph.D. and become an internationally recognized artist and writer in San Francisco. "But they were either afraid to come forward for fear of being arrested themselves, or when they did come forward, the police didn't believe them over the 'upstanding family man,' Gary Ridgway," Sprinkle writes. "It seems as though police weren't working very hard to find the Green River killer."[7]

In her moving essay for the collection *Hos, Hookers, Call Girls and Rent Boys,* Sprinkle touches on one of the most persuasive arguments for decriminalizing prostitution: if sex workers knew they would not be arrested for calling the police, many more would come forward and work with police in targeting violent predators, who often end up killing sex workers *and* women who are not in the sex trade. According to an in-depth examination of prostitute homicides by researchers at John Jay College of Criminal Justice, men who assault prostitutes often have a record of assaulting other women as well. Violence against sex workers, the researchers concluded, is part of a continuum of violence against women in general.[8]

Indeed, researchers have found that countries with the most restrictive laws against prostitution (such as the United States and many countries in Southeast Asia) have the greatest violence against sex workers and other women, while countries with the least restrictive legal systems (such as the Netherlands and Germany) have the least violence.[9]

In the Netherlands, where sex work was decriminalized in the 1970s and has been legal since 2000, many workers in the sex industry feel that they can report crimes against them to the police. The result: an unusually low incidence of violence against sex workers, and red-light districts in Amsterdam and other cities that are safe places to walk around at all hours of the night. In a 2004 study of women working in legal brothels, clubs, and window units in the Netherlands, conducted by the Dutch Ministry of Justice, most of the women surveyed reported that they "often or always feel safe."[10]

Yet because prostitution is illegal in the United States, sex workers can't go to the police, even when they've been robbed, raped, or otherwise physically threatened. Kimora, the striking African American transsexual whom I met at HIPS in Washington, D.C., said she was robbed by a client who lured her into a downtown alley and then pulled a gun on her. "I had already made about $200 and he took all my money," she says. "What am I going to tell the police? They'd just arrest me."

Another time, Kimora says, she was brutally raped by a john near the Trinidad area of Washington, D.C., and decided to press charges. But when she went to the Fifth District police station to file a complaint, "The police officer said, 'Being you're dressed this way, you pretty much lured him,'" she says. "He wouldn't take the report."

Many streetwalkers like Kimora are actually more afraid of the police than they are of johns. She says she heard about one Washington, D.C., cop who patrolled the streets and pretended to arrest streetwalkers. "Instead he'd take the girls to an alley and rape them himself," she says. "The laws don't protect people like me."

In a phone interview, Melvin Scott, commander of the Narcotics and Special Investigations Division of the Metropolitan Police Department in Washington, D.C., said he hadn't heard of any police officers who prey on sex workers in that manner. "If that's something we found, we'd arrest the cop," Scott insists. During his thirty-three-year tenure with the department, Scott says he recalls a few instances when police officers were accused of soliciting sex from prostitutes in exchange for dropping charges. But he couldn't recall any cases in which specific criminal charges were lodged against the officers.

Columbia University sociologist Elizabeth Bernstein found a similar pattern of police misconduct when she interviewed San Francisco streetwalkers in the 1990s. A number of streetwalkers shared stories about police officers who wanted blow jobs in exchange for dropped citations or who revealed their identity as cops after sexual services had been rendered. Some streetwalkers said the police even stole money from them.[11]

Another Columbia University sociologist, Sudhir Venkatesh, studied 160 streetwalkers on the South Side of Chicago between 2005 and 2007. Of all the tricks turned by the prostitutes he surveyed, roughly 3 percent were freebies given to police officers. As Venkatesh concluded, a Chicago street prostitute is more likely to have sex with a cop than to be arrested by one.[12]

In some states, the men in blue are the biggest customers of commercial sex. In Ohio, for instance, law enforcement topped the charts of the listed occupations when it came to buying sex (indoors and outdoors), according to a 2012 report on domestic sex trafficking by Ohio's Human Trafficking Commission. Police even beat out politicians for that distinction, and it didn't matter whether or not the women were selling sex voluntarily. According to the Ohio report, law enforcement officials were the number one customers even when the women they frequented were found to have been trafficked into the trade.[13]

Then there are the cops who abuse their authority in more insidious ways. Jennifer Reed is now a Ph.D. candidate at the University of Nevada, Las Vegas, doing research for her dissertation on adolescent sex workers in Sin City. When she was a divorced single mother raising two children on her own in eastern Ohio, she danced in a strip club just over the border in Weirton, West Virginia, to make ends meet. She soon started doing sex work as well.

"Guys would pay a lot of money for fetishes, like splashing food on girls or mud wrestling. I've done a lot of two-girl shows [two women having sex], bachelor parties, birthday parties," she says matter-of-factly over lunch one day at the Desiree Alliance conference in Las Vegas. Reed, forty-three, is a tall, plainspoken woman with long brown hair and a no-nonsense manner. She is unapologetic about her past; strip dancing and doing outcalls allowed her to finish college and earn a bachelor's degree in psychology and a master's degree in sociology.

What Reed and the other working girls feared most was law enforcement. "The police would come in and solicit women for sex in order to bust them," she recalled. "They ran my [license] plate and knew where I lived."

There was one police officer on the Cuyahoga Falls, Ohio, force who kept pressuring Reed to have sex with him. When she refused, he showed up in the neighborhood where she lived and harassed her children while they played outside. "He threatened to have them arrested," she says. One day, she got calls from the middle school her son attended and the elementary school her daughter attended; the police were at both schools, searching her thirteen-year-old son and her eleven-year-old daughter for drugs.

"I went to my son's school first and talked to the principal, who was female," Reed says. "She knew my son wasn't a problem, he was a good kid, and she understood what was going on." Then Reed went to her daughter's elementary school. When she walked into the principal's office, the same cop who had pressured her for sex was there, "grinning from ear to ear." He held up a bag of what he claimed was marijuana and said he had found it in her daughter's school locker. "It turned out to be a bag of spices, and it had been planted," Reed said. "My daughter is an honors student, but the principal said my daughter would either get suspended or be sent to an alternative school."

Reed put her eleven-year-old daughter in the alternative school and sought a lawyer's advice. "He sent a cease-and-desist letter to the city, saying this is harassment," Reed said. But the attorney also advised her to get out of town. "So I pulled my kids out of school and homeschooled them until we could move," she said.

Most police officers are not like that, but the minority who harass sex workers and other vulnerable citizens tend to be habitual offenders. "They harass a lot of people; my only hope was that he messed with someone who has more power than I did. And that happened to this cop. He messed with someone who knew someone at city hall, and he got taken down," she said.

When the officer harassed Reed's children, however, her attorney said that because she was a sex worker, she had no power. "Sex workers are treated like they are not human," she says.

Norma Jean Almodovar, a former traffic cop with the Los Angeles Police Department, pretty much summed it up at the 2010 Desiree Alliance conference. "We have bad laws, and bad laws lead to bad cops," she said in her keynote speech. Almodovar left the department in 1982 after injuring her back in a traffic accident. She went on disability and decided to become a call girl. As she explained in her 1993 memoir, *Cop to Call Girl*, she felt that it was time to get paid for the sex she had been giving away all those years to her fellow officers. In 1982, she was arrested in a sting operation and served three years in prison for pandering (or recruiting someone into prostitution). In 1986, she made an unsuccessful bid for lieutenant governor of California on a platform that called for the decriminalization of prostitution. As Almodovar told the crowd at the conference, "There are good cops out there and they don't want to have to arrest prostitutes. They want to arrest people who are murdering people or raping people. But what happens when you have laws which allow police to pick and choose who they will arrest and who gets to go free? How do they make their choices? By those who cooperate with them."

## The Long Island Murders

Little wonder that in this toxic atmosphere of harassment and mistrust few American sex workers come forward when they see or experience an act of violence. That reality may have hampered the investigation into the murders of the five escorts whose bodies were discovered buried on Long Island in 2010 and 2011.

The Long Island murders received national attention. But even though several escorts had gone missing after arranging assignations with clients on Long Island as far back as 2007, police did not begin poking into the case until May of 2010. That's when a twenty-six-year-old escort named Shannon Gilbert disappeared after calling police from a house in Oak Beach, a village on the southern peninsula of Long Island near Fire Island. Gilbert was described by family and friends as a smart, engaging woman with olive skin and chestnut-brown hair streaked with blonde highlights. For much of her childhood, Gilbert had cycled in and out of the foster care system, one of four daughters of a struggling single mother in upstate New York, according to the 2013 book, *Lost Girls: An Unsolved American Mystery*, by *New York* magazine writer Robert Kolker. As soon as Shannon graduated from high school, she headed to New York City. She dreamed of becoming a famous actress. Until then, she had worked as an escort, first with a service called World-Class Party Girls and then on her own, placing ads on Craigslist.[14]

In the early-morning hours of May 1, 2010, Michael Pak, Shannon's regular driver to and from appointments, took her to a gated compound in Oak Beach and parked outside Joe Brewer's home. Brewer was a former Wall Street financier whose family has extensive real estate holdings on Long Island. Just before 5 a.m., Brewer tapped on the window of Pak's black Ford Explorer and told Pak that Shannon wouldn't leave his house. When Pak went inside with Brewer, Shannon said, "You guys are trying to kill me." Seemingly high on drugs, she crawled behind a couch. Then she started talking to someone on the phone, and Pak, fearing it was the police, ran out of Brewer's house. According to transcripts, Shannon stayed on the call with the police even as she ran out of Brewer's house and started frantically knocking on the doors of nearby dwellings, calling for help. Pak told police he followed her in the car, shouting her name. But he says he lost her and finally gave up and drove back to Manhattan.[15]

Several other people in the gated compound said they also saw Shannon running from house to house, pounding on doors and shouting for help. But when two residents told her they were going to call the police, she started running again. Even though Shannon stayed on the call with the police for twenty minutes, Kolker says the state police were unable or unwilling to trace her location. "Even though she said, 'They are trying to kill me,' they weren't able to locate her or they didn't put the effort into locating her," Kolker said in a phone interview. "The 911 response was from neighbors' calls." The local police arrived eighteen minutes after the first 911 call from a neighbor. They found no sign of Shannon.

Her disappearance, and her family's efforts to locate her, stirred up a hornet's nest of publicity. When the families of the other escorts who had gone missing also began talking to the press, the furor only intensified. The Suffolk County police began searching the area around Oak Beach, and in December 2010, they unearthed the skeletal remains of four women along Ocean Parkway (all four were wrapped in burlap bags), just three miles from Oak Beach. Using DNA, the police identified the four women as escorts who had disappeared after arranging assignations via Craigslist with clients on Long Island. At that point, the Suffolk County police acknowledged they might be dealing with a serial killer, and during the months that followed, they unearthed more remains buried along Ocean Drive, a highway that runs along the southern peninsula of Long Island and links Oak Beach with other beaches, including Jones Beach, a popular destination for many New Yorkers. Shannon Gilbert's body was not among those found.

In 2011, Suffolk County drained a thickly overgrown and mosquito-infested marsh behind the compound on Oak Beach, and police started searching the marsh. In December, they finally found Gilbert's body. First, they stumbled upon her purse, then her cell phone, shoes, and a torn pair of jeans. On December 18, on the far side of the marsh, not far from where the bodies of the other women had been found, they discovered her skeletal remains. Even then, Suffolk County Commissioner Richard Dormer insisted that Shannon had drowned or died of natural causes.[16]

His claim prompted other forensic experts, such as former New York Chief Medical Examiner Dr. Michael Baden, to state that Gilbert clearly had been killed, just like the other escorts before her. Baden told reporters that it was absurd to think that a woman who weighed not much more than a hundred pounds could thrash her way through a marsh that the police were afraid to walk into. "The circumstances are very impressive that the mother is right and she was murdered," Baden said.[17]

Kolker, who interviewed many police officers and forensic experts for his book, agrees. "Why would Shannon call 911 in the first place, which is something an escort would never do," he says. "Why would she knock on strangers' doors and run away from her driver? Why would she stay on the phone with the police for twenty minutes? All of this indicates she was in fear of her life."

The case, however, remains unsolved to this day. Rumors within the sex work community offer one speculative explanation: that an ex-cop is one of the possible suspects. (In his book, Kolker mentions a former Suffolk County cop who lived in Oak Beach and was a friend and neighbor of Dr. Peter Hackett, an Oak Beach resident whom police questioned because he had lied about calling Shannon's mother shortly after she disappeared.) A number of amateur Internet sleuths and several residents of the Oak Beach compound where Gilbert was last seen offer another theory: that she and four other escorts were killed by Hackett as part of a conspiracy involving Brewer and perhaps other residents of the compound as well. After several months of denying that he had called Shannon's mother a few days after she disappeared and offered to help search for her daughter, Hackett reversed himself. In an interview with the TV show *48 Hours Mystery* in July 2011, he acknowledged that he had called Shannon's mother a few days after her daughter disappeared. (Gilbert's mother has the cell-phone records to prove that Hackett called her.) According to this theory, which Kolker lays out in some detail in his book, Hackett, whose house backs up to the marsh, could have killed Gilbert and the other escorts and kept their bodies in his shed. But then, tipped off to the police search by his ex-cop neighbor, he could have moved their bodies to shallow graves along Ocean Parkway. These amateur sleuths also argued that Hackett, who was a member of the Oak Beach neighborhood association, could have been the person who erased the security video taken by the automatic camera that is always mounted on the entrance to the gated compound.[18]

Hackett has since moved to Florida, and the Suffolk County police have yet to name any suspects in the case. Kolker and others believe that the unsolved mystery has a lot to do with the fact that the victims were sex workers and therefore disposable.

"If this was the daughter of a judge or Son of Sam killing middle-class women, it would be a different story," Kolker says. "One of the big takeaways is that if you're a sex worker and you're in trouble and you call 911 and say someone is trying to kill you, they won't give a shit. And if you do disappear, they'll say you're not one of the victims. And even when your body is found, they'll say you died of fright. We're dealing with very retrograde views of women and prostitution here."

Such retrograde views no doubt hampered the investigation. In 2011, after the first four bodies were found and the news media swarmed the case, Commissioner Dormer rushed to reassure reporters. No sex worker who had volunteered information on the case, he said, had been charged with a crime.[19] But he refused to give sex workers blanket amnesty in exchange for their cooperation. That refusal and the entrenched bias against prostitutes may help explain why the case remains unsolved. The Long Island serial killer is still out there, no doubt laughing at law enforcement's ineptitude.

## The Main Street Woodsman

Even though the serial killings in Massachusetts didn't grab the same attention that the Long Island killings did, the police inquiry into who murdered Carmen Rudy and the other Worcester streetwalkers yielded better results. In 2007, four years after Carmen's body had been discovered in the woods near Marlboro, the skeletal remains of a fifth sex worker from Worcester were found on land abutting a central Massachusetts state park. Shortly afterward, forensic specialists from the New Jersey–based STALK released a profile of the possible killer. (Besides John Kelly, the forensics team included a former chief of criminal investigations for the Seattle sheriff's office, a psychologist, an addictions specialist, and a psychiatric nurse.) The profilers said the serial killer was probably a construction worker or truck driver between the ages of twenty-eight and forty-one years who drove a pickup truck or SUV and liked to hunt and fish. They dubbed him "the Main Street Woodsman" because all his victims had strolled Worcester's Main Street and because the killer was clearly comfortable in the woods (most of his victims were buried there).

A few months later, police homed in on a man who had recently been arrested and jailed for allegedly raping and trying to strangle a woman, who was *not* a sex worker, in a West Boylston motel. The man, Alex Scesny, a thirty-eight-year-old construction worker who drove a white pickup truck, had a criminal record of assaulting women. His parents (and he himself at one point) lived very close to where Rudy's body was found. The real break came when DNA found on the rape victim matched DNA recovered in 1996 from the body of a thirty-nine-year-old woman who had been strangled to death in Fitchburg, Massachusetts, twenty-four miles north of West Boylston. That victim, Theresa Stone, was known to have been a sex worker.[20]

In September 2008, Scesny was convicted of assault and battery against the woman he had attacked in the West Boylston motel. The same day, police charged him with Stone's murder. Four years later, after an extended legal battle, Scesny was convicted in the 1996 rape and murder of Theresa Stone and sentenced to life without parole.[21] While police were unable to tie him to the other murders, John Kelly, president of STALK, told local reporters that Scesny was a "significant person of interest" in the deaths of Carmen Rudy and the four other young women who had walked the streets of Worcester.[22]

This is of little comfort to Elle St. Claire and Jackie Rudy. While Scesny may remain behind bars for the rest of his life, the sad reality is that Carmen Rudy's friends and family will never know for sure who took the life of their flawed but beautiful "wild child."

# Busted in Sin City

NEVADA'S TWO-FACED APPROACH TO SEX WORK

The Great Recession hit Anna and her husband hard. They had recently purchased a house in South Florida, and when the automotive company she worked for went bankrupt, Anna lost her job. Her husband was in graduate school and couldn't help out much. "I still had $50,000 in student loans to pay off and a mortgage," she says. "The economy was so bad, I couldn't even get a job at Wendy's."

Anna had seen the HBO series on the Moonlite Bunny Ranch in Nevada and was intrigued by the idea of getting paid to do something she already enjoyed. "One night, I said to my husband, 'If they're having that much fun and making that money, maybe it's something I should look into,'" she recalls. She and her husband had been together since college, and they often enjoyed recreational sex with other couples. "Being swingers, sex was never something that we attached to love," Anna says. "So I figured I might as well get paid for doing it."

Her husband was supportive of the idea. "He actually finds it exciting," she says. "It turns him on a bit." So Anna, who was then twenty-seven, did some research online and discovered that Sheri's Ranch, one of Nevada's largest and most upscale brothels, garnered the best reviews from women in the trade. She sent the brothel a brief bio and pictures of herself; Sheri's Ranch management liked what they saw and hired her in 2009.

"The first time I came here, I felt like I was on vacation. I didn't have to cook for two weeks, and I could lay out by the pool," Anna says.

I met Anna the day I drove out to Sheri's Ranch, which sits in the dusty desert town of Pahrump, an hour west of Las Vegas. She had been asked by the madam to give me the grand tour.

Anna (her brothel name) is pretty, with radiantly clear skin, a sweet smile, and long, witch-black hair. She is dressed in a short, low-cut cocktail dress that hugs her butt and shows off her figure. Yet her legs are not particularly toned and she is not big-breasted. What catches your attention are her eyes, dark green and strikingly luminous. She exhibits a sweet perkiness reminiscent of the girl next door.

Indeed, Anna *is* the girl next door. She grew up in a middle-class home in a suburb of Philadelphia. Although her father is an engineer and her mother a beautician, she comes from a large family and her parents weren't able to contribute much to her college education. So she took out substantial loans to pay the tuition at a private liberal arts college in New York, from which she graduated with double majors in communication studies and psychology.

For the past four years, she has been working at Sheri's Ranch, two weeks on and one week off. In the beginning, she commuted between Florida and Las Vegas; she was picked up at the airport in Las Vegas and transported to Pahrump via the brothel's free limousine service for customers and workers. After a few months, her husband came to live with her in Las Vegas and transferred to the University of Nevada. They rented out their house in Florida.

Her family, she says, has no idea what she does for a living. "The misconceptions [about sex work] are so numerous, they wouldn't understand," she says. "The public thinks we're all uneducated drug addicts, and that's not true."

At Sheri's Ranch, each woman works a five-day-a-week shift. For the first two days, the women are on call for twenty-four hours, and then, for the duration of their shift, they are on call for twelve hours, Anna says. She sees an average of two or three customers a day, although there are also days when she sees no one.

"I'm going to be on the lower end of what most girls make because I'm pretty picky," Anna says. "I might have one or two big parties versus lots of little ones. My parties generally last a couple of hours to all night. It's more of a girlfriend experience than slam bang, thank you, ma'am." Even so, Anna clears between $2,500 and $5,000 a week in take-home pay. She has already paid off the bulk of her student loans.

"I wish I'd known about [Sheri's Ranch] sooner, I could have made more money," Anna says, as she shows me a room that she calls the "formal dining room," where "a gentleman can take us out to dinner and clothing is optional." In the center of the room is a small, oval table draped with an elegant tablecloth and set for two; a still-life hangs on the wall behind the table, and two brass light fixtures on the mantelpiece complete the Victorian parlor effect.

Anna smiles sweetly. "If he wants a blow job under the table, there is a kneeling pillow and a splatter platter," she says and then adds, "although now that everyone has to wear condoms, there's no splatter."

Mandatory condoms are one of the non-negotiable rules at Sheri's Ranch and indeed at all of Nevada's legal brothels. The women who work in the state's brothels also must get tested for sexually transmitted diseases every month; they can't get a license to work without clean test results. Since that law went into effect during the AIDS scare in the 1980s, no brothel worker has tested positive for HIV.[1] (Nevada state law has required condoms in the brothels since 1988.[2])

"What draws customers here is that they know they're not going to bring something home with them," says Chuck Lee, a Las Vegas businessman who has co-owned Sheri's Ranch since 2001. In fact, the major drawing card for Nevada's brothels is the safe environment they offer—for both clients and sex workers. While Sheri's Ranch is more opulent than the Chicken Ranch (the brothel next door whose name was made famous by the movie, *The Best Little Whorehouse in Texas*), its focus on safety is shared by the state's other brothels. Nevada is the one state in the United States that has officially legalized prostitution, but only within the confines of heavily regulated brothels restricted to sparsely populated counties well outside resort areas such as Las Vegas and Reno.

Contrary to what many visitors believe, all other forms of prostitution remain illegal in Nevada, even on Las Vegas's gaudy Strip, where scantily clad women pose for pictures with tourists and Mexican immigrants hand out cards advertising "hotassescorts" and free admission to the city's many strip clubs. Sex is everywhere in Sin City, and it is a big part of the resort's draw for traveling businessmen and tourists. According to the sex workers I interviewed, the casinos usually look the other way when elegantly dressed escorts pick up men at the casino bars and night-clubs. The yellow pages in every hotel room contain pages and pages of escort service ads for "Barely legal flawless thin and busty blonde" or "Beautiful soccer mom to your room, busty, slim, discreet."

Despite the carefully cultivated atmosphere that anything goes in Las Vegas, the city spends a lot of money enforcing its laws against prosti-tution. Like other local police departments, the Las Vegas Police De-partment receives funding from the U.S. government's antitrafficking task force. In 2012 and 2013, for instance, the department was awarded a million dollars from the Department of Justice for "antitrafficking," according to a University of Nevada researcher. But police use the yellow pages and online ads not to go after traffickers but to entrap the many sex workers who are working in Las Vegas by choice, sex workers and researchers say. The vast majority of sex workers arrested in Sin City are not trafficking victims, although once in custody, some claim they are victims to avoid prosecution.

Under the new antitrafficking laws, "police have to ask [the sex work-ers they arrest], 'Are you a trafficking victim?'" says Jennifer Reed, who is involved in a multisite study of Las Vegas sex workers as part of her Ph.D. dissertation in psychology for the University of Nevada, Las Vegas. "And so some say they're trafficked so they won't get put in jail. And, of course, that inflates the [trafficking] statistics." Las Vegas police are so vigilant about prostitution that they recently stopped two young African American sisters (who were in Sin City on vacation) when the women tried to hail a cab to take them home from a nightclub one night. "They thought we were prostitutes," said one of the sisters, both profes-sionals, who were eating at the same Bavarian restaurant as I was that evening. Such harassment is hardly an isolated incident in Las Vegas, many say. "The police target minorities," Reed says.

They also target anyone who is out late at night wearing provocative clothing. Cris Sardina, a fifty-three-year-old grandmother and former sex worker from Arizona who was in Las Vegas in July 2013 for the fifth annual Desiree Alliance conference, was arrested with a friend for jaywalking while walking back to their hotel late one evening. Her friend, an African American woman from Washington, D.C., who was attending the same conference (and is not a sex worker), refused to pay for the jaywalking ticket and kept asking why she was being ticketed. So police handcuffed her and took her to the local jail, where she had to spend the night. (She was released the next morning with no charges.) Sardina, who needed to be at the conference the next morning (as one of the co-organizers), decided to pay the fine so she wouldn't get hauled off to jail too.

"The Vegas cops knew we were in town and they treated us like dogs," Sardina said. "The cop practically begged me to come after him so he could use his violence on me, but I couldn't afford to go to jail."

Reed says that what sex workers in Las Vegas complain about most is harassment from police officers demanding sex from them. "They say, 'If you service me, I won't bust you,'" Reed says. "But then you have to continue servicing that officer to stay out of jail." The Las Vegas police declined repeated requests for interviews.

To many researchers and advocates, the bifurcation of Nevada's prostitution laws is hypocritical and discriminatory. Most of the legal brothels are owned by businessmen with close ties to the state's political infrastructure, according to Barbara Brents, the sociology professor at the University of Nevada, Las Vegas. Chuck Lee, the co-owner of Sheri's Ranch and a former homicide detective from Chicago, for example, was the chief investigator for the district attorney in Clark County (which envelops Las Vegas and its exurbs). Lee owned several successful car dealerships before he bought into Sheri's Ranch. The brothels are quite profitable for their owners, most of whom are male. (Of the eighteen brothels currently in operation, only two have female owners, Reed says.) The owners receive 50 percent of the sex workers' earnings.

The women who work at the brothels are required to pay room and board and various licensing fees, and at many of the brothels, including

Sheri's Ranch and the Chicken Ranch, they must work shifts that usually run two to three weeks long.

At Sheri's Ranch, sex workers can leave the premises for only four hours on one designated day a week to run errands and do their banking in Pahrump. Lee insisted that such restrictions are mandated by Nye County regulations. However, Brents says she has never seen anything in the Nye County code that stipulates that women can leave the brothel only once a week for a few hours. "I think it's [the owners'] interpretation of what the county says they'll tolerate," Brents said in an interview. "I don't think it's written in the code."

Some of the brothels in northern Nevada, outside Reno, do allow sex workers to leave after their daily shifts. And they do not require the twenty-four-hour on-call shifts that Sheri's Ranch does, Brents says. But all the sex workers must also sign a contract stipulating that they cannot ply their trade outside the brothel walls.[3]

Anna says she doesn't mind the restrictions—in fact, she chose to work at Sheri's Ranch because it was a "lockdown" facility and she felt safer knowing that customers couldn't get in (without permission) and workers couldn't slip out. However, she acknowledges, "Sometimes I feel stir-crazy, so [on her designated day out], I put on my jeans and T-shirt and go to Walmart."

Many sex workers, however, chafe at the brothels' restrictions and at having to share so much of their hard-earned wages with management. "You don't have the ability to be independent and call your own shots," Reed says.

She and others note that the women working at Nevada's brothels have few legal rights. They are hired as contractors, not employees, which means the brothels don't have to pay for their health care or any other benefits.[4] That also makes it easier for management to fire women who cause trouble or don't earn their keep. Many sex workers are adamantly opposed to laws that might legalize prostitution per Nevada's brothel model. Sociologists who study the industry agree that Nevada's institutionalized brothel model wouldn't work in urban areas, mainly because many sex workers value their independence and the flexibility it gives them.

"Just exporting the brothel model to other cities and then cracking down on escorts, that won't work," Brents says. "You'd still have the illegal prostitution you had before. In the most successful [government-legislated] models [for prostitution], like New South Wales in Australia and New Zealand, they allow both independent escorts and brothels."

The irony is that Nevada's approach to prostitution was not always so paternalistic. The state's history of tolerating, indeed welcoming, ladies of the night stretches back into the mid-nineteenth century, before Nevada had even achieved statehood. As the stories of Molly b'Dam and Veronica Baldwin in Chapter 2 illustrate, many women worked as prostitutes and brothel owners in the booming mining towns of the Old West—not only in Nevada but also in other western states such as Colorado, Wyoming, Idaho, and Montana.[5] There were many more men than women in the sparsely populated West, and women who sold sex and ran saloons earned a certain status, even respectability, among the mostly male residents.

Indeed, at least part of the reason that Nevada carved itself out of the Utah territory in 1861 was the Mormon Church's attempt to impose moral constraints on the mining towns, according to Brents and her coauthors in *The State of Sex*.[6] Even when the feds cracked down on prostitution throughout the country on the eve of World War I, local officials in Nevada resisted the purge. While the storied red-light districts in Chicago, New Orleans, San Francisco, and Denver were shuttered, a number of brothels located on the outskirts of mining towns and small supply towns such as Las Vegas and Reno remained open.

In 1919, Prohibition succeeded in closing saloons throughout the state, but the brothels remained open. In fact, Brents and her coauthors argue that while Prohibition squeezed out the women who worked independently as prostitutes and saloon-keepers, it actually helped to cement the power of Nevada's brothels, which plied customers with bootleg alcohol as well as pretty women. After Prohibition ended, it was Nevada's brothels, along with the rise of gambling and the nation's fascination with the bygone days of the "Wild West," that played a key role in creating that state's tourism industry.[7]

During the 1920s and 1930s, prostitution continued to flourish openly in Nevada's urban and rural areas. But with World War II looming, Congress passed the May Act in 1941, prohibiting prostitution within a reasonable distance of military and naval bases.[8] The Nevada state attorney general closed Reno's red-light district, an area of town known as the Reno Stockade, and the state's small rural brothels went underground, serving civilians and soldiers stationed in Nevada on the sly. After the war, the politically connected men who owned the casinos in Las Vegas and Reno decided that prostitution would impede their efforts to market their cities as glamorous destinations for gambling and leisure. By 1947, gaming had surpassed mining as the state's number one industry, and as Brent and her coauthors note, "The casino industry sacrificed open prostitution to make gaming look legitimate."[9] The last openly operated brothel in Las Vegas closed its doors in the mid-1950s, and the only brothels that stayed open were hidden in rural areas, at least a half-hour's drive from Las Vegas or Reno.

In 1971, Nevada's casino interests lobbied the state legislature to ban all brothels, but their efforts backfired. Rural legislators fought the ban —after all, county coffers benefited mightily from brothel licensing fees—and in 1971, a compromise bill was passed, which allowed brothels only in counties with a population of fewer than 200,000 people. In 1980, Nevada's supreme court ruled that counties with fewer than 400,000 residents could regulate and license brothels.[10]

By the 1990s, Nevada's larger brothels were on their way to becoming corporate-run businesses, increasingly operated by businessmen who came from outside the sex industry.[11] The rules governing Nevada's brothels were (and still are) mostly implemented by city and county officials. These locally elected officials have the power to inspect brothels in their jurisdiction whenever they choose, and they hold absolute sway over decisions about who can get a brothel license and whether it can be revoked. Consequently, it is difficult for outsiders who don't have political connections in the state to operate brothels. At one point, Julie Moya, the Manhattan madam, considered moving to Nevada and opening up a legitimate brothel. But she says she was told she would never get a license there—she didn't have the right political connections.

Like Chuck Lee, Dennis Hof, who owns the Moonlite Bunny Ranch and another brothel near Reno, and Joe Richards, who used to own the Chicken Ranch, many of the businessmen who own brothels not only have an in with the powerful county commissioners who govern the brothels in their rural fiefdoms but also have become respected members of those communities. They donate equipment to firefighters, money to charities, even uniforms for Little League teams in their respective locales.[12]

The same, however, does not hold true for the sex workers themselves. Like Anna, the vast majority of these women don't live in the communities in which they work—many come from out of state—and their involvement in the community outside the brothel gates is restricted. Some counties even require brothel workers to leave the county when they are not working.[13]

Nevertheless, conditions at most of the brothels today are better than they used to be. In 1991, a nineteen-year-old single mother who now goes by the professional name of Joi Love went to work at the Old Bridge Ranch outside Reno, Nevada. Joi had enlisted in the Air Force right out of high school, met a handsome airman, and gave birth to a girl two years later, in April 1991. A few months later, she was dancing on the side at a Sacramento strip club when she overheard some of the other girls talking about how much money they made at Old Bridge. Her mother agreed to watch the baby, and Joi drove to Old Bridge, a brothel twenty minutes outside Reno. She returned home a few weeks later with $5,000 in cash.

This wasn't the first time Joi had sold sex. In one sense, she says, she has been doing it all her life. A beautiful woman, slender, with full breasts and smooth ebony skin (she's biracial), Joi says she has always used sex to get what she wanted. "When I was a teenager and I wanted to go to a party on the other side of town, I'd sleep with someone who was going to the party," she says. After she joined the Air Force, at the age of seventeen, Joi was stationed near Seattle and remembers going with a friend to a bachelor's party. The two women stripped and had sex with several men at the party—for pay. "I slept with my sergeant to get out of a work detail," she says. "Getting paid for sex is no different."

Joi didn't like the restrictions at Old Bridge; she and the other sex workers were not even allowed to leave the premises during their nine- to ten-day shifts. The health professionals who checked them regularly for venereal disease came to the ranch, as did vendors hawking wares the women might be interested in, such as cosmetics, hair products, and lingerie. But she did appreciate the tight security and the fact that everyone was "on their best behavior."

"There is so much security at the brothels, you can't get away with anything," she says. "You're locked in there along with the girls, and if you act the ass, you're in big trouble. The bouncers, the bartenders, the chefs, the manager, and all of the girls—everyone is on the girl's side. So [the customer] can't step on somebody's toes."

Joi remembers one occasion while she was working at Old Bridge Ranch. A twenty-four-year-old geek from Sacramento had hit the jackpot while playing blackjack at one of the Reno casinos, and he came to Old Bridge to party. He hung out at the bar for a while, and Joi went up and started talking to him, so he chose her and two other girls and paid $1,000 for each girl to leave the brothel and come back with him to his Reno hotel to party. (Outcalls are allowed by law in Storey County, where Old Bridge is located, but not at Sheri's Ranch or the Chicken Ranch because of different regulations in Nye County, where these two brothels are located.)

For Joi, the evening did not end well. She and the other girls accompanied their newly flush client back to his lavish suite at the hotel and started drinking and dancing to music. But then, she says, one of the other girls wanted to have sex with her, even though the customer wasn't pressing for it. "He wasn't even going there and she was putting it into his head," she says. "It felt like a pressure tactic and I didn't like it." An argument ensued, and Joi was sent back to Old Bridge.

The brothel's management, she says, was furious at her for causing a ruckus. "They can be pretty nasty. It's kind of like a mob mentality. Once one person is angry at you, they have everyone treating you really bad," she says. "One minute you're being squired around in a limousine, the next moment you can't even get a cab to leave the place." Joi left Old Bridge a few days later and never went back.

Four years later, married and the mother of two daughters, Joi was living in Petersburg, Virginia. But money was once again tight. Her husband had been kicked out of the Navy for lending an underage sailor his ID so the young man could buy liquor. Her mother, who had brought her two younger children to live with Joi and her family, was ringing up burgers at a nearby McDonald's. Joi could have done the same but she wanted more — for herself and her family. So she made a deal with her husband — she would go back to Nevada and work in a brothel, if he would take care of the children. This time, she chose the Chicken Ranch, whose famous name was transplanted from Texas to Nevada in 1973, two years after brothels were legalized there. At the time, Joi says, the Chicken Ranch was considered a more upscale brothel than many of the others, including Old Bridge. "The whole environment was more like a resort and spa," she recalls.

Today, the Chicken Ranch seems like a down-at-the-heels remnant of its former glory, particularly when compared with the much grander Sheri's Ranch, a stone's throw down the road. The brightly painted façade of the Chicken Ranch resembles the Disneyland version of a Texas ranch, but slightly before noon one sweltering July day, there are no cars or trucks parked outside and the supposedly locked gate stands ajar, propped open by a stone. Inside, the empty Longhorn bar is much smaller than the bar at Sheri's Ranch, and the entire space feels forlorn, as if time has passed it by. Judy, the current madam at the Chicken Ranch (she asked to be identified by her first name only), gives me a quick tour of the premises. We start in the lounge where the lineup takes place and then walk down a hallway with a low ceiling to a small lounge with a TV set. Sequined stiletto sandals line the wall, waiting for their owners to step into them and become some man's fantasy.

"That's the cat room where the ladies hang out," Judy says. "They have access twenty-four hours a day to the kitchen and cat room." She shows me the dining area and country-style kitchen, a spacious, well-lit space lined with windows. "They have their meals cooked for them," Judy explains. "Lunch is at noon, dinner at 5 p.m."

On the morning of my visit, I see only one sex worker up and about, rummaging through the refrigerator, who appears to be in her midtwenties and is beautiful, blonde, and busty. She regards me with friendly curiosity and says, "Hi." Judy, however, has made it clear that I am not to talk to specific workers without prior permission, so we move on. She shows me a room with a hot tub and a pole for strip dancing, "where customers can party."

"Our clients come from Germany, Alaska, Canada, all over the United States," she says. The sex workers also hail from all over: Florida, New York, Hawaii, California, Panama, Tennessee. At both the Chicken Ranch and Sheri's Ranch, the women range in experience from seasoned escorts, porn stars (who are a big draw because of their films), and erotic dancers to young women, like Anna, who have never worked in the trade before.

While working at the Chicken Ranch in the '90s, Joi says she "dated" an NBA basketball player (now playing with the San Antonio Spurs). Joi also partied (sex workers call the process of selling sex "partying") with a number of well-known musicians and rap stars, judges, defense attorneys, and a smattering of Fortune 500 CEOs. Many of Joi's customers were older men. They had been married a long time, and their wives weren't into sex any more, she says. Or the men were bored with the sex they were having and craved variety. Many of her clients requested sexual intimacies that they were afraid to request from their wives. "They might say, 'I want you to put a finger in my butt,'" Joi says. "Some wives don't want to hear that." Or they'd tell her secrets they wouldn't tell their wives, such as the fact that they like to wear high heels in private or that a son from a previous marriage was hooked on heroin. "The wives don't want to know, so they tell me," Joi says. "A good prostitute is paid to keep secrets."

Joi says she never saw any women who were being coerced into prostitution when she worked in Nevada. "If the girls were there, they wanted to be there," she says. Working in the brothels, after all, "was a safer, more lucrative environment" than working the Las Vegas Strip, she says.

At the Chicken Ranch, some of the women didn't get along—there was jealousy and fighting over petty things such as who was favored by management. But many of the women got along just fine. Joi remembers one woman who called herself Dallas because that's where she was from: Dallas, Texas. She was about sixty, the oldest worker there, "a big-breasted blonde who was just a good person, funny, entertaining, pretty," Joi recalls. "She was good at what she did." Dallas taught the twenty-three-year-old novice a lot about how to live. "She always said, 'Kick ass and take names,'" Joi recalls. "Meaning utilize what you have, don't worry about your age, or what anyone else thinks. If you're happy with you, you'll be successful. To this day, I still live by what she taught me."

Dallas's wisdom helped Joi deal with the daily stress of the lineup. When the bell rang to announce the arrival of a customer, all the women on shift at the time—between ten and twenty—would stand in a lineup for the customer's inspection. The women could introduce themselves —their names and a quick "Hi"—but they weren't allowed to say or do much else. The customer would pick a lady solely on the basis of looks and what he was in the mood for that day. Customers who were too nervous or couldn't make up their minds could go to the bar and have a drink. At that point, the women could go up and engage them in conversation. Joi was good at conversation, so she usually did better at the bar than in the lineup. Sometimes the women worked the bar in pairs; Joi would go up and talk to the customer, see what he wanted, did he like black or white girls, and then if the answer was a white girl, she would send in her friend. "We were just trying to get him to spend his money," she says.

Once the man made his choice, the two might take a tour of the facilities—to see the hot tub, the dungeon, and other specialty attractions the brothel offered. Then they would go to the woman's room, where they negotiated the sexual activities desired and the rate. Once there was agreement on the rate, the customer paid up—cash or credit, please—and the girls took the money or card to the front desk. The brothel managers made a practice of listening in on the negotiations, according to Joi, so they knew exactly what was agreed to, and while managers insisted they then turned off the intercom, Joi says she wouldn't put it past them to continue listening in.

"[The managers] seem all friendly—we're here for you and all that —but as soon as you do something wrong, drinking on duty or drugs, they're mean," she says. "'You got to go, you fucking whore, you're not clean.'"

Joi says drug use was rampant at Old Bridge while she was working there. "There was a heavy biker influence in Reno," she says. "They had the Hell's Angels; they ran a lot of drugs and women through there."

Joi says she herself didn't use drugs while working in Nevada. "That's just not my thing," she says. The only child of a black preacher's son and a white woman of French ancestry, Joi grew up in Sacramento watching her parents get drunk and smoke crack, and she vowed to do things differently. "My dad used to beat on my mom," she says. "They were always fighting and he was an abusive guy." She says her father never laid a finger on her—he took it all out on her mother. "She left him when I was five, but then they got back together for my sake," she says.

When Joi was in sixth grade, she came home from school to find her mother bruised and bleeding from yet another beating. Her father had disappeared—"probably down to the liquor store," she says, so Joi took her mother by the hand, and together they crawled through an overgrown field near her house to a pay phone, which Joi used to call the police. The police took them both to a battered women's shelter in Sacramento. A few months later, Joi went back to live with her father because, as she says, "I didn't like it [at the shelter]; I was on the dance and baton team at school and I missed that. So I went back to my dad. I mean, in my neighborhood, everyone's dad was a drunk. It wasn't something to be ashamed of."

When she was fourteen or fifteen, Joi says, her mother's father would French-kiss her and try to fondle her. "He tried to make out like it was his French background," she says with disdain. Joi herself started having sex with older men when she was fourteen. "I was a wild child," she says. "No one forced me to do it. But I think it's abusive for twenty-two-year-old men to have sex with fourteen-year-old girls."

After her childhood, Joi found life working in the brothels pretty tame. For each of the two months she spent at the Chicken Ranch, she cleared $14,000. She didn't enjoy sharing her earnings with management, but she did like the feeling that she was safe inside the brothel walls. "I knew I wasn't going to be harassed," she says.

Joi, who is now an independent sex worker running her own escort service, says there is still drug use among women working in and outside the brothels in Nevada. "I still keep up with things, and from what I'm seeing, they have a heroin problem really bad in Reno. Heroin and meth are kind of taking over," she says.

At Sheri's Ranch, however, management says it has zero tolerance for illegal drugs. "The girls know that drugs are totally illegal at the ranch; their luggage is subject to be searched when they come to the ranch," owner Chuck Lee says. "And we check the entire premises with trained dogs," including the women's private rooms. Their alcohol intake is also restricted. According to Anna, she and the other ladies are allowed six drinks a day, one per hour. And that's fine with her. "That helps keep us sharp and not make silly decisions while we're negotiating," she says.

If management does find drugs in the workers' rooms or luggage, they are asked to leave, says the madam at Sheri's Ranch, a plump, maternal-looking woman in her forties who wished to be identified by her first name only: Dena. "Some brothels are more tolerant," Dena says. "I know we lose certain girls because we are so strict about it. But we don't want them here anyway."

Dena first came to Sheri's Ranch on a tour with her then mother-in-law, who was a member of a senior women's group called the Red Hats. Dena had been working in the Las Vegas casinos and was a stay-at-home mother at the time. But she seemed so curious about life at the brothel that the general manager asked if she would like to work there part-time as a hostess.

"It eventually evolved into a full-time job," Dena says. The job of a hostess is to chat up the customers who walk in the door and see what they'd like. Some have already been corresponding by email with a specific woman (the women's work emails are posted with their profiles on the Sheri's Ranch website), so they will ask for her directly. Other customers might venture into the dimly lit bar, where they can sit and drink with several of the ladies and make their choice that way. And still others prefer the old-fashioned ritual of the lineup.

The day I was at Sheri's Ranch, a twenty-something couple dressed casually in jeans and T-shirts strolled in, the woman hanging nervously onto her partner's arm. Dena greeted them in the bar and later told me they asked for a lineup. "Threesomes are one of our specialties. Usually, there's a lot of correspondence between couples and a particular woman, but this is a very young couple and they may not have known they could do that," she says. "They wanted to base their decision off visuals. They've done this before; they're from Iceland."

The lineup takes place in the main lounge at Sheri's Ranch, a large, elegant room with high ceilings, ornate light-yellow couches, and a wall of windows open to the pool and waterfall in the backyard. Several large paintings of Rubenesque nudes adorn the walls, and a black baby grand piano sits in one corner of the lounge, right next to a mounted poster explaining the services that Sheri's offers, everything from a "straight lay" to a drag party and a ménage à trois.

The lineup for the Icelanders occurred while I was having lunch with Dena and two other staff members in a red-leather booth in the bar. Several of the scantily dressed ladies who had been sitting in the bar began strolling out into the main lounge, although I didn't really take note until the music was turned off and the bar grew very quiet. When I asked if I could take a peek at the lineup, Jeremy Lemur, the spokesman for Sheri's Ranch, who had arranged my visit, said it was fine. But when I approached the curtain, a tanned security guard playfully barred my way. Dena shook her head and put a finger to her lips. She later explained why she didn't want me peeking: "It's a couple, and they were nervous."

During lineups, the bar music is routinely turned off so customers can hear each woman introduce herself. Just as they did in Joi's days at Old Bridge and the Chicken Ranch, the women in the lineup step forward and are permitted only to say "Hi" and give their names before returning to the line; they have to rely on eye contact and smiles to convey the rest. According to Lemur, Sheri's Ranch usually has twenty women in the house each day, and all of them have to come to the lineup, unless they are already with a customer. "But today it's a small lineup—only eleven women," he said and shrugged. "A lot of the ladies are on vacation."

Several times during lunch, Dena was approached by a tall, model-gorgeous woman with platinum blond hair and a short black dress that showed off her cleavage to advantage. The woman looked very young and seemed upset by something. Dena excused herself for a few minutes, and when she came back, she said, "You become their mom, their confidante, everyone goes through bouts of insecurity and depression. Having a good support system is very important."

Dena, who has six of her own children, the youngest age three at the time, did not want to discuss the private problems that the girls bring to her every day. But she did say that she had one newly arrived woman who had never done sex work before. "I will connect her with individual girls who can help her along," she says.

Anna says she was given the same tutelage when she arrived with no experience in the trade. "You're set up with a Big Sister, and she teaches you the ropes," she says. "I was very nervous about my first party. I felt like I was fumbling through the negotiation process. But then it was fine, and I felt much better afterwards."

At every brothel, it's up to the woman to set the price for her services. After she has given the customer a tour of the facilities (which gives her a chance to find out where the man is from, what he's looking for, and what his financial situation is), she takes him back to her room to negotiate. "When I get a gentleman in my room, I ask what he's interested in doing today, how long he is interested in doing that, and what budget he is working with," Anna says. The customer's occupation and income don't always factor into what he's willing to pay. "One customer might be a doctor and drive a Corvette and then he offers you below house minimum," she says.

Anna says she and her client come to an agreement over price and services 75 percent of the time. The other 25 percent of the time, she lets the hostess know they couldn't come to an agreement. "If he's way off [in terms of price], the hostess will explain to him that it isn't going to work," Anna says. "But if he's not that far off, she'll find somebody who is more in his price range than I am. And if he wants something that I don't do, she'll find someone who will do that." Anna, for instance, says she doesn't do anal sex, domination parties, or foot fetishes. "That's not my personality," she says. "But we have girls here who are trained in domination [they are known as dominatrix] and they have their own whips and paddles."

Like Sheri's Ranch, most of the brothels prominently display posters with a menu of all the possible services customers can buy (without the prices listed, of course), and some of the women create their own menus, which are parodies of restaurant menus, with appetizers, entrées, and dessert. These individualized menus often have prices on them, but there is usually room for negotiation. A $1,000 party, for instance, might include friendly conversation, a tour of the facilities, drinks, a strip tease or sexy lap dance, and/or a romantic bubble bath, some foreplay (with a sensual massage), oral sex, and then intercourse with one ejaculation — all within an hour. Also included are the condoms, lubricant, oils, and various sex toys. Unlimited orgasms can be negotiated for an additional price, as can extended parties, which last for more than an hour or even overnight.[14]

After the price has been negotiated, Anna says she will take the customer's money down to the office (and if the customer doesn't want to part with his credit card, he can come along too). Finally, she performs a "dick check" to make sure the customer has no visible disease. (If he does, he is asked to leave.) Then the party begins.

At Sheri's Ranch and the Chicken Ranch, extended parties often take place in private bungalows set back from the main building. During our tour, Anna, who is wearing black stiletto sandals that add at least three inches to her 5'4" height, gestures out the windows toward a cluster of cabins in the rear of the large fenced-in yard. "Those are themed bungalows, and they come with a steak and lobster dinner," she says. A series of photos mounted on the wall show off the interior of these bungalows.

"There's the King Arthur room [replete with a statue of a knight in armor], the safari room, where you can take a walk on the wild side," Anna says with a straight face. "We also have a Roman room, a room with the theme of Arabian nights, and a '60s room."

A 1960s room?

"You know, it comes with a shag rug, lava lamp, we call it our Austin Powers room," she says, with a hint of a smile.

Walking down a hallway with sun-lit windows lining the back wall, Anna shows me the "bubble bath room" and then a second room, which also features a hot tub and is lathered with signs promoting Anheuser-Busch's Landshark Lager. "We're the only brothel that has a corporate sponsor," she says proudly.

Next up is the favorite room on the tour: the dungeon. The dungeon has black padded walls, on which chains and an assortment of other painful-looking equipment are mounted. In one corner stands a large black leather chair that Anna calls the "fem-dom worship chair for naughty girls"; in another corner is the "forced orgasm chair," where customers can be tied up and dominated. "It's a form of pleasurable torture for the client," Anna explains. A large black leather couch squats in the center of the room in front of a small stage with a single shiny pole for pole dancing. "[Customers] have to sign our waiver that we're not responsible if someone gets hurt," Anna says. "You can also book this room for bachelor parties."

Although Sheri's Ranch seems geared to fulfill any man's sexual fantasy, both management and the workers insist there are limits. "We're not forced to sleep with anyone," Anna says. "If you get a vibe that something is off about a guy, you can hint with your conversation that you're not interested and he'll pick someone else." Anna says that there have been times when customers said something rude or inappropriate to one of the girls, and the staff admonished them to be more respectful, even asked them to leave.

"There is a small percentage of men who come in here to put down women to make themselves feel better," Anna says. "They might say, 'You're not very hot,' or 'Your boobs aren't big enough.' If that happens, I just excuse myself and I walk away."

For the most part, however, Anna enjoys her job. Like Joi, she sees a lot of older men who are either divorced or have lost their wives, and she says she finds it rewarding to be able to give them pleasure. "They get all emotional and they leave feeling happy. It makes me feel good too," Anna says.

Half the men who spend time with her don't want to have intercourse. Sometimes they just want to talk or have a massage. "Many of them are lonely," she says. "They just want to snuggle up and have a date. It's therapeutic on both ends."

Indeed, Anna's experience at Sheri's Ranch has pointed her toward a new career. She says she is going back to school to get a master's degree in psychology so she can be a marriage counselor or a sexual surrogate. She has already been accepted into a master's program at a school in Florida. "Some people view sex surrogates as glorified prostitutes," she says. "But the ultimate goal is to get people feeling comfortable with being touched."

Anna says she will be working at Sheri's Ranch for only five more months, so she can begin graduate school in January. She says she has made "amazing friendships here" and will leave her stint at the brothel with mixed feelings. "It's like a big family and it's my second home," she says.

We are now back in the airy main lounge, sitting and talking on one of the velvet couches. Soon Jeremy Lemur reappears to tell me that "things are picking up" in the bar and Anna's services are needed. Earlier, he had promised that I could talk to another brothel worker, a twenty-something who goes by the name of Tatiana and has worked at the brothel for several years to pay for her schooling while she was in college. Tatiana now works as a biologist, but she still comes to the brothel for several weeks at a time to supplement her income. A bottle-blonde beauty with a gorgeous body and dark come-hither eyes, Tatiana was the woman picked by the Icelandic couple for their threesome. Jeremy now says she is still occupied and won't be able to talk to me after all. It is clear that he wants my visit to end, even though I still have many questions to ask Anna and she seems happy to chat. But when Jeremy reappears, she stands and so do I. She shakes my hand, smiles, and then, ever the perfect hostess, she waits for me to leave before resuming what she calls "just a job."

# Misguided Laws and Misuse of Resources

When Julie Moya arrived at the police precinct on the Lower East Side on January 31, 2005, to turn herself in, she found the media camped outside. Wearing jeans and black stiletto boots, she walked inside arm in arm with her attorney, Dan Ollen, as flashbulbs went off and microphones were thrust in her face. On her attorney's advice, she said nothing. She was handcuffed, booked, and put in a holding cell jammed with other women.

"I was in shock," she recalls. After a sleepless night sitting on a hard bench in the cell, Julie was brought in front of a judge, who listened as prosecutors painted a sinister picture of her, one in which she scarcely recognized herself. She was a manipulative madam, the prosecutors said, who ran a $3-million-a-year prostitution ring in which she trafficked in underage girls who were brought to her for the specific purpose of taking their virginity. Her attorney tried to rebut the accusations, saying Julie never knowingly hired underage prostitutes. He explained that one of her son's friends had brought in a teenage girl and told Julie she was nineteen. A few weeks later, when Julie discovered the girl was actually fifteen, she fired her immediately.

The prosecutors asked for a bail of $2 million. Ollen countered that Julie could not afford more than $25,000 in cash; she had spent most of her money supporting her family and rescuing stray animals, he said. But the judge set the bail at $500,000 in cash, and Julie, knowing she could not raise that amount even with the help of family and friends, resisted the urge to cry. She was not going to let those bastards see how devastated she was. "That's when I started to understand that something really bad was going to happen to me," she recalls. "But I was determined to hold my head up and not let people know how I felt."

On the bus to Rikers Island, she was seated next to some rough-looking women who sported gang tattoos and glared at her. One big African American woman wearing shackles leaned toward Julie and said, "We're going to 'madam' you when we get to Rikers."

"I was really scared," Julie says. "I had always feared Rikers Island —people get murdered at Rikers."

After sitting in a cell at Rikers for a week, Julie was brought to the Manhattan District Attorney's Office, where she and her attorney met with Assistant District Attorney Matthew Bassiur. He was a good-looking young man with an air of arrogance, Julie recalls. When he started ticking off the state's litany of accusations against her, she felt like slapping him in the face. But her attorney had warned her to sit tight and say nothing unless asked a specific question. The first thing Bassiur wanted to know was whether she knew where the kiddie porn houses in New York City were. Julie stared at him in astonishment. "If I did, I would have turned them in a long time ago," she replied. "I would never condone something like that. You don't really know me."

Bassiur then changed tactics. He said the underage girl who had worked for Julie for a short period of time had told them she partied with a New York State Supreme Court judge. He wanted Julie to tell him who that judge was. Julie knew exactly whom he was talking about. The judge, an older married man, had come to her brothel for many years, and she was not about to give him up.

"I could only imagine what they would do to this man," she says. "He thought the [underage sex worker] was nineteen years old. The stories [in the press] would totally destroy his life and family as well. I decided I could not destroy this man's life to get a lower sentence for myself. I said no and that was that."

A few days later, the Manhattan District Attorney's Office unsealed an indictment charging Julie with three counts of promoting prostitu-tion, twenty-five counts of third-degree rape, and twenty-eight counts of criminal sexual acts for facilitating sex between adults and minors.[1] The judge hearing the case refused to lower her bail.

Julie spent the next three months in a cell on Rikers Island, wondering if she was going to survive. She says she saw some "pretty horrible things," such as inmates having sex with the correctional officers and unwarranted violence. "I saw a captain kick a girl because she wouldn't have sex with him," she says.

A friend of Julie's snuck her some opioid pills in a makeup container, and the knowledge that she could swallow them was the only thing that kept Julie sane. "I knew I could check out if I had to," she says.

Finally, in late May, the District Attorney's Office offered Julie a plea bargain. If she would plead guilty to one count of promoting prostitution, they would dismiss the other fifty-five charges. She agreed, and on July 27, she was sentenced to two and a half to five years in prison, including time served. (Although she was convicted only of a misdemeanor, because she had been convicted of an earlier drug charge, the state was able to ramp up her prison time.) The *Daily News* headline screamed, "Madam on Hook for 5 Yrs." The story went on to say, "In addition to prison time, Moya was ordered to forfeit her Freeport, L.I. [Long Island], home, two cars, a boat and all the money in her bank account, which attorneys say is down to $3,500."[2]

Julie Moya, ironically, is one of very few sex workers in the United States who has done significant time. Like Heidi Fleiss, the Hollywood madam who gained notoriety in the 1990s for her celebrity clientele, Julie ended up doing prison time because she refused to divulge client names. (Fleiss's original conviction for prostitution was overturned by an appeals court in 1996, but she eventually served twenty months of a seven-year federal sentence for tax evasion.)

What happened to Julie Moya and Heidi Fleiss is highly unusual. The overwhelming majority of sex workers who have been arrested in recent years are not held for prosecution or convicted; most are released within hours after their arrest, research shows. (Cook County, Illinois, is a notable exception to this rule, because in recent years its police department has hewed to a strict interpretation of an old law, allowing a repeat prostitution misdemeanor to be upgraded to a felony, which often carries jail time.)

The most comprehensive study on the efficacy of U.S. prostitution laws was done by Julie Pearl, a graduate student at the University of California's Hastings College of the Law in San Francisco. Pearl compiled crime data from the FBI Uniform Crime Reports and the Bureau of Justice between 1985 and 1987 and then conducted extensive interviews with police officials in twenty of the twenty-two U.S. cities with populations greater than 300,000. She found that approximately 80 percent of those arrested for prostitution were not held for prosecution, and only half of those held were found guilty as charged. That essentially means that 90 percent of arrested prostitutes escaped judicial sanction, Pearl concluded in her study, published in the *Hastings Law Journal* in April 1987.[3]

A decade later, the San Francisco Task Force on Prostitution, which also examined local criminal justice records, found much the same thing: the vast majority of arrests made in that city in 1994 were never prosecuted. After spending several hours in jail, the women, mostly streetwalkers, were typically dismissed. They would immediately catch a cab back to the strip to try and make up for their lost earnings. Yet that didn't stop police from doing repeated sweeps. In her field study of San Francisco streetwalkers in 1995, Bernstein found that the same streetwalker "might go to jail as often as four times a week," particularly if she was on the stroll in the city's fashionable shopping and tourism district.[4]

A similar pattern holds true today in many large cities. Of a total of 3,645 arrests for prostitution-related offenses in New York City in 2013, only 403, or 11 percent, resulted in charges with served time, according to the New York State Division of Criminal Justice Statistics.[5]

Arrest statistics in San Francisco and New York also reveal larger societal biases at work. Nationwide, female sex workers are arrested four times as often as male sex workers and are much more likely to be subject to prosecution, despite evidence suggesting that there are roughly as many male as female sex workers.[6] Arrest patterns also reflect an inherent racist bias on the part of law enforcement. Although women of color constitute 40 percent of streetwalkers, they make up 55 percent of those arrested and 85 percent of those incarcerated, according to one 1993 study.[7] Consider New York City for a more recent example. Even though whites make up 47 percent of the city's population, blacks 13 percent, and Hispanics 26 percent, police in 2013 arrested 1,567 blacks and 1,007 Hispanics for prostitution-related charges, as compared with only 397 whites.[8] A 2014 study found that nearly 70 percent of defendants facing prostitution charges in Brooklyn are black, and 94 percent of those arrested for loitering are black.[9]

The U.S. criminal justice system's strikingly uneven enforcement of prostitution laws may also have something to do with the laws themselves. While there is a federal law prohibiting the interstate movement of people for the purpose of prostitution—the Mann Act—the legal status of prostitution is largely determined on the state level, and states have different laws governing the sex industry and they enforce them differently.

While certain forms of sex work, such as child pornography, pimping, pandering (procuring a prostitute for someone else), and exchanging sexual acts for pay, are prohibited in most states, other types of commercial sex, such as phone sex, stripping, erotic dancing, and adult pornography, are permitted (and regulated to some degree.) In California and many other states, the pimping law prohibits people from living off the earnings of a prostitute, essentially criminalizing all domestic partners of sex workers, including roommates.

While most states consider the act of selling sex a misdemeanor, in several states (such as Illinois), repeat prostitution misdemeanors are often upgraded to felonies. Promoting prostitution in the second degree (compelling someone by force or intimidation to engage in prostitution) is also a felony, as are trafficking and profiting from underage prostitution. Many states, including New York, New Jersey, California, Colorado, and the District of Columbia, also regulate prostitution through vagrancy and loitering statutes, which chiefly target streetwalkers.

In many states, police are allowed to use condoms as evidence of prostitution. Service organizations have long opposed that policy on the grounds that it discourages sex workers from practicing safe sex. In 2012, the group Human Rights Watch interviewed 197 sex workers in New York, Washington, D.C., Los Angeles, and San Francisco and found that many limited the number of condoms they carried because they feared being arrested by police.[10] "Because of this policy, people are afraid of carrying condoms around," says Cyndee Clay, executive director of HIPS (Helping Individual Prostitutes Survive), the nonprofit organization that does outreach to streetwalkers in Washington, D.C. "So workers are at greater risk of their health. If you can't make a case with or without a condom, I question whether you can make a case at all. Is the impact on public health worth it?"

In May 2014, advocates for the Urban Justice Center, a nonprofit organization that provides legal services to marginalized populations in New York, were finally able to convince New York City police and prosecutors not to use condoms as evidence in building cases against persons charged with prostitution and loitering. However, condoms can still be used as evidence against johns and in charges of facilitating prostitution. "Many of our clients are arrested for that because they work with other sex workers or share space," said Sienna Baskin, codirector of the Sex Workers Project for the Urban Justice Center, in a June 2014 interview. "So we're pushing for something more comprehensive. We have a state bill we're trying to get passed."

The states also define illegal sexual activity in starkly different ways. For instance, North Carolina requires sexual intercourse for the definition, while other states include fellatio, assisted masturbation, and any physical contact of the genital areas, buttocks, and breasts as sexual activity for the purposes of prostitution.[11]

State laws also differ on when police can make a binding arrest. Some states require that sexual activity or contact actually take place, while in most states, including New York and Massachusetts, the mere offer or agreement to perform acts is sufficient. Some states also require proof of compensation in addition to the agreement to sell sex, but most do not.[12] Jillian, the Jewish escort from western Massachusetts, was arrested minutes after she accepted some cash and verbally agreed to give an undercover police informant a blow job in a Springfield motel.

For Jillian, that sultry August day in 2004 had begun auspiciously enough. Before she met with two scheduled clients, Jillian and Jack, her lover, security guard, and driver, stopped by a friend's house to shoot up. Jillian, then twenty-three, was a heroin user, "a junkie ho," as she sardonically described herself in her blog.

That afternoon, Jillian remembers flying down Interstate 91 on the way to her first assignation, Jack at the wheel, both of them high and singing along to oldies on the radio. Her first assignation is with a new client who has seen her ad in the local weekly, the *Valley Advocate*, and wants a half-hour with her. But when Jillian and Jack pull into the parking lot of the River Inn in West Springfield, something doesn't feel right. The two-story motel looks seedy; Jack mentions that he used to bag dope in a room here. Oh, Jillian thinks, that kind of place. She gets out of the car and notices that someone is watching her from the balcony. Alarm bells go off, but she ignores them. It's just her paranoia, she thinks. The caller said he would pay $150 for a half-hour, and she needs the bucks. When she started doing heroin, the other call girls were angry with her. She was giving them a bad name, they said; they wanted her to be this wholesome all-American girl who just happened to have sex for money. They saw her as a smart, articulate activist who could speak for them all. She is all of that, she knows. But right now, she's coming off a heroin high and she needs some quick cold cash.

Inside, she is greeted by a skinny, sloppily dressed black man who starts asking her questions, the kind of what-do-I-get-for-this questions that an undercover cop would ask in an effort to get a hooker to admit she is being paid for sex. But the guy's eyes are red-rimmed, and he seems too jumpy and drug-addled to be a cop. At first, Jillian answers his insistent queries with her usual response: "I can't answer that question for obvious reasons, but I think if you call a service like this you know what it's about. . . ." But he keeps nattering on. "Will I get a blow job, will I?" Jillian doesn't like his tone, so she starts walking toward the door, and the man suddenly changes tactics. "Whoa, whoa, you're getting frustrated." He hands her $160, which she takes. Mistake number one. "I got to go get you change," she says and starts walking back to the car. But then she remembers, we don't keep change in the car, so she goes back into the room. The man asks her again, "Will I get a blow job?" and in exasperation, she growls under her teeth, "Yes, you will get a blow job."

He asks her to take off her clothes, which she does, slowly, seductively, draping her heart-patterned dress over a chair. Then, he tells her to turn around and show him her ass, and at that moment, two detectives walk in and flash their badges. Stunned, Jillian looks at her Judas client, who simply shrugs, as if to say, "Who me?"

The cops tell her to dress, and as soon as she does, they cuff her and lead her out the door, commenting on the track marks on her arms. Jillian wishes she had thought to slather foundation on her arms, which she usually does before going on a call. And then it dawns on her: her heroin habit has gotten the best of her. If she hadn't been so high and greedy to make more dough, she might have seen and heeded the warning signs. Shoulda, woulda, coulda. She is furious with herself and with the cops, especially the one who has radioed in, "We think she just used."

The police, she knows, couldn't care less that she first started shooting up two years ago for fun. It was a social activity, and it had nothing to do with being an escort. But then her boyfriend, Peter, broke up with her — for the last time — and her best friends blew town. Jillian felt abandoned, and she started shooting up every day, to forget the pain, forget Peter and her loneliness. Before long she was hooked. And this is where her addiction has landed her, handcuffed and defenseless in a stinking motel room, flanked by smirking cops.

Outside, several other cops have surrounded Jack, who is still sitting in the car, his window down. They put a gun to his head, and he tells them to put it down before they hurt somebody. They bark at him to get out of the car, keep his hands up, he's under arrest. "What for?" he asks. "Oh you know," one cop replies.

Jillian can't hear the rest because she is shoved into the police cruiser, where her two guards start asking questions. Jillian tells them she won't talk until she sees a lawyer. But as they drive off, she can't resist one little dig. "Wow," she says, "it must feel so productive arresting people for nonviolent crimes. Right now, someone could actually be getting hurt." The cop in the passenger's seat turns around and snaps, "You asked for a lawyer to be present, so just shut up."

Jillian keeps her mouth closed for the rest of the ride, but having read a shelf-load of books on sex work, she knows she has statistics on her side. And she does, to a large extent. Research shows that U.S. laws criminalizing prostitution are counterproductive and a huge waste of resources. In her study, Julie Pearl found that each of the cities she surveyed in 1985 spent an average of $7.5 million enforcing prostitution laws, more than some of these cities, such as Los Angeles, Dallas, Phoenix, and San Diego, spent on municipally funded health services the same year. Half the city governments studied spent more on prostitution control than on either education or public welfare.[13] In 1985 alone, sixteen of America's largest cities spent more than $120 million on prostitution arrests.[14] That translated into an average of almost $2,000 ($1,989) to bust just one sex worker, Pearl found.[15]

Over the last three decades, from 1980 to 2012 (the most recent numbers available online are for 2012), total prostitution arrests in the United States have fluctuated widely, reaching a high of 111,400 in 1990 and dropping to a low of 55,374 in 1999. In 2000, total arrests shot up again, to 87,620 (largely in response to the federal antitrafficking law passed that year), but by 2012, they were back down again, to 56,575, according to the federal Bureau of Justice Statistics. If you multiply 56,575 arrests by $2,000, the total amounts to more than $113 million in taxpayer money spent each year on arresting prostitutes, most of whom are never prosecuted.

Pearl also discovered that law enforcement agencies in America's largest cities spend more time and resources arresting prostitutes than they do pursuing and solving violent crimes. On average, she found, police in these cities made as many arrests for prostitution as they did for all violent offenses combined. In 1986, police in Boston, Cleveland, and Houston arrested twice as many people for prostitution as they did for all homicides, rapes, robberies, and assaults combined. In Dallas, residents and visitors reported over 15,000 violent crimes in 1985, only 2,665 of which resulted in arrest. The same year, Dallas police made 7,280 prostitution arrests, which cost local taxpayers over $10 million.[16]

Police in these cities spend most of their time indoors trying to entrap sex workers like Jillian and Joi Love. For example, vice officers typically spent thirty to forty minutes in massage parlors before making an arrest, Pearl found. Yet such efforts provide no additional protection for the public.[17]

Indeed, dozens of researchers in recent years have criticized enforcement of prostitution laws on the grounds that it diverts the attention of law enforcement agencies from more serious crimes. Most police officers who arrest streetwalkers are not out there patrolling for other types of crime. As Pearl found in her interviews with law enforcement in the nation's largest cities, undercover vice officers who make most of the prostitution arrests "have neither the time nor responsibility to search for and arrest perpetrators of violent and property crimes."[18]

And that remains true today. Melvin Scott, the commander of the Narcotics and Special Investigations Division of the Metropolitan Police Department in Washington, D.C., says the members of his vice squad focus on arresting prostitutes and traffickers, not other kinds of criminals.

HIPS's Cyndee Clay says that arresting sex workers does not help them get out of prostitution or improve the communities in which they stroll. "It's a massive waste of resources," Clay says. "If we weren't spending this much money on law enforcement, we could spend more resources to help people get to the point where sex work becomes a choice, one of many options, as opposed to an economic necessity."

Many researchers agree that refocusing law enforcement efforts on violent crime, property theft, and underage prostitution would be a much more effective use of taxpayer dollars. Ronald Weitzer, the George Washington University sociologist and longtime scholar of the sex industry, notes that the United States has been arresting sex workers and clients for decades, yet prostitution continues to flourish. Indeed, it is on the rise in the United States, as it is globally. In an essay he wrote for the *Annual Review of Sociology* in 2009, Weitzer argues that it is time to recognize that law enforcement is not an effective solution to what is essentially a socioeconomic problem.[19] As he and others note, criminalization is a failed strategy that clearly harms sex workers and lets violent predators off the hook.

"What we're doing is fueling a law enforcement machine," Clay agrees. "I would rather use that money stopping violent crime and arresting people who actually hurt others." Clay says the same holds true for arrests of clients, known in the trade as johns. When police spend a lot of time setting up stings to arrest johns in hotels, brothels, or even on the street, she notes, they are usually "arresting regulars who are not violent and have good jobs." HIPS, she says, compiles a list of clients reported by street workers to be violent, and the organization shares that information with other sex workers. "If sex workers were able to talk to police, we could get violent people off the street," she says. "That's where our resources should be going, not toward arresting adults involved in consensual sex."

Despite dismal conviction rates (for both sex workers and clients), police acknowledge that laws against prostitution have a direct payoff for them—in public relations and increased funding from federal antitrafficking task forces. They can use prostitute arrests, which are relatively safe and easy to make, to bolster crime statistics and improve their image as effective crime fighters. Yet such statistics engender a false sense of security among the public. Consider New York State's breakdown of reported complaints and arrests in 2011: while almost 90 percent of reported prostitution cases were closed by arrest, only 58 percent of complaints about violent crimes yielded an arrest that year, according to records obtained from New York State's Division of Criminal Justice Services and the 2011 New York State Statistical Yearbook online.[20]

Some police openly acknowledge that they prefer arresting prostitutes to pursuing more dangerous criminals. As one Las Vegas metropolitan police lieutenant told a reporter, "You get up in a penthouse at Caesar's

Palace with six naked women frolicking in the room and then say, 'Hey, baby, you're busted!' That's fun."[21]

Such busts are a huge waste of resources that do little to deter prostitution. Moreover, arresting sex workers (most of whom are streetwalkers) further marginalizes vulnerable women, making it more difficult for them to obtain housing and other kinds of employment. Once they've been arrested for prostitution, women have tremendous difficulty getting a job outside the sex industry. They also face discrimination in housing and child custody cases, according to advocates who work with the homeless. And such marginalization occurs even when there are no convictions. In most states, all it takes is an arrest to launch this vicious cycle. When someone is arrested for prostitution, that arrest goes into the state's bureau of criminal identification and becomes part of the public record that is available to employers and housing managers who routinely do background checks, according to an analyst for the federal Bureau of Justice Statistics and a New York defense attorney.

A few years after her arrest, Jillian obtained a copy of her Criminal Offender Record Information (CORI) and discovered, to her chagrin, that her 2004 arrest for prostitution was included in that publicly available record, even though she was never convicted. "That goes against the whole innocence until proven guilty thing, don't you think?" Jillian says.

In her 2002 book, *Prostitution Policy*, Lenore Kuo, a professor of women's studies and philosophy and chair of the Women's Studies Program at California State University, Fresno, argued that once women are arrested for prostitution, they often cannot obtain regular employment or housing because of the criminal record checks many employers and low-income housing managers do. She concluded, "Arresting prostitutes often serves only to heighten their isolation and estrangement, not only from friends, family and the community but also from the very . . . services they may need in order to access alternative means of income."[22]

The repercussions of criminalization don't end there. "Not only does the arrest of prostitutes permanently and officially stigmatize [women], it also often results in the loss of child custody, deportation, housing and other forms of discrimination," Kuo notes.[23]

The specter of discrimination is the last thing on Jillian's mind as she sits in the back of the police car, her wrists chafing under the cuffs. She is much more worried about the possibility of going through withdrawal alone, in a filthy jail cell. The year before, Jillian had read about a young woman who had died of heatstroke and withdrawal complications after being locked up for hours in a Framingham, Massachusetts, jail cell. Could something like that happen to her, too?

At the precinct, the police rifle through Jillian's purse, looking for drug paraphernalia and drugs. They come up empty-handed. Even so, they give her the dirty junkie routine. "If I catch anything from you . . ." one cop says. Jillian tries to keep her cool and heckle them as much as possible. Every officer she sees gets the how-productive-to-arrest-people-for-nonviolent crimes line. The captain loses his temper. "This isn't Northampton, sweetheart, so save it for the judge and spare us your beliefs."

Jillian is thrown into an empty cell, and a wave of nauseating power-lessness washes over her. She sees the words "I want to go home" carved high up on the plaster wall of her cell and wants to cry. The trick, she remembers reading somewhere, is to keep your mind occupied, so you don't have to think about what might happen to you, all alone in this godforsaken place. She racks her brain to come up with a good protest song. The only one she can think of is "We shall overcome." She starts singing it at the top of her lungs and learns later that Jack heard her all the way down in the men's cells. Finally, a policewoman comes in and tells her she'll be there all night if she doesn't shut up.

A little later, she is joined by another hooker, whom she recognizes as Constance, of Constance and Anastasia in the *Valley Advocate* ads. Constance tells Jillian that she didn't agree to anything, didn't take the money or remove her clothes; they have nothing to make the arrest stick. Even so, since she is from Connecticut and crossed state lines, her bail may be set too high for her to get out before court in the morning. So she asks Jillian to please call her boyfriend if she makes bail. "Of course," Jillian says, and the two women bond over war stories about their work.

Finally, the same policewoman returns to take Jillian to the booking area, where she has the opportunity to make the one phone call that could spring her—until her court hearing in the morning. She desperately tries to remember what numbers she'd memorized for just this situation (the police confiscated her cell phone during the arrest). She knows she can't call her parents; her father would probably get on the phone and start yelling that this is where she belongs, in jail, until she cleans up her act. And her mother wouldn't know what to do. Jillian stays in regular contact with her mother, an Orthodox Jew who constantly prays for her, but doesn't speak very often to her father. He disapproves of her occupation and wants nothing to do with her.

She calls one friend's number, but there is no answer; the same thing happens when she calls two other names high on her memorized list. It *is* 2:00 in the morning after all. On the next try, she gets through to a friend of Jack's, a drug dealer, and he says he can get the bail money but doesn't have a car. The bail bondsman, whose time is just about up, agrees to make one final phone call for Jillian, and she gives him the number for another hooker by the name of Ruth, who is at the very bottom of her list. Hallelujah, Ruth answers the phone. Yes, she says, she has a car and she will pick up Jack's friend and bring him and the money to Springfield. They arrive just in time, with enough loot to spring her and Jack. Jillian feels so grateful and humbled. As she walks out of prison, a free woman, she muses out loud, "Who among all your friends can you count on when you need bail? A drug dealer and a ho."

In addition to taking Jillian's cell phone, the police have confiscated all the money she and Jack had on them. So Jillian asks Ruth to drive her to one last assignation, which she got off her voicemail from the day before. The customer is more than happy to party with her, but the money Jillian collects from him doesn't last long. "We spent the money so we could be high just in time for court, because that's the kind of shallowly rebellious prick I am," Jillian writes in her blog a month later. "I just want everyone to understand that this [arrest] is no deterrent, only inspiration for greater heights of criminal activity."

# The Rhode Island Story

The morning after Jillian is sprung from jail by "a drug dealer and a ho," her case is continued without a finding. Jillian is hopeful that the prostitution charges will eventually be dismissed, since it's her first offense. But then her father writes a letter to the Hampden County District Attorney's Office, telling prosecutors that his daughter is hooked on heroin and pleading with them to mandate that she receive treatment in exchange for a lighter sentence. Jillian is furious at him, but the die is cast. In February 2005, she pleads guilty to a prostitution misdemeanor and agrees to enter a methadone maintenance program in exchange for the promise of getting the prostitution charge cleared from her record. That evening, Jillian, with characteristic sass, updates friends on her online journal: "If only my estranged father hadn't fucked me in court by sending a hysterical please-incarcerate-and-forcibly-rehabilitate-my-crazy-junkie-daughter letter to the DA, drugs wouldn't even have been an issue in this case, but oh well. Anyway, it gives me a few months of freedom to, er, Get it Out of My System, and eventually clean my record. Darlene reminded me that as soon as I get on the program I'll be earning shitloads of cash once again, which I can spend spoiling my friends, being a self-righteous philanthropist, creating even more self-righteous communes, and saving up for my next habit."

In the end, Jillian does no prison time and completes her year of probation without further incident. But she has become hooked on methadone, which she considers "100 times more addictive than heroin." In an interview a few years later, she says she is still trying to wean herself off methadone but finding it incredibly difficult. In the meantime, the authorities have a "sword of Damocles" over her head. "If I don't follow every bureaucratic rule in the program, they cut off my supply and I'm in horrible torture for months," she says. "Forced treatment is nothing better than mind control."

Julie Moya has her own sword of Damocles to deal with upon her release from prison in 2007. She is still on probation and completely broke. "I didn't know how I was going to face the world again," she recalls. "I had an arrest record and no high school education. What could I possibly do?"

In prison, at least, there had been some structure to her days. After a few months in Bedford Hills, a maximum-security prison for women in Westchester County, Julie was transferred to Beacon, a minimum-security facility in upstate New York, which was essentially a working cattle farm. The farmer in charge saw that Julie had a way with animals, so he put her in charge of the cow pod. "I made friends with everyone there," she says. "I was working with the calves. They would send the baby calves in with their umbilical cords hanging off, and I would take care of them until they were six months old. I took care of one little blind calf for a long time."

At Beacon, Moya worked from 8:00 in the morning until 8:00 in the evening and was exhausted by the end of the day. Even so, she loved it. "The work farm was like being in paradise," she says. "You could see the rivers and beautiful mountains in the distance."

Her release from prison was a rude awakening. She felt angry and adrift in a city in which she had once felt embraced. It took her a long time to regain her footing. Several co-workers whom she had bailed out when they were all arrested in 2005 repaid their loans. Other friends came around and told her that she had to open up her place again. "They missed the place," she says and then laughs. "Half of the guys at NBC had our website on their computers. It really was the best little whorehouse in New York."

But deep inside, Julie was hurt and angry—at the lies that law enforcement had spread about her and the people who had turned on her to save their own skins. She decided to write a blog about her experiences—

to get the truth out there, she says—and also to make the case for legalizing prostitution in the United States. "I used to not want legalization; I thought it would lower prices and allow the government to get their hands on it," she says over lunch one day at an Italian restaurant in midtown Manhattan. "But now I do. I think it would make things safer for the girls and clients too."

Many sex workers are afraid their families will find out what they do, she says. If sex work were legal in the United States, they wouldn't fear being arrested and having their families find out and ostracize them. Julie envisions a system in which brothels would be licensed and sex workers would receive certificates or cards and would be tested regularly for sexually transmitted diseases. If prostitution were legal, she says, sex workers would also be eligible for social security and health benefits, which they currently don't have access to. "Women should have control over their own bodies," she says. "They can get an abortion, but they can't have a transaction involving sex. That doesn't make any sense."

Legalizing or decriminalizing adult consensual sex work, Julie says, would also make it easier to crack down on traffickers and places that are run by criminals, because sex workers would be more likely to come forward and report abuse to the police. "Robbers and extortionists know we are easy targets because we won't go and report them." Julie's own employees have been robbed a few times, usually late at night, when they were carrying cash from the day's transactions. One time, her son was robbed of $4,000 in the lobby of their brothel by two men pretending to be clients. Julie did report that crime to the police (and she wasn't arrested), but the money was never recovered. "I think it was an inside job, and all we could do was fire the security person who I think was in on it," she says.

Julie hopes that legalization might also help lift the long-standing stigma around being a sex worker and allow sex workers to pay taxes and receive benefits as other workers do. When she was released from prison, Julie herself was eager to erase the stigma and shame she had felt operating in the shadows of the law. She decided to become a chauffeur—she has always felt comfortable driving a big car around New York—so she went back to court to get permission for a driving permit. But the judge refused her request. A few months later, out of options and desperate for money, she reopened Julie's of New York under a new name. By 2009, she and her son Jerry were running two busy brothels in midtown Manhattan, and Julie was once again able to start saving toward retirement.

The same month that Julie Moya went back to working as a madam, Joi Love, the single mother who worked in Nevada's brothels in the 1990s, decided to move to the one other state in the nation that permitted indoor prostitution: Rhode Island. After Joi's two months at Chicken Ranch in 1996, she had returned to Virginia, kicked out her cheating husband, and enlisted in the Army, where she started as a pay clerk and worked her way up to financial services. Along the way, she earned associate degrees in information technology and business management. In 1999, Joi got a job with the Commonwealth of Virginia Department of Information Technology as a contracts manager and was soon promoted to a contracts administrator for the state. By then, she was the mother of three daughters and a respectable member of the Petersburg, Virginia, community. She worked on the gubernatorial campaign of Mark Warner and attended his inaugural festivities in 2002, and in 2003, she was appointed to the Petersburg Commission on Community Relations Affairs.

In 2004, Joi took a better-paying job as a purchasing manager and budget analyst with Virginia State University. She received an excellent performance review after her first three months at the university. "Mrs. [Joi's real last name] is meticulous with details, energetic and drives toward excellence," the reviewer writes in the August 9, 2004, report (a copy of which Joi gave me, along with other pertinent documentation about her life.) "She formulated and loaded the budget for FY05 in her first week on campus and has excellent organizational skills. She is a solid performer with great potential."

A few weeks later, Joi was hired by the Georgia Institute of Technology for a better-paying position in its accounts payable department. Money was tight, and Joi needed to pay the mounting medical bills for her youngest daughter, who had been hospitalized with a severe skin condition. Joi's mother, who was still living with her, agreed to watch her daughters so that Joi could commute between Virginia and Georgia.

By the beginning of 2006, however, Joi was fed up with the straight life, tired of bosses who wouldn't allow much flexibility in her schedule. "I took a few sick days, and when I got back to work on Monday, my boss yelled at me for taking off," she recalls. "I felt disrespected and used. It just wasn't worth it."

So at the end of January, she quit and began dancing at a strip club in Atlanta. She was thirty-three years old and looked much younger. In May, she and her boyfriend (whom she'd met at the strip joint) moved to Miami, where Joi danced in several clubs and did sex work on the side. But after she was arrested, first on Miami Beach for prostitution and then during a trip to Las Vegas (charges were dropped in both cases because the police had no proof that she was soliciting), Joi decided it was time to move to a state where prostitution was legal, indoors at least.

The story of how Rhode Island became the only state other than Nevada where some forms of prostitution were not illegal, and retained that status for almost thirty years, is a fascinating tale, with a cameo appearance by none other than Margo St. James, the founder of the modern sex workers movement. In the mid-1970s, St. James was traveling around the country trying to convince Americans to get the government out of their bedrooms. During a stop in Rhode Island, she met the owner of a downtown Providence strip club who persuaded her to help him challenge the constitutionality of Rhode Island's prostitution law. In 1976, St. James and COYOTE filed a federal lawsuit, arguing that the Rhode Island statute, which made prostitution a felony punishable by up to five years in prison, was so broad that it could prohibit sex between unmarried adults. The lawsuit also alleged discrimination in how the law was applied, citing data that showed the Providence police were arresting female sex workers much more often than their male customers. As in many other states, the criminal justice system in Rhode Island worked like a giant revolving door. Police would round up sex workers, mostly female streetwalkers, only to see them pay bail and hit the streets again.[1]

At a town meeting in 1979, a state district court judge told some Prov-

idence residents who were upset about streetwalking in their neighborhood that the way to get prostitutes off the streets was to change the law
to make prostitution a misdemeanor and thus speed up their prosecution
in the courts. So in 1980, the conservative speaker of the House spon-
sored a bill that made prostitution a misdemeanor rather than a felony.
But in rewriting the law, the drafters somehow deleted a section that
addressed committing the act of prostitution, according to the *Providence Journal-Bulletin*.[2] The omission was not caught, and the General
Assembly unanimously approved the bill, rendering Margo St. James's
lawsuit moot.

The loophole went largely unnoticed until 2003, when Providence
police raided four brothels posing as massage parlors. The lawyer for
the Midori and Oriental Garden Spas argued that no law had been violated. The state supreme court, the lawyer noted, had ruled in 1998 that
Rhode Island's law against soliciting was primarily aimed at outdoor
prostitution and could not be used to convict someone for activity taking place in private.[3] The criminal charges were dismissed, as were later
charges levied against spa owners by police. By 2007, Providence, Rhode
Island, had become a major tourist attraction for men, with numerous
strip clubs, massage parlors, and brothels, which catered to clients up and
down the East Coast. Joi Love wanted a piece of that action.

In June 2007, she moved to Rhode Island, working first at the Sportsman Club, a hotel and bar with a strip club attached to it. "I stayed there
a week, and the door guy gave me the number of a landlord who would
rent to me," she says.

Joi and I are talking on the third floor of bustling Providence Place,
a glitzy three-story mall in downtown Providence. It is the first time I
have met her in person, and I am struck by how beautiful she is, with
a mane of long, curly black hair, big brown eyes, and ebony skin. She
is impeccably dressed in a caramel knit sweater and tight white jeans
that show off her willowy figure. Black high-heeled boots complete the
effect. Joi has already purchased her lunch (Popeye's fried chicken, rice,
and beans), and we sit down near large plate-glass windows overlooking
I-95 and some former textile mills, which have recently been refurnished

into condos. The now-closed Sportsman Club where she got her start in Rhode Island is located right across the street, Joi says. She gestures at the textile mills across the interstate. "I lived in those luxury condos," she says. "But they were really racist; they kept saying, 'Your people this' and 'Your people that.' Just to show them that my people did have money, I paid for four months, and then I moved into the house where that steeple is." She points out the window at a church steeple in the hazy distance.

By the time we meet that afternoon in December 2009, Joi has moved to a six-bedroom house with a pool on a quiet residential street in North Providence. Her oldest daughter is an honors student on an athletics scholarship at Wake Forest University. Her middle daughter lives with her and goes to high school in Providence; she's on the cheerleading team. Her youngest daughter is living with her father in North Carolina but visits Joi on the holidays and every summer.

So what does she tell her children about the dungeon she has recreated in the basement of her house, complete with handcuffs, paddles, whips, and ropes? Or the medical exam room and tiny classroom where students can get spanked by Teacher? "I tell my kids the age-appropriate truth," she says. "I tell them I use the dungeon to pretend to beat people or that I'm teaching in the classroom. I don't give them details, but I'm sure my eighteen-year-old knows what I do; she's not dumb."

In her two years in Rhode Island, Joi says she has assembled a large database of high-brow clients, including judges and lawyers, military personnel, businessmen, and Brown University professors. She has over a thousand clients ranging in age from eighteen to ninety, but most, she says, are between twenty-nine and fifty. Joi herself is thirty-seven, although she looks no older than twenty-nine or thirty.

"I'd say 75 percent of my clients are married, but I get a lot of singles too," she says. "The married men have sick wives or they've been married so long the wife doesn't want to do it anymore. Or they are bored. Some men like it for the thrill: can they get away with it?"

Joi charges $400 for two hours; one hour is $250. Most of her clients stay at least two hours once a week, she says. Joi says she makes over $10,000 a month. Even so, she is choosy. If a customer seems rude or drunk on the phone, she will not make an appointment to see him. If he just wants to give her money and have sex, she's not for him. "If you want to have some type of conversation, a connection, then I am for you," she says. "This past weekend, I had two couples. The guy [in one of the couples] had been coming to me for a while, and he convinced his girlfriend to come and visit with him. The girlfriend wanted to dress him as a woman and then have a three-way."

Joi says she is doing sex work completely by choice. "I've never felt as free," she says. "I can go to my children's games and take them shopping. In this industry, I can be myself. I don't have to do anything I don't want to do."

Joi is still with the same man she met in Atlanta, and she considers him a partner, not a pimp. "My boyfriend doesn't dictate to me when to work or how to work," she says. "I have my own bank account. I don't cook, clean, or do laundry. He takes care of all of that for me."

A few weeks before my meeting with Joi, the Rhode Island legislature voted to close the nearly thirty-year-old loophole in the state law that permitted indoor prostitution. In the months leading up to the November 2009 vote, religious groups and antiprostitution feminists such as Donna Hughes testified that illegal immigrants were being trafficked into the state's brothels and spas and that Rhode Island's lax attitude toward prostitution was giving the state a bad name.

A month after the new law was passed, making indoor prostitution, like outdoor prostitution, a misdemeanor, the police arrested six female escorts and eight male customers in four separate sting operations at hotels in Providence, Warwick, and Johnston.[4] In February 2010, they raided two spas in Providence that were widely known to be brothels.[5] No one was prosecuted or convicted in either of those raids, and no illegal immigrants were found, according to court records and the Providence police.

Joi herself wasn't sure she wanted to stay in Providence, now that indoor prostitution was no longer legal. "I can't see myself living in New England for the heck of it. I'm not the New England type," she said. "But for now I'm sticking around because of my clients."

What bothered her most was the impact of the new law on many women who are already marginalized and in desperate economic straits. "When they passed the new law, they didn't do anything to help all those sex workers who were out of a job," she said. "There are no programs in place to help them find another job, get retrained. The law is just going to push a lot of hos out onto the street and further hurt women."

That's exactly what happened, according to researchers. As Weitzer notes in his 2012 book, "outlawing indoor sex work in Rhode Island in 2009 resulted in closure of massage parlors, throwing a substantial number of women out of relatively safe workplaces into more dangerous venues. . . ."[6]

When Joi and I meet again at Providence Place three months later, she says one of her newest clients is a Rhode Island legislator. "I'm the third [sex worker] he's seen and the first one since the law has changed," she says. "I asked him why he voted for the change. I told him that he should vote 'the way you actually are.' He told me it was politics and has nothing to do with how he actually feels. It's plain hypocrisy."

Joi says she supports decriminalizing prostitution and has a hard time understanding why so many Americans are opposed to commercial sex. "You can drink and kill yourself and someone else," she says. Joi waves her left hand, and the huge diamond ring on her middle finger glitters in the sunlight. "You can smoke a cigarette at $9 a pack and get cancer and give everyone around you cancer. You can do all those things, but how many people got killed by a ho last night?"

Joi says she regularly gets tested for HIV and drugs and has the test results on hand if clients want to see them. "I would prefer that sex workers be tested and required to have cards," she says. "That way, if you're underage or illegal, you won't have a card. That would prevent child prostitution and illegals. That would be better than having police raid my house and humiliate me and my family."

Like many other sex workers I've interviewed, Joi is adamantly opposed to underage prostitution or trafficking. "If you have a seventeen-year-old in a strip club, that should be illegal," she says. "If you molest or sell a child, you should go to prison. If you beat and force a woman, that too. If a ho robs you at gunpoint with her pimp, I'm in favor of sending them both away for a long time."

In the middle of our conversation, Joi's cell phone rings. It's her youngest daughter, who is living with her father in North Carolina. "Sue Sue, whatcha doing?" Joi asks. Sue Sue, who is in middle school, is apparently calling from her school bus and complaining about some kids who are acting up on the bus. "Tell those kids they have to stop acting like that," Joi says. "Tell them right now. No, you're not supposed to yell at them, just tell them in a calm voice." Joi listens for a few minutes and then says, "I'm going to go shopping for you. What colors do you want? Okay. What size?" Then she says, "All right, I love you. Tell Daddy he doesn't have to call me anymore, 'cause you called me. All right, love you, bye-bye."

Joi says she doesn't have a formal child support arrangement with Sue Sue's father. She pays what she can, and he does the same. "He called a couple of days ago and said [our daughter] signed up for saxophone lessons. It's $55. He asked me to pay for half, and I said 'Fine,'" she says. "It's better for me that way. I agree to pay what I can. When she was living with me, he paid what he could. I don't need to have him support me."

A few months later, Joi invites me to her house in North Providence. When she opens her front door, a white pit bull (whom she rescued from the street) jumps up at me and bangs into my leg. Joi puts him in her bedroom on the first floor and shuts the door. Across from the bedroom is a spacious living room with a huge brown leather sofa and matching chairs clustered around a white-brick mantelpiece. Down the hallway is the kitchen and a dining room with a table set with fancy brown ceramic ware and brown napkins.

Joi leads me down a narrow flight of stairs to a large, cozy-looking den with two big flat-screen TVs and a pair of overstuffed burgundy leather sofas surrounding a wooden coffee table. A young African American woman is vacuuming. "This is my girlfriend, Raven," she says and then gestures at her. "You can just chill if you want to."

Off from the den, like spokes on a wheel, are a series of smaller, private rooms. First she shows me the classroom, with colorful ABC letters taped to the walls and a small writing desk and chair in the center. "I make it up differently depending on who is going to be the student and who is going to be Teacher," Joi says. "I use little ABC blocks, and bring in trikes and bikes."

Next up is the medical exam room with a metal examining table and an anatomically correct body chart on the wall. Two rubber dildos and some jelly sit on a table nearby. "I do body rubs in here, but I'm not a licensed masseuse," she says. "I do a lot of role-playing. It's not about sex; it's about fulfilling someone's fantasy."

We settle down on the sofas, and Joi sounds off about the hypocrisy of most Americans when it comes to sex work. "As a prostitute, I'm not considered a person. If I get bashed in the face by a man, I can't go to the police because I'll be arrested and treated badly before I get the help I need," she says, waving a long slender arm. "But if a rich white man is fucking a twenty-two-year-old blond gold mine and giving her a BMW, how is that not prostitution?"

At one point, Joi says she isn't particularly concerned about Rhode Island's new law. "I don't sell sex for money, I sell time, and legally speaking, my house is what's called an alternative meeting space," she says. But then she waves a hand. "I grew up in the ghetto, so I'm always ready to be arrested for nothing," she says.

When I ask who Raven is, Joi says the twenty-one-year-old was being beaten up by her boyfriend-pimp and she called Joi's boyfriend, Lucky, in desperation. (Lucky's barber was a client of Raven's and had given her Lucky's number.) When Joi and her boyfriend went to pick Raven up, Joi says she told her that she'd take her home to Virginia, but Raven didn't want to go. "She's been here eighty-seven days, and she says no one has ever taken care of her before," Joi says. "I send money to her son and clothes to her sister, who is taking care of her son. She says I've done more for her than her own family has ever done."

A few weeks ago, Joi and Lucky took Raven home so she could visit her son. He was living with her twenty-year-old sister, who has two children and is pregnant with a third, their forty-year-old mother, and the mother's younger boyfriend in a two-bedroom apartment in Franklin,

Virginia. "Everyone is on welfare and flat broke and fighting all day," Joi shrugs. "Raven could have stayed home, but she didn't want to. She's twenty-one and had never run a dishwasher. Can anyone say she's in a worse position now?"

Just yesterday, Joi says, she and Raven set up a scenario at a client's request. Raven played his girlfriend, and Joi was her mother. "We started out in the office, and then we took our clothes off and he wanted to watch [Raven] take a shower, and then I took a shower and he watched me. And then we rubbed him down," she says. "There was no sex involved for me. And I got a tip. That's how I like it."

THREE MONTHS LATER, on October 12, 2010, North Providence police, armed with a search warrant, raided Joi's house. Joi, Lucky, Raven, and a friend were watching television, fully clothed, in the den. The officers cuffed Lucky but not Joi, Raven, and her friend. They searched the entire house, took all three of Joi's computers and some papers out of her desk, and snapped pictures of the pool and specialty rooms. A few days later, after Joi had bailed everyone out, she and her boyfriend packed up and left for Baltimore.

Joi tells me later that no charges were ever filed in the case, but she has no intention of going back to Providence to live. She had three good years there, but after Rhode Island closed the loophole on indoor prostitution, Joi lived every day waiting for the other shoe to drop.

"I had actually been looking to relocate anyway," she later says in an email. "I knew it would be a matter of time. I had too many followers and clients not to be on the radar."

For most of 2011, Joi shuttled back and forth between Baltimore and Rhode Island. "My client base is too great to give up, plus I have weekly regulars," she says. Her oldest daughter was still away at college, and the summer before the raid, her middle daughter had decided to finish high school in Kentucky (where she has relatives).

By early 2012, Joi had resettled in East Greenwich, Rhode Island, a small town near the Connecticut border, where she started an escort service. In an interview a year later, she said, "I've kept most of my clients. Yesterday was Valentine's Day, and I got fifty Happy Valentine emails, cards, and phone calls from clients."

JOI, IT TURNS OUT, is not the only sex worker who stuck around despite the 2009 law making indoor prostitution illegal in Rhode Island. By August of 2014, ten of the fifteen spas that were shut down in the years after the law passed had reopened, according to police, and men from Massachusetts and other neighboring states continued to frequent the city's strip clubs and spas.

The head of Providence's vice squad is Anthony Sauro, an unassuming fifty-seven-year-old of Italian ancestry with a shock of white hair and a fit, athletic build. When we met up, he had been on the Providence police force for thirty-two and a half years and in charge of its vice squad (narcotics, nightclubs, prostitution) for the past two years. Just before Labor Day weekend that year, he gave me a tour of some of the city's notorious hot spots, and the afternoon culminated in a guns-drawn raid on a brothel in the West End.

That morning, Sauro picks me up at the bus terminal, driving an un-marked VW Passat (acquired in a heroin raid.) He is wearing a gray polo shirt with "Captain" embroidered on one breast. A gun is strapped to one side of his belt, and a walkie-talkie to the other. He begins the tour by driving down Main Street and into the asphalt parking lot of what looks like a former motel. It houses an "unbelievably busy" brothel, Sauro says, which charges an entry fee of $60 a customer and supplies body rubs and hand jobs. The women who work there are all Asian, imported from Flushing, Queens. Most of the clients are from Massachusetts.

As Sauro and I sit in the car, a silver truck pulls into the lot and backs into a parking space. But the man at the wheel doesn't get out. He's too busy staring at us. A few minutes later, the truck pulls out again, and Sauro says, "I think we scared this guy off."

A few blocks down, Sauro pulls into another parking lot, where the sign on the door of the squat, one-story building reads, "ABC Spa."

"That's actually the Refresh Spa, it's an old sign," Sauro says. "This place is full service [meaning customers get more than a hand job]. See, both cars [in the lot] are from Massachusetts."

Sauro says the city is trying to pass a "Bodyworks" law that would require spas that do body work to obtain a license and register their employees. Such an ordinance, he says, would make it easier for police to close down spas that do sex work. Without such regulation, Sauro says it's difficult for the Providence vice squad to gather the evidence needed to close down the city's spas or strip clubs (which often permit commercial sex in private rooms). That's because many of these places hire retired cops or police from neighboring cities as security. "The first time I walked into the [Asian] spa on Main Street, I heard from someone on the force who knew I was looking into it within an hour," Sauro says. "The owner had called a Johnston [Rhode Island] cop, and he called one of my guys to find out what was going on."

Foxy Lady and Cadillac Lounge, two well-known strip clubs in downtown Providence, also hire retired Providence police to work as security. "So if we go in there undercover, they're going to know about it," he says.

When Sauro became head of the vice squad two years ago, he started cracking down on the spas more aggressively than his predecessor had. He was soon told to dial it down. Last year, his department executed 157 search warrants, but only 3 or 4 of them involved venues of prostitution, he says. Most of the warrants were for drug searches. Sauro says his squad doesn't have the resources to go after independent escorts or high-end escort services. He himself thinks adult consensual prostitution should be decriminalized. "We're not really stopping it," he says. "If we [decriminalized it], we could focus on trafficking. It's just like marijuana. Marijuana [under a certain amount] is decriminalized in Rhode Island."

At the same time, however, his department is under greater pressure to eradicate trafficking. "We get a lot of people asking what we're doing about trafficking," he says. "A lot of pressure is coming down on us."

All of which explains why shortly after 1:30 that afternoon, I find myself sitting with Sauro in his unmarked Passat in a small private parking lot on Waverly Street in Providence, a few houses up from a run-down

Victorian that apparently houses a brothel catering largely to Guatemalan immigrants. The brothel is in the West End, a poor, largely minority neighborhood, and Sauro wants to close it down because it's in a family neighborhood. "You've got kids biking up and down this street," he says.

The Providence police have raided this particular brothel before, but it always seems to reopen for business after a short hiatus. If the city passes the "Bodyworks" law requiring spas to obtain licenses to operate, Sauro says, city officials could make sure these places don't open up in family neighborhoods. Police could revoke the licenses and shut down the establishments if they found evidence of prostitution or other illegal activities.

A few yards in either direction on Waverly sit two large unmarked SUVs, one white, one black, with tinted glass. Inside are four men from Sauro's vice squad and two women from the U.S. Department of Homeland Security. The women are part of the stakeout, Sauro explains, because the feds sometimes prosecute cases of trafficking across state lines. Sauro had introduced me to the four men and two women when we gathered, before the stakeout, in the parking lot of a nearby police garage. All six officers were out of uniform, dressed casually in jeans and T-shirts, and from their jokes and nonchalant attitudes, it seemed clear they were old hands at this kind of thing. Even so, before getting back into their SUVs, they all (with the exception of Sauro and myself) donned bullet-proof black vests with "POLICE" emblazoned in big white letters across the front of their vests.

All six were carrying handguns, and I could see one or two semiautomatics in the back of one SUV. The game plan was to wait for a customer to walk into the brothel and catch him and a sex worker in the act. As Leo Pichs, one of the undercover cops and the only Spanish-speaking member of the stakeout crew, explained, "We're going to wait till we get a couple of bodies in there, and then we just fucking whack it."

Ten minutes into the stakeout, Pichs's voice crackles over the walkie-talkie: "Two guys going in. Looks good. We'll give it a few minutes."

Five minutes pass, and Sauro speaks into his walkie-talkie: "Okay, Leo, let's go." He wheels out of the parking lot in time for me to see the two SUVs pull up in front of the brothel. The four men and two women jump out and run down the driveway into the back of the building, hands on their guns. Sauro pulls into the driveway after them. "I'd be rushing in with them, but I don't want to leave you," he says. A minute later, he gets a hand signal (which must mean everything's under control) and runs in after them, instructing me to stay in the car. A few minutes later, Sauro comes back and says I can come in.

Inside, two men sit handcuffed in the small spare living room, a stocky Guatemalan immigrant (the unlucky john) and a skinny older man wearing a BOSS T-shirt and a golfing cap who Sauro says is the trafficker, or pimp. Two women (who are not handcuffed) sit on chairs in different rooms, one in a bedroom, the other in what must have once been the dining room. The walls of the first-floor apartment are dirty and bare; rough gray mats are duct-taped to the hardwood floor, and there is a cockroach in the kitchen. A soda bottle lies on its side on a small table, spilling Mountain Dew over a box of Newport cigarettes, in front of a TV that is still tuned to the Spanish channel. One of the undercover cops says the pimp knocked the soda over in his haste to get away.

If this is a brothel, it is a big step down from the establishment that Julie runs in New York City and a world away from the upscale fantasies sold by Sheri's Ranch in Nevada. And yet, the woman who sits on a chair near the spilled bottle, a towel wrapped around her bikini underwear, is pretty and slim, with streaked blonde hair, immaculate French nails, and big green eyes, carefully made up. Her name is Juanita Delacruz; she's twenty-eight, and she comes from the Dominican Republic. She says she is an exotic dancer in New York City and came up to Providence on her own volition, to earn money to pay her rent. She can make $3,000 in five days here, she tells one of the cops.

The women from Homeland Security have rifled through Juanita's purse in the other bedroom and emerge with a fistful of cash and some blue poker chips. They want to know what's with the poker chips, but Juanita doesn't understand what they're asking. Pichs comes over and asks her a few questions in Spanish. He then translates what she says:

"They're tips. They are each worth $5, and they are like an IOU from clients who will come back to pay her in cash and retrieve the chips."

The other woman, dark-haired and stockier, sits in a nearby bedroom, next to a tousled queen-size bed that takes up most of the room. On the bureau opposite the bed sits her bag, clothing spilling out, paper towels, makeup, lubricating liquid, the tools of her trade. A pair of fake-diamond–studded high heels lie discarded on the floor. The woman, who says she is from Mexico, is wearing capri pants and a low-cut tank top. She doesn't appear to understand much English. When I look in the room a few minutes later, she is slumped over, her head in her hands.

One of the undercover cops, a wiry young man named Greg Scion, announces, "We have one stain and one condom." Sauro laughs and adds, "He's also got a timer. We can use that as evidence as well."

Sauro takes me aside and says that they don't plan to arrest the women. "We treat them as victims," he says. But he adds that they may be taken down to the police station so that detectives can try to get information out of them about the pimps who operate the brothel. Pichs briefly talks in Spanish to both women and then asks the female officers from Homeland Security to take Juanita into the other bedroom so she can get dressed.

While all of this is going on, two other young men saunter into the back of the apartment. They have no idea they've just walked into a raid. "What's going on?" asks one of them, smiling. Scion and another undercover cop quickly usher them outside and demand their IDs. The men, who are also Guatemalan, deny that they are here to see prostitutes, but it is clear they are lying. Scion reassures them, "As long as you're not wanted, you're fine. No problem."

A few minutes later, the word comes back: they're not on any Homeland Security databases. Expressions of pure relief sweep across their faces, and without another word, they disappear. "They're illegals; they work in a restaurant in East Providence," Scion says. "They weren't wanted, so we let them go."

Back inside, Pichs reappears in the living room, holding a sack.

"We've got the money, the ledgers, photographs, we just have to get the girls downtown." The two handcuffed men are ushered out by two uniformed policemen who were summoned after the raid, and the two women from Homeland Security take the girls outside.

As Sauro and I get back in his car and drive off, he says, "We still have a lot of investigating to do. We're trying to find out who's running the operation."

When I ask if raids like this one are the best use of police resources, he responds, "It's a quality-of-life issue. It's in a neighborhood where kids are riding bikes." Even though Sauro readily acknowledges that both of the sex workers in the brothel came to Providence voluntarily, he says that sometimes trafficking is involved.

A few days later, Sauro tells me that the Dominican sex worker was not arrested. But the Mexican woman was found to be an illegal immigrant, so the Providence police turned her over to the immigration authorities. Her name is Edith Palacio Miguel; she is thirty-five, and she was deported a couple of years ago, only to slip across the border again a short time later.

By the time I catch up with Sauro again a few months later, he says the city of Providence has passed the "Bodyworks" law, enabling police to shut down a number of Asian spas, including the one on North Main Street. Meanwhile, the john arrested in the brothel raid has pleaded guilty to a misdemeanor prostitution charge and is back at work. The pimp in the BOSS T-shirt is still sitting in a jail cell in Rhode Island, charged with trafficking and other prostitution-related charges. Sauro says he is awaiting trial.

The Mexican sex worker who Sauro originally said would be treated as a victim has been deported. As for the brothel on Waverly Street, it remains closed—for now.

# Sex Work Overseas

## PROHIBITION IN SWEDEN VERSUS LEGALIZATION
## IN NEW ZEALAND AND THE NETHERLANDS

t is after 7 p.m. on a sweltering July evening in Las Vegas, and the pool party at the Desiree Alliance conference is well under way. Dozens of sex workers in bathing suits and sarongs are clustered around one of the outdoor pools at the Alexis Park Resort, chatting and splashing in the bath-warm waters. Michelle Christy, the forty-four-year-old escort I met earlier in the day, beckons me over. "I have someone I think you should meet," she says, and gestures toward a pretty blond woman in a tank top and shorts, sitting by the side of the pool, her legs dangling in the water. The woman looks young, in her late twenties perhaps, and her light blond hair is bound into a single braid behind her back. Another sex worker, I assume.

"This is Ida Kock," Michelle says. "She's from Sweden, and she's doing some very interesting research." Kock, as it turns out, is a Ph.D. candidate in ethnology (the study of races and peoples) at Umea University in northern Sweden, and she is studying a very distinct group of people: sex workers in Sweden. I am curious about the impact of Sweden's 1999 law, which prohibits the purchase of sex (criminalizing clients) but not the actual sale of sex by individual sex workers. (Known as the Nordic model, the Swedish approach has since been adopted in Norway, Iceland, and most recently, Canada.)

Kock says the Swedish law, which was designed to protect sex workers from predatory men, has actually had the opposite effect, making their work less safe. I am eager to hear more, but since I haven't brought my notebook to the party, we agree to talk tomorrow. I am thus caught off guard the next morning, when shortly after the conference kicks off, around 10:30 a.m., Ida Kock skips up the steps to the stage. (As conferences go, Desiree's daily kick-off is on the late side, but one of the organizers tells me, "A lot of our attendees are working after hours, so we have to keep them in mind." From talking to conference participants, I discover that a number of the sex workers who have flown into Las Vegas from around the country do indeed have dates with regular clients who just happen to be in Sin City this week as well.)

Leaning into the microphone and speaking in excellent English, Kock announces that she would like to give a short testimonial to a friend of hers, "Jasmine," a one-time sex worker in Sweden who was recently killed by her ex-boyfriend.

"Due to the fact that she was a former sex worker, Jasmine was deemed an unfit parent and her ex-boyfriend received custody of the children, even though he had several convictions for drugs and other crimes," Kock says. "He was deemed to be a more fit parent than she was, so even a criminal is considered a better parent than a sex worker."

After Kock finishes speaking, there is a moment of silence to honor Jasmine's memory, and then the audience erupts into wild applause. The Swedish ethnographer later gives me a fuller account of her friend's tragic story. Jasmine, whose real name was Eva-Marree Kullander Smith, had a troubled childhood and spent much of her adolescence in state care (foster homes). She became pregnant with her first child, a girl, when she was twenty-one. A year later, when she was pregnant with her second child, a boy, she decided to leave their father, Joel Kabagambe, a Uganda émigré who had a history of substance abuse and was physically abusive toward her.

Kabagambe also had a criminal record, a conviction for drug possession and another one for assault. Eva-Marree and Joel agreed to share joint custody of their children, but he wouldn't help her financially. To support herself and her one-year-old daughter and infant son, Eva-Marree began working as an escort in Stockholm, meeting clients discreetly in hotels there. In 2009, her ex-boyfriend lodged a complaint with the state social services, claiming that their son, then only six months old, had a burn on his arm and that his mother had deliberately harmed him. A Swedish social services agency took the kids away from her, and shortly after that, a cousin of Eva-Marree called the agency to report that she was working as a sex worker.

"The cousin claimed that she was selling sex from the apartment while the kids were there, which wasn't true," Kock says. The social services agency investigated and found that there was no merit to the father's complaint, but by then he had been granted temporary custody of the children and was suing for full custody.

Kabagambe, furious that Eva-Marree was doing sex work, refused to let her see the children, even though she had joint custody. "He was fined for that, but he kept denying her access to the kids," Kock says. And this is where "social services started to get weird," Kock says. "They questioned her ability to parent and accused her of having a self-harming behavior, even though she had stopped selling sex."

To Kock, the reaction of the state agency in Eva-Marree's custody battle is intrinsically bound up with the Swedish government's moralistic approach to prostitution. The government views sex workers as victims of male violence and patriarchal oppression[1] and thus does not explicitly penalize them for selling sex. Instead, anyone who obtains or attempts to obtain sex in exchange for payment can be charged with an offense punishable by either a fine or imprisonment for up to one year.

"The Swedish law is very connected to the idea of selling sex as male violence toward women," Kock explains. "People who sell sex aren't doing anything illegal whatsoever. Yet if they sell sex, it's considered a self-harming behavior." This approach essentially treats women as children who must be protected from themselves at all costs, Kock says.

At the same time, other Swedish laws criminalize those who "promote" or "improperly financially exploit" sex work. Such legislation effectively criminalizes sex work indoors (unless the sex worker owns the space in which he or she works). Since it is illegal to share any income derived from sex work, sex workers are often forced to live and work alone (which makes them more vulnerable to violence from clients.) It also forces them to lie, in order to rent the premises in which they work.[2]

While the 1999 Swedish Purchasing Act was intended to protect sex workers, it has actually harmed them, research shows. Streetwalkers have reported increased violence, in part because regular clients avoid them for fear of arrest and have turned instead to the Internet and indoor venues for sex. The clients who remain on the street are more likely to be drunk and violent, and they often demand unprotected sex.[3] As two Swedish researchers, Susanne Dodillet and Petra Östergren, found in a recent study, when clients are in a hurry and frightened of being arrested, it is more difficult for the sex worker to assess whether they might be dangerous.[4]

Since the passage of the law, Swedish police have also become more aggressive toward sex workers. In their study, Dodillet and Östergren found that instead of police being a source of protection for sex workers (as the law intended), many women feel hunted by them and are subject to invasive searches and questioning.[5] More intensive police patrols have resulted in the disbanding of informal networks that sex workers had formed to protect themselves.[6] Some sex workers say that police have reported them to their landlords, causing them to be evicted, according to a 2014 study. In other cases, police have informed hotels that sex workers were selling sex on their promises, leading to the deportation of migrant workers. As the researchers of this 2014 study note, "Such reports are strikingly at odds with government claims that 'the women . . . who are victims of prostitution and trafficking do not risk any legal repercussions.'"[7]

The Swedish National Police Board, which examined the new law after it was implemented, also found that clients are no longer willing to assist in cases against profiteers who exploit sex workers. Previously, legal cases against traffickers or pimps could sometimes be supported by the testimony of sex buyers, the police report noted, but that is no longer happening because clients fear being arrested themselves.[8]

Despite more aggressive policing, the 1999 law has not put much of a dent in the Swedish sex industry; all it's done is displace streetwalkers, forcing them into more isolated, dangerous spaces, researchers have found.[9] In the meantime, the number of convictions for purchasing sex has remained low, amounting to around 500 in the ten years since the law was enacted.[10] The majority of police investigations against clients are discontinued because of insufficient evidence, according to several studies.[11] Fear of arrest and prosecution has also resulted in clients' being unwilling to give sex workers their contact information, making it more difficult for workers to screen their clients, according to the 2014 Swedish study.[12]

Nor is there evidence that the Nordic model has reduced trafficking in the region. Indeed, since the Swedish law was passed, the total number of foreign prostitutes in Denmark, Norway, and Sweden has increased, according to a 2010 report by the Swedish government. After the Swedish law went into effect, the number of women from Nigeria who were being trafficked in Norway (which borders Sweden to the east) rose dramatically. After Norway passed a similar law against purchasing sex, in 2009, Gothenburg, a Swedish city close to Norway, experienced a dramatic increase in trafficked prostitutes from Nigeria. The Swedish government's report acknowledged that the total number of foreign prostitutes in all three Scandinavian countries has increased since the Swedish law was first passed.[13]

The rise in trafficked sex workers throughout Scandinavia was cited by two New York University law students in a 2012 research paper arguing that criminalizing prostitution tends to reduce the number of voluntary prostitutes and increase the number of those involuntarily trafficked into the trade. It all has to do with supply and demand. Workers who sell sex by choice are more likely to exit the trade when faced with the risk of arrest, and that drives up the price, making it more lucrative for traffickers to step in and fill the demand.[14]

The 1999 law has had negative public health consequences as well, according to surveys of sex workers and reports from Swedish authorities.[15] Because clients are so rushed and afraid of being arrested, sex workers have less time and power to screen them and demand safe sex (that is, use condoms). "You have to get into a car really fast rather than having time to talk and screen the client, as you did before," Kock says. A report from the Swedish National Board of Health and Welfare and a separate 2014 survey of Swedish sex workers found much the same thing: female sex workers are now exposed to more dangerous clients and cannot take the time to negotiate condom use or evaluate the risks involved.[16]

In addition, Sweden's prohibitionist approach discourages the distribution of condoms to sex workers, according to a recent survey by HIV Sweden, a nonprofit health group, and the Rose Alliance, a sex workers group in Sweden. Of the sex workers surveyed, 68 percent said they had never received condoms from social services providers who work with sex workers to prevent the spread of sexually transmitted diseases.[17] This has led to reports of an increase in unprotected sex between prostitutes and their clients.[18]

In large part because the Swedish law impedes sex workers' ability to practice safe sex, the Global Commission on HIV and the Law, an independent group convened by the United Nations, released a report in 2012 denouncing the Nordic model. "Since the enactment in 1999, the law has not improved—indeed it has worsened the lives of sex workers," the commission's report concluded.[19]

That was certainly the case for Eva-Marree Kullander Smith. In August 2012, Eva-Marree lost custody of her children to her ex-boyfriend, despite his criminal record and the fact that he had restraining orders placed on him by two previous girlfriends. Social workers testified that Eva-Marree was an unfit parent because she had once done sex work. She appealed the court's decision and lost again in March of 2013. The second time around, Kock says, the court didn't question Eva-Marree's ability to parent because she had once sold sex; instead, a judge ruled that the kids had been away from their mother for so long they were detached from her. The judge didn't seem to understand or care that the separation was not Eva-Marree's fault, Kock says.

A few months later, she finally arranged a supervised visit with her four-year-old son. The date was July 11, 2013, and it was to be the first time she had seen her son in eighteen months, Kock says. Eva-Marree was on her way to meet her son at a family social care facility in Sweden when she bumped into her ex-boyfriend, Joel Kabagambe, on the same bus (even though he wasn't supposed to be at the visitation.) They started arguing, and when they got to the facility and were walking through its gardens, Kabagambe pulled out a knife and stabbed Eva-Marree thirty times in the back, neck, and chest. The social worker who was there to supervise the visit tried to intervene and was also stabbed in the neck. "She survived, but Eva-Marree died in the ambulance on the way to the hospital," Kock says. "Her son, who was waiting inside the house, heard her screaming." Eva-Marree was twenty-seven years old when she died.

Her murder and the circumstances surrounding it became nationwide news. At the October 2013 trial of Joel Kabagambe, the defense claimed that he was mentally unstable and was on medication at the time of the stabbing. Kabagambe was found guilty of murder and sentenced to eighteen years in prison.

"If he had these mental problems, how was he seen as the fit parent?" Kock asks. "She had no convictions and had done nothing illegal, yet she was still considered to be the unfit parent. It shows what people who sell sex are treated like in custody battles."

The 1999 law itself didn't cause Eva-Marree's murder, Kock says, but it has certainly heightened the stigma surrounding sex work in Sweden. "The [1999] law is often portrayed as helping women in the sex industry, but that's nonsense," Kock says. "It doesn't help them; it makes their lives more difficult."

Laura Agustin, a well-known anthropologist and author of *Sex at the Margins: Migration, Labour Markets and the Rescue Industry,* agrees. As she wrote in a blog for *Salon* shortly after Eva-Marree's murder: "The lesson is not that Sweden's law caused a murder or that any other law would have prevented it. Whore stigma exists everywhere under all prostitution laws. Sweden's law can be said to have given whore stigma a new rationality for social workers and judges, the stamp of government approval for age-old prejudice."[20]

## A Sea Change in Sex Worker Safety

In 2000, the Netherlands, long a bastion of tolerance, took an entirely different approach. After decades of tacitly allowing prostitution under a policy of de facto decriminalization, the Dutch government legalized sex work in certain indoor venues, such as brothels, massage parlors, and window units, and began regulating those venues as regular businesses. Owners were required to obtain licenses and become subject to regular inspections, much like the owners of brothels in Nevada's rural counties. In the Netherlands, the licensed brothels and parlors are taxed and treated like any other business. Sex workers also have to register if they want to be considered legal and have access to health care and social security benefits.

The 2000 law also allowed street prostitutes to work in specific outdoor parks, known as *tippelzones*, in major cities throughout the country. In 2003, some of the *tippelzones,* including the largest one in Amsterdam, were closed in response to complaints from Dutch citizens about overcrowding and drug abuse in these parks. A few *tippelzones* in Utrecht and other Dutch cities remain open, according to Dina Siegel, a professor of criminology at Utrecht University.

The 2000 law also stipulated that only Dutch citizens could be considered legal sex workers, making at least 12,000 migrant workers illegal almost overnight.[21] As sociologist Elizabeth Bernstein notes, a sizable proportion of the illegal workers left the country for Germany or Belgium, while those who remained relocated to the *tippelzones* or resorted to working for underground escort agencies or through the Internet.[22]

In an interview on Skype, Dina Siegel explained that the whole idea behind legalization was to make prostitution more visible and stem the rising tide of non-European women migrating into the Netherlands. "It was more of a migration issue than a prostitution issue," says Siegel, who has studied sex workers migrating from Russia, Eastern Europe, and Latin America into the Netherlands. "[The government was] trying to control the migration of non-European women."

The 2000 law also stiffened penalties for traffickers or anyone found guilty of forcing people to engage in prostitution or employing the services of minors; it mandated prison sentences of up to six years for such offenders. Brothels and window units discovered to be employing illegal migrants or underage workers or breaking other existing laws could be shut down under the new legislation. In 2007, the city of Amsterdam closed down thirty different sex businesses, accusing them of breaking the law. Siegel, however, says the crackdown was largely an effort by municipal officials to refashion the red-light district into a shopping mecca for tourists. "They don't want tourists who go to prostitutes; they want tourists who go to the Van Gogh museum," she says. In 2008, after a new administrative decree permitted authorities to deny permits or contracts to any organization in which criminal activity was suspected, the Amsterdam city council shut two of the most famous sex clubs in that city and also closed a number of other brothels and window units.[23]

According to a major study commissioned by the Dutch government and published in 2007, the new law appears to have enhanced the safety of sex workers working in the legal sector.[24] In another study, sociologist Ronald Weitzer found that since legalization, there has been a sea change in the way that Dutch police treat sex workers and the owners of brothels and window units. "The police are our best friend at the moment; we work together with the police," one owner of a window unit in Amsterdam's red-light district told Weitzer.[25]

Decriminalizing the Dutch sex industry has also made it safer for the general public. For decades, the red-light districts in Amsterdam and other major cities have been safe places for tourists and residents to wander through at virtually all hours of the day or night. When I visited the city in the 1970s with several classmates (I was spending my junior year abroad at the time), we happened to stay in a cheap hostel in the middle of the red-light district, right next door to one of Amsterdam's famous window units for prostitutes. These window units resemble one-room storefronts with large windows open to the street. The sex workers sit or stand in front of the windows dressed in bikinis or sexy lingerie. They pose provocatively or shake their bodies and call out to people passing by. When a client goes inside, they shut the red-velvet curtains lining the windows and get down to business.

One day during my visit, several tourists stopped in front of the hostel's smaller front-facing windows and peered in at me as I was doing homework. They were probably wondering why a lady of the night was wearing a turtleneck and jeans. Apart from living in a fishbowl, my compatriots and I felt completely comfortable wandering around the district. Indeed, after an afternoon visit to the Heineken Brewery to sample the free beer, one of the men in our party (another American college student) disappeared for several hours, no doubt to taste the pleasures of Amsterdam's red-light district.

Now that prostitution has been legalized, the sex industry in the Netherlands has boomed, and an even greater proportion of its clients are tourists. Elizabeth Bernstein visited the famous red-light district in Amsterdam, which lies in the center of town and is hard to miss. As she describes it, "The district is safe and well-policed, but the roaming packs of libidinous male tourists, rowdy and drunken crowds, wafting aromas of cannabis, ubiquitous fluorescent lights, and dense multi-directional foot traffic are overwhelming to the senses, to say the least. From the fragments of dialogue my ear casually perceives, it is clear that the buyers — like the sellers — hail from many different countries across Europe, North America, Africa, and Asia. Amsterdam's red-light district is a dense microcosm of the global sexual marketplace."[26]

Bernstein also described her visit to a live sex show at one of the numerous sex theaters in the red-light district:

> I stood in a massive line behind a group of some forty or fifty sari-clad women and their husbands, who had just piled out of the tour bus that was parked in front. There were also several coed groups of well-scrubbed North American, Australian and British college students on package holidays, already excited and in giggles. . . . [Inside] the members of the audience sat sipping beer, rather than munching popcorn, but otherwise it was quite like going to the movies. All watched politely as a young

blonde woman dressed as a nun fellated a slightly older and darker Surinamese man dressed as a priest, while Gregorian chants played softly in the background. Then they went out in the audience, the robes came off and they proceeded to have full intercourse, splayed across the laps of giggling audience members.[27]

As Bernstein concludes, "the Netherlands' pragmatic recognition of the sex trade as a legitimate sphere of commerce and employment has resulted in greater social legitimacy and working conditions for at least some parties"—that is, sex workers in the legal sector who are now free of police harassment.[28] It has also improved the lot of brothel owners who can afford to pay the licensing fees and high taxes required of such businesses.

While the legal approach in the Netherlands has undeniably improved some sex workers' lives, one big question remains: what has the impact of legalization been on the trafficking and exploitation of underage sex workers and illegal immigrants? Let's start with underage prostitution. Several studies have found the presence of minors virtually nonexistent in both the legal and illegal sectors of the Dutch sex industry. The 2007 study commissioned by the Dutch government found that "scarcely any underage prostitutes seem to be working in the licensed sector, and there are no signs of a large presence of underage prostitutes in the non-licensed [sector] either." [29] In a 2010 survey of 94 window workers in Amsterdam, none was found to be underage.[30]

According to a recent report issued by the National Rapporteur on Trafficking in Human Beings and Sexual Violence against Children, an independent government-funded Dutch agency, the percentage of reported underage trafficking victims (in relation to the total number of reported victims) declined from 28 percent in 2007 to 16 percent in 2011. Most of these underage victims have Dutch nationality, the report found.[31]

The overall trafficking picture is muddier. While there is no question that sex trafficking does exist in the Netherlands, Dutch officials and researchers who monitor human trafficking say there is no solid evidence of an increase in trafficking since prostitution was legalized in the Netherlands. The 2007 study commissioned by the Dutch government found that the number of foreign prostitutes working without valid papers had decreased in the years after legalization.

But in the past five years, there has been a substantial uptick in the number of Eastern European women (from Bulgaria, Romania, and Hungary) entering the Netherlands. There are currently about 25,000 to 28,000 sex workers in the Netherlands, and between 65 and 80 percent of the women are not from the European Union, according to Dutch government estimates.[32]

However, most of these women are not being forced into the sex trade against their will. According to social services agencies that work with sex workers in Amsterdam's red-light district, most of the migrant women know beforehand that they will be working in prostitution in the Netherlands. Many of the women from Eastern Europe (where the economy has been in a tailspin with the European debt crisis) were persuaded to move to the Netherlands by female friends who were already working there.[33]

Dina Siegel, who has studied and interviewed dozens of migrant sex workers throughout the Netherlands, found much the same. "These are girls from Romania and Bulgaria, and they come for a few years to help their families," she says. "They invest the money they make in houses or their studies or a business. They are all here voluntarily. I haven't seen one who was forced. There are probably a few [who have been trafficked], but I didn't see them."

In a 2011 article published in the *European Journal on Criminal Policy and Research*, Siegel cites a number of different studies finding that the overwhelming majority of the non-European women, including those from Nigeria and Latin America, choose to work in the Dutch sex trade and travel to the Netherlands in order to improve their economic situation. She concludes, "Given these findings, the problem of human trafficking often seems exaggerated and misinterpreted in the EU [European Union] as well as in other parts of the world. In . . . public debate, it is much more fashionable to talk about human trafficking, violence and exploitation than it is to approach the phenomenon of prostitution as a career path chosen by women themselves."[34]

The number of possible trafficking victims "registered" by Dutch police in 2011 (1,222) was 71 percent higher than the number registered in 2007 (716), according to the 2012 report by the National Rapporteur. But that doesn't mean that trafficking is actually on the rise in the Netherlands, as the report itself noted: "An increase in the number of reported victims could mean that human trafficking is increasing in the Netherlands, but is more likely an indication that more victims are being identified and that the reporting and registration of victims has improved. For example, a partial explanation of the sharp increase in 2011 could be the fact that in that year CoMensha [Coordination Centre for Human Trafficking] made agreements with regional police forces on the structural reporting of victims."[35]

As Weitzer notes, the number of persons convicted of trafficking offenses in the Netherlands has remained fairly stable in recent years: 79 in 2003 and 23 in 2007. He argues that these numbers cast doubt on the claim by some antiprostitution groups that trafficking has skyrocketed since prostitution was legalized in 2000. Several studies commissioned by the Dutch government concluded that it is likely that trafficking has become more difficult under legalization (because indoor venues that hire illegal migrants are penalized). As one National Rapporteur report concluded, "Before the lifting of the general ban on brothels, THB [trafficking in human beings] and other (criminal) abuses were taking place in all sectors of prostitution. Some of these sectors are now under control and can be assumed to have rid themselves of their former criminal excesses. . . . It is possible that THB is increasing in the illegal, non-regulated or non-controlled sectors. If this were the case, it still cannot be assumed that the extent of THB is now at the same or even above the 'old' level it was before the ban on brothels. It is in fact likely that this is not the case."[36]

Even if trafficking, or the transporting of migrants across borders for involuntary prostitution, does not appear to have increased, that doesn't mean that sex workers in the Netherlands (and elsewhere) are not being exploited or coerced into the trade. The 2007 Dutch study found that despite legalization, pimps are still a common phenomenon there, controlling many sex workers, particularly those who work in the window units or as escorts.[37] The researchers who conducted that study observed that a great majority of the window prostitutes work with a so-called boyfriend or pimp and that some of these workers are forced to hand over their earnings to their pimps.[38] Problems with pimps occur relatively frequently among Eastern European, African, and Asian prostitutes, but also among Dutch prostitutes, the researchers found.[39]

While no amount of coercion in the sex trade is acceptable, the numbers of prostitutes who are being trafficked and exploited under the Dutch system of legalization is much lower than the local media claim, researchers in the Netherlands say. Among the prostitutes interviewed in the licensed sector, only 8 percent indicated that they started doing sex work under some form of coercion, the 2007 study found.[40] As Siegel concludes, "The image of the Netherlands as a country where almost everything is permitted with its legalized prostitution and which attracts and facilitates human traffickers from all around the world is a myth. . . . As a social phenomenon human trafficking is limited in Dutch media and in public debate to a vague generalized abstraction, which does not distinguish between voluntary independent sex work and the cases of violent exploitation."[41]

What the media also fail to report is that there actually seems to be less violence against sex workers in countries that have legalized and regulated the sex trade. For example, a comprehensive 2005 study of prostitution throughout the continent, commissioned by the European Parliament, found that countries (such as Denmark and Spain) that have an abolitionist approach to prostitution (in other words, it is decriminalized but not regulated as a form of work) appear to have a higher level of violence than countries that have legalized prostitution, such as the Netherlands and Germany.[42]

Despite such findings, the Swedish ethnographer Ida Kock and many sex worker advocates are critical of Germany's approach. In 2002, Germany decriminalized prostitution and allowed its municipalities to decide whether they wanted to legalize and regulate the trade. (Cities and towns with a population of less than 50,000 were allowed to completely ban prostitution.) Sex work is thus legal in a number of Germany's major cities, including Frankfurt, Berlin, Hamburg, and Bremen. Sex workers can legally work in hotel-brothels, sauna clubs, and their own homes, and as in the Netherlands, most of the women working in the sex trade come from Eastern Europe. Only 40 percent are of German background.[43] In the decade since Germany decriminalized the trade, prostitution-related crimes have declined markedly and trafficking has also declined, according to German government statistics.[44]

However, all sex workers in Germany are required to register as prostitutes, and Kock says that most don't register because they don't want the stigma of wearing the Scarlet S. "The German model is so unsuccessful because so many sex workers don't register," she says. "No one wants to be known as a sex worker in public."

The German approach is "similar to the Nevada model: paternalistic, corporate, and dominated by men," Koch says over a box lunch on the second day of the Desiree Alliance conference. "The Nevada model is very demeaning for people who work in the industry; there is mandatory testing and the brothels take 50 percent of the women's earnings. The giant brothels in Germany are the same."

Even though Germany's 2002 law granted adult sex workers the right to enter into contracts with brothel owners and sue clients for nonpayment, in reality, the vast majority of sex workers in Germany don't sign contracts or press for greater rights. "Prostitutes fear that employment contracts will jeopardize their anonymity," reports Weitzer in his 2012 book. "Owners dislike contracts because they would then have to pay insurance premiums for their employees, who also would be entitled to holiday pay, pregnancy leave and social security benefits."[45]

## New Zealand's Successful Approach

To Kock (and many sex worker advocates), the safest and most successful governmental approach to prostitution can be found Down Under—in New Zealand. In 1995, New South Wales, the highly populated region in Australia that contains the country's capital, Sydney, was the first in that area of the world to decriminalize brothels and street prostitution, allowing local councils to regulate where brothels could be located and in what form. However, living on the earnings of a prostitute remained illegal (except for those running a brothel), as did advertising for prostitution and procuring prostitutes. In 2003, New Zealand officials went much further, removing criminal prohibitions against solicitation, living on the avails of adult sex work, and operating indoor venues where sex work takes place.

The New Zealand Prostitution Reform Act, as the 2003 law is known, retained prohibitions on underage prostitution and made it a serious offense to compel anyone to sell sex or arrange for or receive commercial sexual services from someone under the age of eighteen. The act, which some researchers argue is essentially legalization, requires brothels, escort agencies, and other venues to be licensed and allows for periodic inspections of the premises by law enforcement, health, and social services agencies.[46] In both New Zealand and New South Wales, sex workers themselves do not have to register as prostitutes; if they want to pay taxes and obtain health and social security benefits, they can register as a service worker or an independent contractor. "That's a huge deal," Kock says. "That means that when you go to the tax office, you don't have a stranger asking you questions about your sex work."

According to several studies, lifting the ban on prostitution has improved working conditions for both indoor and street workers in New Zealand and New South Wales. It has made it easier for streetwalkers to insist on condom use and has enabled indoor workers to refuse clients without being penalized.[47] Indeed, in February 2014, the New Zealand Human Rights Review Tribunal awarded a sex worker sizable damages for sexual harassment by a brothel owner.[48] In a 2006 study of 772 sex workers in five locales around New Zealand, the majority said they feel safer since decriminalization; the police no longer harass them and they feel more comfortable reporting crimes.[49]

Decriminalization has also made it more likely for sex workers to practice safe sex, an undeniable public health benefit. In a 2010 study that compared sex work in three Australian cities, researchers found that women who worked in licensed brothels in Melbourne, where prostitution is legal and those who worked in New South Wales, where it is decriminalized, were much more likely to have access to free condoms than sex workers in Perth, where all forms of prostitution are criminalized.[50]

Neither New Zealand nor New South Wales requires mandatory testing of sex workers for HIV infection and other sexually transmitted diseases. Instead, their governments rely on community-based health education programs that encourage safe sex and educate sex workers about AIDS and other diseases. As a result, sex workers in New Zealand and New South Wales have "very high condom use rates" and a very low incidence of HIV transmission, according to a 2012 report issued by the United Nations Development Programme.[51]

In contrast, the U.N. report found that countries in Asia and South Pacific that criminalize some aspects of sex work or heavily regulate it in certain locales (with mandatory testing) have not been nearly as effective in preventing HIV epidemics among sex workers. The problem, the report noted, is that the majority of sex workers in countries such as Cambodia, China, Taiwan, Thailand, and the Philippines operate illegally or outside the regulated sector. And because these workers fear arrest, they are much less likely to use condoms and practice safe sex. The report concluded, "Criminalization increases vulnerability to HIV by fueling stigma and discrimination, limiting access to HIV and other sexual health services, condoms and harm reduction services, and adversely affecting the self-esteem of sex workers and their ability to make informed choices about their health."[52]

The report also found that antitrafficking laws in Cambodia, India, Malaysia, and the Philippines have been used to justify raids on brothels that result in the abuse of sex workers and undermine efforts to reduce the spread of HIV.[53] In Cambodia, for example, Human Rights Watch documented cases in which sex workers (who were not being trafficked) were "rescued" from brothels and detained at police centers, where they were beaten up after trying to escape. One woman told Human Rights Watch that the guards threatened to "slit our throats" if she and other sex workers tried to escape again.

In what some consider a supremely ironic twist, one of the leaders of
the antitrafficking movement in Cambodia who encouraged these brutal
crackdowns was recently forced to resign from her own antitrafficking
organization amid allegations that she had lied about being a child trafficking victim herself and had encouraged other young women to fab-
ricate trafficking stories. Somaly Mam has raised millions of dollars to
combat trafficking (the foundation bearing her name raised $2.8 million
in 2012 alone from wealthy Western donors). Mam's antitrafficking work
was frequently cited by *New York Times* columnist Nicholas Kristof, and
indeed, Mam's foundation was listed as a "partner" of Kristof's own antitrafficking movement, Half a Sky, on his website.[54]

In February 2012, while speaking at the White House, Mam said
that she had been sold into sex slavery at the age of nine or ten by a
man she knew as Grandfather. However, acquaintances and teachers
who knew Mam as a child said that she had come to their Cambodian
village with her parents and stayed there until she graduated from high
school, according to a 2014 *Newsweek* cover story. One of the women
Mam coached, Meas Ratha, gave a chilling performance on French television in 1998, describing how she had been sold to a brothel and held
against her will as a sex slave. In late 2013, according to *Newsweek,* Ratha
finally confessed that her story was fabricated and carefully rehearsed for
the cameras under Mam's instruction. She also said she had been chosen
from a group of girls who had been put through an audition.[55]

Mam's ex-husband, Pierre Legros, who helped her start her first antitrafficking initiative in the 1990s, acknowledged that the lure of big
money provides incentives for antitrafficking nonprofits, such as Mam's
foundation and an organization he cofounded with Mam to rescue trafficking victims, to inflate statistics and distort the truth. "If you have no
story, you don't have money," he told the *New York Times.*[56]

While Mam has stepped down from her own foundation, "the consequences of her fables will prove harder to correct," wrote one former sex
worker in a *New York Times* op-ed piece that ran the same day as the news
of her resignation. "Ms. Mam and her foundation banked on Western
feel-good demands for intervention, culminating in abusive crackdowns

on the people she claimed to save," wrote Melissa Gira Grant, the author of *Playing the Whore: The Work of Sex Work.* "In brutal raids on brothels and in parks . . . women were chased down, detained and assaulted."[57]

Not surprisingly, it was antitrafficking zealots such as Mam and Legros who criticized New Zealand's move toward decriminalization, warning that it would bring a flood of prostitutes to New Zealand. But since the passage of the 2003 act, the number of sex workers in the country has remained relatively stable. In addition, there has been no increase in the number of underage workers, according to a government-funded 2008 study done by the Prostitution Law Review Committee, a commission of eleven experts appointed by the Ministry of Justice to review the impact of the Prostitution Reform Act. Trafficking remains a relatively minor problem in New Zealand, which retains one of the most favorable rankings in the U.S. 2013 Trafficking in Persons Report. Overall, the 2008 Ministry of Justice study concluded that the "majority of individuals involved in the sex industry [in New Zealand] were better off now than under the prior system."[58]

Given New Zealand's isolated location (its closest neighbor, Australia, is 2,583 miles away), it is not surprising that trafficking is not a major problem there. In contrast, Germany and the Netherlands, by virtue of their central European locations, are much more vulnerable to the migration of both voluntary and involuntary sex workers from other parts of Europe, Latin America, and Africa.

## The Stigma of Sex Work

Many researchers and sex worker advocates prefer the New Zealand approach because it recognizes the entrenched stigma involved in being a sex worker and does not force sex workers to declare their occupation publicly. The government has also made an effort to include the voice of sex workers on the committee in charge of implementing the 2003 law.

Even Down Under, however, sex work remains stigmatized. Sex workers are looked down upon by the general public and are often estranged from their families. Of the 772 New Zealand sex workers surveyed in a national study done by the University of Otago's Christchurch School of Medicine, most felt that the stigma attached to sex work was a greater risk to their health than the risks from violence, exploitation, and unsafe sex. While decriminalization has made it possible for sex workers to practice safe sex and better protect themselves from violent clients or pimps, it has not significantly lessened the impact of the stigma on the sex workers' mental health, the study found.[59]

Much of the existing stigma against sex workers comes from entrenched views of marriage and female sexuality, as discussed in Chapter 4. In a 2010 book about the New Zealand prostitution reforms, Gillian Abel, a public health researcher at the University of Otago at Christchurch, and Lisa Fitzgerald, a public health sociologist at the University of Queensland, Australia, cite the same problem: "Sex workers and most especially female sex workers do not conform to ideals of 'normal' sexuality with its accompanying presumptions of female passivity in the sexual domain. They are, therefore, as Sibley has termed 'othered'—different from 'normal' decent citizens, framed as 'deviant' and generally stereotyped as involved in drug use, gang activity, crime, spread of sexually transmitted infections and with threatening the moral fabric of society."[60]

In a Skype interview months after we met by the pool in Las Vegas, Ida Kock also connected the stigma surrounding sex work to "ideas about female sexuality and female chastity" and warned that such entrenched stereotypes will not change quickly. "I think we all overestimate the value of changing the law," the Swedish ethnographer says. "We can have better legislation that protects sex workers' rights, but the stigma won't go away overnight."

In the meantime, Eva-Marree Kullander Smith's young children are in the care of Swedish Social Services, the same agency that refused to let her raise them. They will never know their mother or how hard she fought for them.

# 11

## Canada's Public Health Experiment

W hen Valerie Scott was a child growing up in New Brunswick, the northeastern province of Canada just over the border from Maine, she would watch old westerns on rainy afternoons. And that's when she fell in love with saloon girls. "The cowboys running around killing each other bored me, but I lived for the moment when the saloon girls came on," Scott recalls. "The cowboys couldn't pull the wool over their eyes, and sometimes they'd get their own saloon. I knew that's what I wanted to be: a saloon girl."

This was, of course, years before Valerie understood exactly what saloon girls did, but even when she gleaned the truth (from a friend at the age of eleven), she wasn't deterred. After graduating from high school, she majored in science at the University of Guelph in Ontario (near Toronto) and began working as an exotic dancer to pay her way through school.

"One of my first costumes was a nineteenth century saloon girl," Scott says. "I danced for seven years and worked up to feature status." By the early 1980s, she had dropped out of school and was performing burlesque in a different city every night, from Philadelphia, Miami, and New York to Toronto, Vancouver, and San Juan, Puerto Rico. She eventually tired of the constant traveling and, at the age of twenty-four, discovered a new way of working in the sex industry.

"I put a companion ad in the *Globe and Mail* [a major Toronto newspaper] and ran it for one week," Scott says. "I received ninety-three replies, and I threw out the ones with poor grammar, reasoning [that] they probably wouldn't have a very good job. And then I began to work." She would meet clients in a public place, and if they passed her screening test, she would take them to her apartment or a hotel. Most of her clients were men from Toronto, many of them married. "I remember standing in the hallway of my apartment after the third or fourth client I'd seen and thinking, 'I could kick myself for not getting into the business sooner,'" she says. "This is a good job. I don't care what everyone says."

By the mid '80s, however, Scott was disgusted, not by the sex work, but by the stigma surrounding it from every facet of society. "I couldn't handle being treated like I was a disposable person," she says. "I couldn't handle my colleagues being treated like that. And I hated lying to my parents and friends about what I was doing."

In 1985, the conservative government then in power in Canada passed a law that prohibited communicating in a public place for the purpose of engaging in prostitution. Known as the communicating offense, it made life on the streets much more dangerous for streetwalkers, who, because of the fear of being arrested, could no longer take the time they needed to assess clients before they climbed into their cars. What Scott saw politicized her.

"I didn't work on the street, but too many of my colleagues who did were getting hurt," Scott says. "I would take women to the police station to have them report the violence, and the police would say to my face, 'It's part of their job.'"

One day, Scott was listening to the CBC (Canadian Broadcasting Corporation), and she heard John Crosby, then Canada's justice minister, talking. "He was carrying on about sex workers like we were vermin," Scott says. "That was it. That was the moment."

Scott joined the Canadian Organization for the Rights of Prostitutes (CORP) and became active in the sex workers' rights movement. The first lawsuit she and CORP filed challenged, on constitutional grounds, the new law making communication for the purpose of prostitution a criminal offense. But in 1990, the Supreme Court of Canada upheld the law. Scott wanted to carry on the fight, but her group didn't have the money. "Challenging all the [prostitution] laws was a $200,000 case," she says. "We had $40 in our legal fund."

In Canada, unlike the United States, selling or buying sex itself was not a crime. Instead, Canadian authorities relied on three laws to curb prostitution: a law prohibiting the operation of a bawdy house or brothel; a law against living on the avails of prostitution, which was aimed at pimps but also was used to arrest sex workers' domestic partners, security guards, and business agents; and the law against communicating for the purpose of prostitution.

In the years after the Supreme Court of Canada upheld that last mandate, Canadian researchers amassed a body of research showing that all three criminal codes increased the risk of violence to sex workers and made it more difficult for them to practice safe sex and access health care. Several studies showed that violence against sex workers increased dramatically in the 1990s after the passage of the communicating law, according to a 2006 report by the Canadian House of Commons.[1] Sex worker advocates say the 1985 law against communicating made life particularly dangerous for streetwalkers.

One study, for instance, showed that up to 98 percent of women who worked the streets of Vancouver's poorest area, the Downtown Eastside, experienced violence from clients, pimps, and others.[2] Another, more recent study, published in the *British Medical Journal* in 2009, found that of 237 streetwalkers throughout Vancouver, more than half (57 percent) had experienced physical or sexual violence at least once in an eighteen-month period.[3] As lead researcher Kate Shannon said, "These women continue to be pushed to work in isolated spaces, with limited access to housing and drug treatment, which further compounds their risk of being physically assaulted or raped."[4]

What this research revealed was that violence was not intrinsic to sex work—women working indoors were much less likely than street workers to be assaulted. Rather, it showed that the laws prohibiting women from working in brothels, communicating with clients, and living on the avails of prostitution were largely responsible for the violence against sex workers. For example, a 2011 study of Vancouver sex workers found that Canada's prostitution laws made it more difficult for them to secure housing and practice safe sex.[5] Published in *Social Science & Medicine*, this study found that criminalization made it difficult for sex workers to live and work together in indoor spaces and thus forced them out on the streets, where it was harder for them to negotiate safe sex. In addition, restrictive curfews and guest polices at many rooming houses in Vancouver's Downtown Eastside forced low-income women out onto the street, where they were at greater risk of being subject to physical violence and contracting sexually transmitted diseases, the study found.[6]

"Normalized violence in street-based cultures often leads women into relationships with older men for protection . . . and these relationships can be physically abusive and economically exploitative," the researchers noted. They concluded that Canada's prostitution laws led to discriminatory and exploitative housing practices that target the most marginalized populations (poor minority women.) The researchers called for the development of women-only housing, which would "promote women's agency and ability to negotiate health, safety and risks of HIV infection."[7]

The Canadian findings echo earlier research in Miami, which found that homelessness and marginal housing increase the risk that sex workers will have unprotected sex. Women who are either homeless or sleeping on a friend's couch are more likely to be desperate for money and have sex with clients who refuse to wear condoms, the Miami studies found.[8] In yet another study of street-based workers, by the Urban Justice Center of New York, sex workers themselves said that the single most important public health intervention would be stable and affordable housing. As the researchers noted, "Homelessness creates a cycle of deepening impoverishment that may be almost impossible to escape. The lack of a fixed address or a telephone number hinders attempts to find other employment. The high cost of even substandard short-stay accommodation imposes a financial burden that may be hard to meet without resorting to the 'fast money' offered by illegal activities such as prostitution. Temporary accommodation creates an environment that is often not conductive to resolving other contributory problems such as substance dependency."[9]

Since other research shows that drug addiction increases the risk of HIV infection, decriminalizing prostitution and providing more stable housing for sex workers would reduce the spread of HIV infection and other diseases. (Perhaps this is a good place to point out that the Netherlands, where prostitution has been decriminalized since the 1970s and legalized since 2000, has the lowest rate of HIV infection in the world.[10]) The intrinsic link between eliminating laws against prostitution and improving public health is one of the primary reasons why groups as far-flung as the World Health Organization, the United Nations AIDS Advisory Group, Human Rights Watch, and the National Association of Social Workers support the decriminalization of consensual adult prostitution.

While such emerging evidence helped bolster the policy argument against Canada's prostitution laws, what really turned the tide of public (and judicial) sentiment was the discovery that a serial killer had been systematically butchering Aboriginal streetwalkers in Vancouver. Many of these women were part of the generation of Aboriginal Canadians (native Indian, Inuit, and Métis) who had been molested as children after they were taken away from their parents and put in residential schools. According to a recent class action suit against the Canadian government, thousands of Aboriginal children in British Columbia were removed from their own homes and put in non-Aboriginal homes across North America between 1962 and 1996.[11]

"It was during a period when we wanted to destroy their culture," explains John Lowman, a professor of criminology at Simon Fraser University in British Columbia. "And some of these children were preyed on by pedophiles over and over again. And that's part of the generation that was involved in survival sex. They are the most victimized women in our society."

By the late '90s, dozens of these streetwalkers had gone missing, and everyone on the street knew that a serial killer was on the loose. But police ignored the mounting concerns, Lowman says. In 1997, Robert William (Willy) Pickton, a wealthy pig farmer, was charged with the attempted murder of a sex worker whom he had stabbed on his farm after having sex with her. The woman survived, but because prosecutors believed she would not be a believable witness (she had drug problems), they stayed the charge. (A stayed charge can be dismissed after one year.) Furthermore, crucial evidence against Pickton was left unexamined in a police storage locker for seven years.[12] In 1999, Canadian police were tipped off that Pickton had a freezer filled with human flesh on his farm. Although police interviewed Pickton and obtained his consent to search his farm, they never did a search.[13] Not until 2004 did lab testing show that DNA from two missing women were on the clothing and rubber boots seized from Pickton in 1997.

Pickton was finally arrested and brought to trial in 2006. He was convicted of killing six women; another twenty murder charges against him were stayed, although police believe the sixty-four-year-old farmer may have murdered as many as forty-nine women, mostly street-based prostitutes.[14] He was sentenced to life in prison with no possibility of parole for twenty-five years. "It was a national disgrace," Lowman says. "But it created a sea change in attitudes—a woman doesn't deserve to die because she's involved in sex work."

Lowman, who wears his long white hair in a ponytail and has a mischievous twinkle in his blue eyes, began studying sex workers even before he obtained his Ph.D. His dissertation focused on the effects of law enforcement on crime patterns, including the displacement of sex workers from indoor locations onto the street. That research developed into a career-long interest in sex work and the law, and starting in the early 1980s, Lowman received federal funding to do a series of studies on how Canada's laws were affecting sex workers. Between 1984 and 2002, Canada's Department of Justice provided funding for Lowman to conduct eight studies of prostitution law enforcement.

In 2002, Lowman was introduced to Alan Young, a law professor at Toronto's York University, who was thinking of mounting a constitutional challenge to Canada's prostitution laws. In the late 1990s, Young had represented a dominatrix by the name of Terri-Jean Bedford, who had been arrested for running a bawdy house in Toronto. Bedford, who went by the name of Madame de Sade, dressed in black leather, and often brought her whip to court, was ultimately convicted of the charge after a long legal battle. But Young realized there just might be a case for challenging the laws themselves on the grounds that they violated sex workers' rights to liberty and security of the person under the Charter of Rights and Freedoms, adopted as part of Canada's constitution in 1982.

I caught up with Young by phone one day in July 2014. He was holding court with his students and said he had only twenty minutes to talk. Young explained that he had decided in 1990 that he would systematically challenge every consensual crime under the Canadian criminal code—as an academic exercise. But it wasn't until police caught Robert Pickton and "were digging up bodies on the farm" that he turned his attention to the laws against adult prostitution. "I felt it was time to take on the prostitution laws," Young says. "The criminal law is a blunt instrument; it's not a good panacea for social problems."

Around the same time, Valerie Scott and her organization, now renamed Sex Professionals of Canada (SPOC), were searching for a lawyer who would take on a legal challenge on a pro bono basis. One day, Young came across SPOC's newly posted website, found Scott's phone number on it, and called her. "We were looking for him and he was looking for us," Scott says.

By 2006, Scott and Terri-Jean Bedford had agreed to be plaintiffs in a constitutional challenge to Canada's prostitution laws. By then, however, both women had pretty much retired from sex work—Scott was forty-eight and Bedford forty-seven—and they needed to find someone who was still doing sex work and willing to go public as the suit's third plaintiff. Scott, who has long wavy brown hair, strong cheekbones, and a dancer's poise, was making a living rehabilitating sick and injured wildlife at wildlife centers in and around Toronto, but she continued to devote most of her spare time to sex workers' rights activism. Given the enormous stigma of working in the sex trade and the fact that the families and friends of many sex workers have no idea how they earn a living, Scott knew that finding a third plaintiff who was willing to weather the publicity around the case would not be easy. She decided to approach a twenty-seven-year-old sex worker by the name of Amy Lebovitch, who was already active in SPOC and had been in the public eye to a certain extent as a spokeswoman for the organization.

At the time, Lebovitch, a sultry blonde with blue come-hither eyes, was working as an escort in Toronto. She had grown up in Montreal, the offspring of middle-class Jewish parents, and had left home at the age of eighteen because of family problems that, in an interview, she said she would rather not talk about. By the time she walked out, she had gone to the Canadian equivalent of community college for two years and was thinking of going on to a four-year university. Without a place to live or means to support herself, Lebovitch began doing sex work on the streets of Montreal.

"I needed money quickly and it just made sense," she says. After a few months, she moved to Ottawa, about two hours west of Montreal, and began taking classes at the University of Ottawa. She also began doing mostly indoor sex work. Occasionally, when she didn't have money to advertise, she would go back on the stroll.

"It's not the safest way to work and I didn't enjoy it," she says. "But without criminalization, without the fear of the police and not being able to properly screen clients, it could be safe. We need to make it safer so people are able to have a conversation with someone before getting into the vehicle."

A year later, Lebovitch moved to Toronto and began taking social work classes at Ryerson University. And that's when she met Valerie Scott. "I did an interview with her about SPOC for one of my social work papers," Lebovitch says. "We talked for hours, and it was sort of like this world opened up in my mind about activism and organizing. I was really intrigued about the idea of meeting and working with other sex workers, so I emailed Valerie and said, 'I didn't tell you at our meeting but I am a sex worker and I'd like to come to your meetings.'"

Lebovitch joined SPOC in 2003 and became a spokesperson for the organization. Her family, of course, had no idea she was doing sex work, and she wasn't about to tell them. "I didn't think the little publicity I did would get to Montreal, so they wouldn't see it," she says. "And they didn't." But all that changed a few years later, when Valerie Scott approached her about being the third plaintiff in their case.

"Alan [Young] did a pretty good job explaining the magnitude of what might happen," Lebovitch says. "But I don't think I truly appreciated how big the impact could be."

As the three plaintiffs worked with Young and others to prepare the paperwork for the lawsuit, a subcommittee of Canada's House of Commons released a report that examined the country's laws against prostitution and concluded that they did more harm than good. Prostitution was "above all a public health issue," the subcommittee concluded, and it recommended that the Canadian government engage in a "process of law reform" and move toward a more pragmatic, decriminalized approach that recognized the importance of prevention, education, treatment, and harm-reduction measures for people involved in selling sex.[15]

"The 2006 report was the most important in a series of government reports that came out [on the issue of Canada's prostitution laws]," Lowman says. "It spelled out the one thing that all the parties agreed on — that the current laws are unacceptable."

In 2007, Alan Young filed the constitutional challenge, which argued that Canada's prostitution laws violated sex workers' charter rights to liberty and security of the person and that these charter violations were not in accordance with the principles of fundamental justice (as set out by the charter). The lawsuit also argued that the communicating law violated sex workers' rights to free expression and that none of these violations were justified in a free and democratic society.

In September 2010, Ontario Superior Court Justice Susan Himel ruled that all three laws violated the rights of sex workers to safety and security and that they could no longer be used to arrest people involved in sex (except in cases of underage prostitution and trafficking). Canada's conservative government appealed the ruling, and in a March 2012 decision, the Ontario Court of Appeal agreed with Himel on the bawdy house law but did not strike down the laws against living on the avails of prostitution and muddied the language of the living-on-the-avails law. Young's team appealed the ruling, essentially kicking the ball up to the Supreme Court. As it proceeded through the courts, the Bedford case (named after Terri-Jean Bedford, the first plaintiff in the case) stirred up a hornet's nest of publicity, thrusting its three plaintiffs into the national media glare. The families of Valerie Scott and Terri-Jean Bedford were already aware of the two women's occupations. Scott says that when she came out to her family, her mother was upset, but mostly because of concern about her daughter's safety. Indeed, Scott, whose family is of Scottish ancestry, attributes her fighting spirit to her mother, who was a schoolteacher and set up the very first home for battered women in New Brunswick "in the days when people didn't want to talk" about domestic violence. And while Scott has a son (whom she raised as a single mother), he was grown by the time she mounted the constitutional challenge. She says he is proud of his mother's activism and accepted her livelihood a long time ago. "He's fine with it," she says. "He was raised to be fine with it."

While all three women were mocked in the media, the publicity surrounding the case exacted the biggest toll on Amy Lebovitch. Sometime after the Court of Appeal ruling, her family connected the dots, and in 2012, decided to cut all ties with her. "My last name is not that common," Amy says.

In June 2013, the Supreme Court heard arguments from both sides of the case, including dozens of witnesses who testified about the pros and cons of criminalizing prostitution. On December 20 of the same year, the court issued its momentous ruling, striking down all three laws governing Canada's sex trade as being in violation of sex workers' right to security. In a unanimous seventy-one-page decision, Chief Justice Beverley McLachlin wrote, "Parliament has the power to regulate against nuisances, but not at the cost of the health, safety and lives of prostitutes. . . . [The prohibitions] do not merely impose conditions on how prostitutes operate. They go a critical step further, by imposing *dangerous* conditions on prostitution; they prevent people engaged in a risky—but legal—activity from taking steps to protect themselves from the risks."[16]

The night before the ruling was due, Amy Lebovitch says she couldn't sleep. "I was in an Ottawa hotel room waiting for the verdict, and in my mind, I was moving around all the possibilities of what might happen," she says. "But one of those possibilities was not that we would win."

When the Supreme Court announced its decision, Lebovitch said it felt like a dream, "very emotional and shocking." But reality soon set in. The court had suspended its ruling for one year to give Parliament time to respond, and officials in the conservative ruling party soon made it clear they had no intention of allowing prostitution in Canada to be decriminalized.

They made good on that threat. In early December 2014, the Canadian Parliament passed a law that prohibits the purchase of sex (akin to the Swedish model); bans the sale of sex near a playground, school, or day care center; and prohibits anyone from directly profiting from commercial sex. The law essentially makes it illegal for any sex worker to hire a bodyguard, driver, or business partner, much as the previous living-on-the-avails law had done. In a new twist, the legislation also bans the advertising of sexual services, although a sex worker would not be prosecuted if she advertised herself. (The sale of sex itself also is not prohibited per se.) But anyone who posts a prostitute's ads on websites or in newspapers such as Toronto's *NOW* (which had eleven pages of sex-related ads in a 2014 issue) could face jail sentences and fines.

Joy Smith, the conservative MP (member of Parliament) who cosponsored the new legislation, says the law is designed to curb the demand for commercial sex by criminalizing buyers and penalizing pimps and traffickers. "I'm against criminalizing the prostitutes," she said in a July 2014 phone interview. "This bill recognizes that prostitution is an unsafe and violent thing, and it requires that $20 million be put in place to help with exit services."

Smith contended that more than 98 percent of Canadians involved in prostitution are victims and only 1 percent are doing it by choice. However, a number of Canadian studies contradict her claim and suggest that, for many sex workers, the decision to do sex work is a rational economic decision.[17] Many of these women choose sex work over minimum-wage jobs in the service sector and see themselves not as victims but as entrepreneurs.

In our interview, Smith also claimed that the majority of Canadian prostitutes begin sex work when they are underage. Her assertion is undercut by several studies showing that the average age of entry among

both street and indoor prostitutes in British Columbia is between eighteen and twenty-two.[18]

Smith is certain the new legislation will withstand a court challenge.
Some researchers and sex worker advocates, however, say it simply re-
produces all the safety and security problems for sex workers that caused
the Supreme Court to strike down the previous laws. And the ban on the
purchase of sex will violate Canada's Charter of Rights and Freedoms
in a completely new way as well. "Section 15 of the charter guarantees
equality, but when you have two consenting adults involved in a sexual
transaction in which only one of them will be penalized, you have a
classic case of inequality and discrimination," Lowman says.

Advocates for sex workers agree that the new law will simply force sex
workers from the relative safety of their homes or brothels into spaces
that are less safe. "They will go where the clients are, but because they are
being criminalized, the clients will want to be less visible. So sex workers
will be forced into those clandestine, in-the-shadow spaces where sex
work is less safe," says Jenn Clamen, thirty-eight, a community mo-
bilizer for Stella, a Montreal-based sex worker advocacy group run for
and by sex workers. Clamen, a longtime advocate for sex workers' rights,
also teaches part-time at the Simone de Beauvoir Institute, a college of
Concordia University that studies feminism and issues of social justice.
Clamen says the new law will inevitably expose Canada's sex workers to
more violence. "It means they will have to deal with the same kind of
thing that was demonstrated with the Pickton [murders]," she says.

Alan Young agrees. "By criminalizing the purchase of sex, the government will make it impossible for sex workers to move indoors. Johns
are not going to go indoors and be sitting ducks for law enforcement.
They're going to circle around with their cars in the dark," he says. "So
the new law will create more problems, more violence, and result in the
one outcome that not one Canadian wants, which is a burgeoning street
prostitution problem."

Advocates say the conservative government is deluded if it thinks that
prostitution can be eradicated by criminalizing buyers; this didn't work in
Sweden and it won't work in Canada. "Women decide to work in the sex

industry for a variety of reasons, whether it is to pay their bills, support their children, get an education, or support their drug habit," Clamen says. "These women will continue to work in the industry, but they will be more likely to be involved in unsafe situations." The new legislation ignores all the reasons why women and men work in the sex industry, she says. "If they were really concerned about prostitution, the government should be targeting issues like poverty, lack of education, drug use," Clamen says. "But the new law doesn't do any of that."

Clamen says Canada's sex worker community is disheartened by the new legislation but determined to fight it. At some point, someone will challenge the constitutionality of the new law in court, she says, and Canada's disparate sex work community will band together to support that challenge.

"People are very disheartened, and it's just going to have to be that way," Clamen says. "Keep in mind the Bedford case was a seven-year process. So we will have to go through that all over again or wait until a government with a more human rights approach comes into office and starts addressing the real issues. You can't just force people to get out of the sex industry, just like you can't force them to stop taking drugs."

# California

EPICENTER OF THE SEX WORKERS'

RIGHTS MOVEMENT

Maxine Doogan doesn't really want to be on the stage of this arid, windowless ballroom at 8 p.m., taking part in a panel on trafficking. For most of the day, the San Francisco sex worker has been on the phone in her Las Vegas hotel room with defense attorneys from around the country, helping them prepare motions to dismiss charges against the sex workers they represent. The San Francisco labor rights organization that Doogan founded, the Erotic Service Provider Legal, Educational and Research (ESPLER) Project, has developed a standard motion to dismiss charges, and attorneys are always calling her for help in fine-tuning it. Maxine, who works as a dominatrix, also spent part of the afternoon partying with a client, a younger man who had called after seeing her online ad. So by this hour, Doogan, a divorced mother of three in her fifties, is ready to call it a day. But because she agreed at the last minute to organize the trafficking panel for the Desiree Alliance conference, here she is, scheduled to speak last in the panel's four-person lineup.

Perusing the crowd from her perch on the stage, Doogan has to admit she's more than a little surprised that so many people have shown up at this hour—as many as forty women and men are clumped around tables strategically spaced to fill the cavernous room. It's the third day of the conference, and the collective energy is starting to ebb. Making matters worse, in less than an hour, conference organizers will kick off a demonstration on Las Vegas's tourist-packed Strip to protest the recent murder of two sex workers. Doogan seriously doubts anyone will stick around long enough to hear her speak.

To her relief, the first three people on the panel don't talk long. The first speaker, a staff attorney with the Sex Workers Project of the Urban Justice Center, has just come from presenting research on how bad-client lists can be a useful safety tool for sex workers, and she seems tired and somewhat scattered as she throws out a few facts about the negative impact of trafficking laws in New York state. The audience perks up a bit for the next speaker, if only because she is holding a tiny shih tzu in her arms. Emi Koyama is a transsexual sex worker and activist from Portland, Oregon, and she talks about how the wave of new antitrafficking laws are making it harder to help teenage runaways and homeless youth obtain the services they need.

"The human trafficking task force is under the gang unit at the FBI. They believe it is Mexican drug cartels that are trying to import young people into the U.S. to sell them. And that's not true," Koyama says, and the little dog in her arms squirms at the frustration in her voice. "The antitrafficking movement calls for criminalization; it doesn't call for more complete responses that deal with the factors that cause runaways and youth homelessness."

Finally, it is Doogan's turn, and before any more people can drift away, she leans forward and starts speaking in a firm, no-nonsense voice that carries to the farthest table in the room. "I'm a prostitute of twenty-two years, and I expect to be working for twenty-two more years," she says, and the audience erupts in applause. At last, someone with some energy.

Doogan, who wears her blonde farm-girl hair in a midlength bob, goes on to explain that she and the ESPLER Project worked hard to defeat the latest antitrafficking statute in California, the CASE (Californians against Sexual Exploitation) Act, also known as Proposition 35. The ballot measure was designed to increase the criminal penalties for sex trafficking, but many advocates believe it will only harm the people it is intended to help (that is, prostitutes). The measure, opposed by the American Civil Liberties Union and even a few antitrafficking groups, imposes heftier fines and prison sentences for anyone convicted of sex trafficking. The CASE Act also expands the definition of traffickers to include sex workers who may be working together for safety and psychological support, according to a report prepared by the San Francisco Human Rights Commission. For example, two sex workers who band together to provide referrals to each other for reliable clients could be viewed as encouraging each other to prostitute and thus be prosecuted for a crime. The CASE Act, the report concluded, creates a disincentive for collaboration and makes sex workers more likely to be exploited by a pimp.[1]

Doogan informs her audience that since the passage of the CASE Act in 2012, it has been employed mostly to punish and harass prostitutes. "One of our members was traveling for work, and she was the target of a sting operation of the antitrafficking task force," Doogan says, her voice rising in anger. "She was a thirty-nine-year-old woman in a hotel room with a naked client who turned out to be an FBI agent. She was arrested for prostitution and put in handcuffs for three hours. The antitrafficking people spoke to her as if she was a twelve-year-old girl who had been forced into trafficking. She obviously wasn't, but if she had been a real victim, this is how she would have been treated. They are violating people's human rights under the guise of antitrafficking."

Doogan tells a few more horror stories about the effects of antitrafficking laws in California and throughout the United States, and then she delivers her denouement. "Our solution is to decriminalize prostitution. We are bringing a federal court case against district attorneys, alleging that antitrafficking laws are violating our civil rights, the right to free speech and the right to privacy," Doogan says. "We have plaintiffs, and we're raising money to file the suit. We need your help. So when I email you, I want you to respond to me, even if it's only to say, 'Fuck you, Maxine.' But I want you to respond. With everyone in this room working together, we can get this thing done. We will get it done." When Doogan stops to catch her breath, the audience erupts into wild applause.

If the crowd's reaction is any guide, Doogan has just picked up the mantle laid down by earlier charismatic leaders of the sex workers' rights movement, such as Margo St. James. In fact, Doogan and the ESPLER Project are really only the latest incarnation of what many people have known for a long time: California is the epicenter of the sex workers' rights movement, and if prostitution is going to be decriminalized, it will be decriminalized first in California and specifically in San Francisco, the golden gate to all things possible.

San Francisco, after all, was the first city in the nation to assemble an official task force on prostitution, in the 1990s, to examine its municipal laws against prostitution. The thirty-person task force included Margo St. James, recently returned from her sojourns in Europe (where she worked with sex workers' rights groups in France, Belgium, and the Netherlands). St. James says she came back to the States to marry Paul Avery, a San Francisco Bay area reporter best known for his coverage of the Zodiac killer, the infamous serial killer who stalked San Francisco in the 1970s. St. James had known Avery since the '60s, when the then-married reporter would wander into Pierre's bar, where she worked. Avery finally proposed to St. James on a visit to the south of France in the mid-'80s. "I was driving him back to the train, and he said, 'I'm not going to bug you about getting married,' and I said, 'Okay, I'll do it,'" St. James recalls. "We were married in 1992 in my favorite café, Malvena's in North Beach."

In 1996, the task force, which included other sex worker advocates, city officials, and representatives from San Francisco's neighborhoods, issued an in-depth report on prostitution in the Bay area. The task force unanimously recommended that the city stop enforcing and prosecuting prostitution laws and instead redirect the estimated $7.6 million it spent annually on the enforcement of those laws toward services for needy constituencies. (As examples of programs that should be more fully funded, the task force cited services for battered women, the homeless, youth runaways, and immigrants.) The task force also recommended that instead of arresting streetwalkers, city officials use existing municipal codes against littering, noise, and trespassing to resolve the quality-of-life problems that neighborhood residents often blamed on street prostitution. Its report noted that despite the millions of dollars spent every year on enforcing antiprostitution laws, these quality-of-life problems had not been ameliorated. Nor had prostitution in San Francisco decreased over time.

In 1996, largely to draw attention to the task force's recommendations, Margo St. James ran for a supervisor's seat on the six-person San Francisco Board of Supervisors. She came in seventh, barely out of the running, and when one of the supervisors stepped down a month later, she applied for the vacant seat. But Willy Brown, the city's mayor at the time, refused to appoint her to the board and instead chose a wealthy and well-connected young man by the name of Gavin Newsom,[2] who would go on to become the city's mayor in 2003 and the state's lieutenant governor in 2010. In 1998, St. James filed to run again, this time for assessor, and as she tells it, Brown was so worried that she would win that in exchange for her not running, he agreed to provide Department of Public Health funding for the St. James Infirmary, the new health clinic she had recently founded for sex workers in San Francisco. (The St. James Infirmary continues to provide free HIV testing and other health services for sex workers in partnership with the city's public health department.)

"Willy didn't want me to have a seat because he couldn't control me," St. James said in a phone interview. "By that time, my crime reporter husband Paul Avery was sick, and I brought him to Orcas Island," a ferry ride from Bellingham, Washington, where her family had a cottage. (Avery, a longtime smoker, died of emphysema in 2000.)

Despite Margo St. James's considerable popularity, city officials never did act on the task force's recommendations to decriminalize prostitution. In 2004, activists in Berkeley brought a measure to the ballot calling for decriminalization there, but only 36 percent of Berkeley residents voted for it. A similar measure made it onto the ballot in San Francisco in 2008, and that one did better (41 percent of the city's residents voted for decriminalization), but it also failed.

Six years later, I caught up with one of the lead writers on the original San Francisco Task Force on Prostitution: Carol Leigh, a longtime sex worker, poet, writer, and aspiring actress who had coined the term sex work. In 2002, Leigh published a collection of her essays and poems, titled *The Unrepentant Whore* and adorned with a voluptuous cover shot of Leigh splayed naked on a bed of rose petals. Since then, she has reinvented herself as a videographer and now makes her living as a video producer and IT guru for several sex education and erotic websites. She is mostly retired from sex work. "I'm sixty-three," she says laughing. "I might need to go back to it, but it's been awhile."

Leigh believes that implementing change at the ballot box would be an uphill battle right now, given the current frenzy over trafficking. Police departments and nonprofit groups in California and throughout the United States that receive funding from the federal antitrafficking task forces have kept up a drumbeat of publicity about the problem of sex trafficking and their efforts to fight it. In the process, much of the American public has become convinced that prostitution is intrinsically linked with exploitation. "There's so much bad publicity about prostitution in the context of antitrafficking," Leigh says. "So much damage has been done."

When I spoke to her by phone, Leigh had just released the trailer for a short film that she made showing how antitrafficking laws are leading to the deportation of immigrants and the violation of sex workers' rights. Instead of being treated as victims and given the services they need, many prostitutes around the world, both adults and minors, are being arrested, charged with trafficking, and if they are illegal immigrants, deported. A twenty-minute version of the movie, called *Collateral Damage,* has been screened in Japan, Austria, Denmark, Germany and India, and Leigh is still working on turning it into a feature-length film.

In a phone interview around the same time, Maxine Doogan spelled out a less obvious form of collateral damage from the antitrafficking movement. The new fines imposed by Proposition 35 on people arrested for trafficking (which can total up to $1 million per case) are slated to be administered by the California Emergency Management Agency, which is supposed to disperse the money to police, prosecutors, and nonprofit groups that work with trafficking victims. Although a system to keep track of and disperse these monies has yet to be set up, sex worker advocates fear that the hefty new fines might create an incentive for law enforcement to inflate trafficking statistics and make the problem look worse than it really is—in order to keep the money flowing in. "We call this profiting from the criminalization of prostitution," Doogan says.

The report by the San Francisco Human Rights Commission, a city-funded group that examines local human rights issues, raised similar concerns. That draft report noted that the way the measure's fines are being dispersed might create an incentive for law enforcement to focus on sex trafficking and ignore other types of labor trafficking, which are actually more common in California and everywhere else. According to a 2012 International Labor Organization study, labor trafficking constitutes 68 percent of trafficking, whereas forced sexual exploitation constitutes 22 percent of the 90 percent of forced labor situations that occur in the private economy. But since Proposition 35 imposes stricter penalties and much higher fines on convicted sex traffickers than on labor traffickers, it may be detrimental to the "victims of labor trafficking, as they can potentially be ignored or given less attention," the commission concluded in its report.[3]

Some prosecutors don't buy that argument. Nancy O'Malley, the district attorney for Alameda County (which encompasses Oakland and other towns across the bay from San Francisco), says her office prosecutes both labor and sex trafficking cases. Indeed, Alameda County (population, 1.5 million) prosecutes fully 50 percent of all the trafficking cases in California (population, 25 million), and O'Malley is known throughout the state as a woman on a mission. "We've been very aggressive about trafficking for a number of years," says O'Malley, who became Alameda's district attorney in 2009. "My consistent effort has been to say that if trafficking is not in your community, you're just not looking."

Yet even O'Malley acknowledges that most police departments do not take labor trafficking very seriously. "I think law enforcement doesn't have the tools to look at labor," she says. "They don't investigate it as a crime. But we're investigating it as a crime."

O'Malley is the first to admit, however, that most of her office's energies go into combatting the sex trafficking of underage youth, through a program she has dubbed HEAT (Human Exploitation and Trafficking)

Watch. Her office is working with a coalition of antitrafficking proponents to further increase penalties and fines against pimps and clients
who exploit underage youth, in a measure known as Senate Bill 1388.
According to sex worker advocates, most of the lobbying support for this
measure has been paid for by Demand Abolition, a group that is aimed
at ending the demand for commercial sex and funded largely by Swanee
and Helen Hunt, Texas sisters who are heirs to the Hunt oil fortune.

"There are very well-funded groups like the Hunt sisters working with
the Justice Department, the FBI, and other law enforcement on an antiprostitution campaign, and [Senate Bill 1388] is just one small piece of
that agenda," says Rachel West, a longtime community organizer with
the US PROstitutes Collective (US PROS), a nonprofit that serves mostly
streetwalkers. West served on the original San Francisco Task Force
on Prostitution in 1996, and her organization is working with Doogan's
group to defeat the bill.

The sex worker advocacy groups recently managed to convince the
sponsors of Senate Bill 1388 to remove the provision that would have
criminalized clients and made it harder for sex workers to negotiate safe
sex. In its current incarnation, however, Senate Bill 1388, like Proposition
35, may still create perverse incentives for law enforcement. In a recent
analysis of the bill, the state Senate Committee on Public Safety concluded that the payment of criminal fines under the proposed law "raises
the issues of an improper bounty—an incentive for law enforcement
agencies to pursue investigations based on financial interest, rather than
public safety."[4]

O'Malley waves aside such concerns. "The challenge is not inflating numbers or creating incentives. It is getting people to recognize the
problem," she says. If anything, she believes the problem of pimps sexually exploiting underage girls (which she considers synonymous with
trafficking) is an under-recognized crisis. "On any given day on International Boulevard in Oakland, you can see kids on the street and traffickers lurking in the background," she says. "It's a real problem."

San Francisco city officials agree that underage prostitution is a
problem that demands attention, but they have a different approach to

dealing with it. "If you acknowledge that these youth are victims of trafficking, we shouldn't be treating them as criminals," says Minouche Kandel, a spokeswoman for the San Francisco Department on the Status of Women, a city agency.

Nonprofit groups that work with sexually exploited youth agree. They say arresting these teenagers simply retraumatizes them and makes them even more distrustful of authority and thus more dependent on pimps. "A lot of [exploited] children have been abused by police, and they don't feel comfortable with you if you work with law enforcement," says Ellyn Bell, executive director of the SAGE Project, the oldest antitrafficking organization in the country (founded in 1992). Her organization, which works mostly with underage sex workers, has received funding from private donors, the city of San Francisco, and the U.S. Department of Justice's Office for Victims of Crime.

Bell says she supports the decriminalization of prostitutes, regardless of their age. "Our goal at SAGE is to provide people with trauma-informed services and options to change their lives, if that's what they want," Bell says. "And if they're not ready to change their lives, we try to give them options to live safer."

In line with this more prevention-oriented approach, San Francisco police make far fewer arrests for adult or underage prostitution than Alameda County does. "We're trying to be mindful of not pursuing policies that would harm sex workers," Kandel says. "Some people feel that all prostitution is by definition violence against women. But if we're honoring women's autonomy and adult women are choosing to do this, then we should respect that and make sure they're not harmed."

## The Legacy of a Corrupt Cop

Maxine Doogan has seen this movie reel before—in her own life. She began doing sex work at age twenty-five in Alaska, as a divorced single mother struggling to make ends meet. She had grown up in Fairbanks, a town in central Alaska, part of a large politically connected family. The Doogans lived in a state where prostitutes, historically, had been a respected part of society (much like in the Old West). Indeed, until the early 1960s, Fairbanks had a fairly visible red-light district, what Alaskans called the "working line." But once oil was discovered, the federal government began pressuring state officials to rein in the brothels and introduce antiprostitution laws similar to those that had already been implemented in most of the other states. Even then, most Alaskans remained pretty laissez-faire about prostitution.

"There's a lot of acceptance in Alaska for different types of people and not as much prying into people's personal lives," Doogan says. She herself had read *The Happy Hooker*, by Xaviera Hollander, when she was twelve and liked the famous madam's adventurous attitude toward sex. So when Doogan found herself divorced and in financial straits, she followed Hollander's lead and began working in the brothels of Anchorage, which she continued to do until the price of domestic oil plummeted and took Alaska's economy down with it. In 1988, Doogan came to Seattle and began exploring the sex trade there. But it was the height of Gary Ridgway's murder spree, and police had also mounted a huge sting of escort agencies around the city. "There was no place to work in Seattle besides the streets, and the streets were really dangerous," Doogan says.

Having obtained some training in construction at a women's center in Seattle, she found a job first as a union pile driver and then as a certified welder. In the process, she learned a lot about labor organizing and the power of working collectively. But although her construction job had great health insurance benefits, she still wasn't earning enough to support herself and her three children. (She was also paying child support to their father, who helped with child care.) So Doogan, who by then had come out as a lesbian, began working as a dominatrix and running an escort service called the Personal Touch (which hired gay men and women doing domination work). Along with dozens of other sex workers, she ended up being arrested in another series of police stings in the early 1990s. But by then she had begun traveling to San Francisco on a regular basis to see whether she wanted to move there.

"I had already started doing some organizing with sex workers in Seattle, and I knew some escorts were working as [police] informants, so

I saw the arrests coming," she says. "And San Francisco had a history with COYOTE."

Doogan was one of only two sex workers arrested in King County's massive sting operation who did not plead guilty. "I never worked with any of the informants," she says. Doogan and her attorneys were thus astounded when, during her first trial on felony charges of promoting or profiting from prostitution, two escorts got up on the witness stand and said they had given her portions of the proceeds from their sex work. "These women all lied on the stand," she says. "I never received any money from them."

That trial ended in a hung jury because most of the jury members didn't find the witnesses credible. Doogan *was* found guilty after a second trial, but that conviction was overturned on appeal, again because of the questionable testimony given by the same female witnesses. Rather than undergo a third trial, which Doogan couldn't afford—"those trials cost me $10,000 a piece"—she agreed to plead no contest to the misdemeanor charge of attempting to promote prostitution. She spent twenty days in jail and another year or two on probation.

"There was this one detective who had wrangled these witnesses to testify against me, and he was really coming after me," Doogan recalls. "Even after I pled, he kept coming after me with probation violations. At one point, my attorneys asked me, 'Why does this guy hate you so much?'"

Ten years later, Doogan finally learned the answer to that question. In 2004, she got a call from an officer with the Seattle vice squad. They were investigating Dan Ring, the King County sheriff's vice detective who had been on her case, and they wanted to talk to her about potential crimes Ring had been involved in, such as theft, drug distribution, and sleeping with sex workers who were informants on some of his escort sting operations. In 2005, the *Seattle Post-Intelligencer* published a three-day series that revealed numerous illegal activities Ring had been involved in, according to a three-and-a-half year investigation by the FBI, the King County sheriff's office, and Seattle police.[5]

As the Seattle newspaper reported, Ring had had sex with two of the women who were key witnesses in the cases against Doogan and

other escort service operators. The King County prosecutor was reviewing those cases, and Ring's alleged misconduct, some attorneys said,
could result in overturned convictions and compensation for court costs.[6]
County prosecutors had charged Ring with a number of offenses, but on
the eve of his trial in 2005, the detective reached a lucrative settlement
with the King County Sheriff's Office, granting him $10,000, a $3,500-a-
month pension, and payment of nearly $200,000 in legal fees. In return,
Ring agreed to retire as a cop.[7]

Doogan suspects that Ring got a good deal because the sheriff's office
didn't want the bad publicity from the public trial of a corrupt cop. "He
was a big whoremonger—he would threaten to arrest women for prostitution and then end up dating them," Doogan says. "Here was the police
who are supposed to be your stopgap for safety, and he was harassing
the women he's supposed to protect. It really exposed for me the kind of
corruption that goes on in vice squads across America."

The King County prosecutor who was reviewing the cases ultimately
came up with a list of cases that had been tainted by Ring's misconduct,
and it included Doogan's case, according to Lewis Kamb, one of the reporters who wrote the *Seattle Post-Intelligencer* series. But when Doogan
filed an appeal to vacate her conviction, the appeal was rejected on the
grounds that she had taken a plea deal and thus had waived her right to
having the conviction overturned. None of the other tainted cases were
contested, and Ring got off scot-free. The last Kamb knew, Ring was
still living with the stripper who had lied on the witness stand in Doogan's case. Indeed, she is listed as the beneficiary on Ring's pension from
the King County Sheriff's Office, Kamb says.

## A Constitutional Challenge

Doogan's personal experience is not the only reason she is so intent on
mounting a constitutional challenge to laws that criminalize prostitution. She has seen firsthand how easily external funding can sway the
public's mind on ballot measures. The success of Proposition 35 had a lot
to do with the millions of dollars that Chris Kelly, the former Facebook

executive and a 2010 Democratic candidate for attorney general, plowed into efforts to make sure the antitrafficking measure passed.[8] Kelly, who lost in 2010, has political ambitions, but the sex workers' rights groups hadn't seen him coming, and they were badly outspent. Many Californians agree that the state's "proposition way" of doing government is not a truly representative approach. "It's about who has the most money and screams the loudest," says Bell from the SAGE Project. "That's who wins these ballot measures."

After Proposition 35 passed, Doogan and other sex workers drew some solace from watching their colleagues to the north take the court battle over Canada's prostitution laws to the highest court of the land. Canada's Supreme Court ruling in December 2013 cemented Doogan's decision to mount a court challenge stateside. "We figured it might cost $100,000 for a lawsuit that brings relief to people throughout the country, as opposed to bringing another ballot measure in California, which would cost at least $300,000," Doogan says.

Compared with sex workers in Canada, however, Doogan and her band are operating under a distinct disadvantage: they haven't been able to find a law professor, like Alan Young, willing to take on the case pro bono. While they are working with a private attorney who is familiar with the country's prostitution laws, they will have to pay him the going rate for his services. The northern California chapter of the American Liberties Civil Union (ACLU) is considering mounting its own constitutional challenge to the prostitution laws. If Doogan's group files first, the ACLU may come in with an amicus brief.

The northern California ACLU chapter has intervened in other issues involving sex workers. Proposition 35, for example, was originally written to require traffickers to register as sex offenders and inform police about their online activity. Right after the law was passed in 2012, the ACLU requested a restraining order against that particular provision, arguing that it would have a chilling effect on free speech. A district judge in the northern California circuit court agreed and issued a restraining order so that part of the law could not go into effect until a formal challenge was heard in the courts.

A constitutional challenge to U.S. prostitution laws must clear yet another hurdle. While Americans have a clear right to free speech, the U.S. Constitution does not confer the same right to safety and security that is spelled out in Canada's charter. It was that basic right that Canada's Supreme Court cited in overturning that country's prostitution laws.

"The Canadian Charter of Rights and Freedoms was written in 1982, and the American Constitution was written by a bunch of slave owners back in the 1770s," Doogan says. "[The Canadian plaintiffs] were able to bring their case based on the issue of safety. We will not be able to make a challenge based on safety because safety is not a value in our U.S. Constitution."

In March 2015, Doogan's group filed a lawsuit in the U.S. District Court challenging Section 647(b) of the California Penal Code, which prohibits compensation for a lewd sex act, on the grounds that it violates people's right to privacy and equal protections under the law. The lawsuit argues that laws making consensual commercial sexual activity between adults illegal are unconstitutional because they infringe on privacy rights protected by the 14th Amendment. There is legal precedence for such an argument. In 2003, in the *Lawrence vs Texas* decision, the U.S. Supreme Court held that a Texas law classifying consensual adult homosexual intercourse as illegal sodomy violated the privacy and liberty rights of adults, under the 14th Amendment, to engage in private, intimate conduct.

Doogan and others believe that ruling could be extended to prostitution. "The *Lawrence* ruling invalidated similar laws throughout the United States that criminalized sodomy between consenting adults acting in private," says Michael Chase, a retired high-tech executive who now devotes his time to human rights issues in California. "It was a great decision because it allows people to live their sexual lives without governmental intervention."

The lawsuit that the ESPLER Project filed also argues that the state's law against prostitution denies individuals the right to free speech and the right to choose how to earn a living. The lawsuit further alleges that the enforcement of antiprostitution laws discourages safe sex because the possession of condoms is used as evidence by prosecutors. Like the Canadian case, the California lawsuit will have multiple plaintiffs, including several sex workers and a client. As in Canada, the lawsuit also argues that criminalization, particularly the recent spate of antitrafficking laws in the United States, has caused all sorts of human rights violations. "One of the issues we have with antitrafficking laws is that they result in the arrest of sex workers themselves," says Chase. "The definition of trafficking is so loose that women who are helping each other be safe are considered to be trafficking."

What got Chase involved in this cause was reading the literature of Proposition 35 supporters. "I was personally appalled by the way they attempted to infantilize adult women," he says. "It reminded me of the civil rights movement in the South and the way they referred to adult men as boys." Chase says he's known in northern California's human rights circles "as the straight guy who understands transgender and sex work issues."

As of this writing, the ACLU had still not decided whether it will file a brief in support of Doogan's group. And that doesn't bode well for the sex workers' rights movement, in large part because Doogan and her group are having trouble rallying other sex workers behind their legal challenge and raising money. "Most of this community thinks they're at low risk of being arrested," Doogan says. "They don't really understand this is a full-on war that has been declared on us by the antitrafficking movement."

Some sex workers' rights groups do avow support. Rachel West, who remains an organizer with US PROS, says her street-based group endorses Doogan's constitutional challenge and will help support it financially. West says her group has worked with the ESPLER Project on a number of recent battles, including a successful fight last year to get the state to pay workers' compensation for sex workers who have been raped on the job.

But the battle is far from over. There are times when seasoned advocates such as West and Doogan feel as though they are alone on a beach

facing a tsunami. West says US PROS has been fighting for decriminalization since 1980, but it is constantly struggling to find funding to survive
and help individual street workers with their legal troubles.

"Prostitution is really in large part about poverty," West says. "A lot
of the women we represent are mothers, and they are doing it to support
children. The people going to jail are mothers." While West herself
attended the 2013 Desiree Alliance conference, the single mothers she
represents were conspicuously absent. They are too busy struggling to
survive on the streets, she says. Most of the men and women who go to
the conference are escorts who have middle- or upper-class clients, and
they are not being arrested or harassed by police. That may explain why
there was not more discussion about a legal challenge at the conference.

Indeed, the day after her rousing speech on the trafficking panel, Doogan again mentioned her plans to mount a constitutional challenge—
at a smaller, standing-room-only session on the history of the sex workers' rights movement. But the only person who approached her afterward
to talk about the challenge was a board member from the California
ACLU. He wanted to discuss legal strategy. "I'm glad he's interested," she
says. "But no one else seemed to be."

# A Saner Approach to Prostitution

**M**addy has a "date" Friday evening in Washington, D.C., with a high-ranking government official who saw her ad on eros.com, a popular website for escort ads. The hazel-eyed twenty-six-year-old from North Carolina (whom I met at the Desiree Alliance conference) is staying at a boutique hotel in Dupont Circle, and she has agreed to meet with me before her date. We decide to rendezvous at Kramer's, a popular bookstore and eatery a few blocks from her hotel. Earlier in the day, she had called to move up our meeting because her client was thinking of booking extended time with her. So I rush over to Dupont Circle on the Metro, and as soon as I walk into Kramer's, I get a text from her: "The timing didn't work out so there's no need to rush." I text her back saying I'm already at Kramer's and will wait for her here. What better place than a bookstore for dawdling?

Ten or fifteen minutes later, I get another text from Maddy: "I'm here." A minute later, I discover her bent over behind a table of stacked books, changing from flats into high-heeled black pumps. She straightens up and grins. "You caught me in the act," she says. Maddy, it seems, takes her persona as an enticing escort seriously.

We grab one of the few unoccupied tables in the back room at Kramer's, but Maddy orders only a coke. "I have serious food allergies," she says. "But that's okay. I'll have a soda."

She is dressed casually, in a light-pink tailored shirt and tight-fitting blue jeans; a gauzy white scarf is wrapped loosely around her neck. She is wearing no makeup, and she has tied back her flyaway blond hair in a loose braid. Even so, she looks model-fresh and exquisite, like a porcelain doll that could easily break.

Maddy says she comes to Washington, D.C., about once a month to see clients. Most of her clients are corporate executives and top government officials who have seen her ads—one recent ad she wrote described her as a "sharp wit in a soft body." "This guy I'm seeing in a few hours, he found my ad a few months ago and finally got around to getting in touch," she says. "According to a survey done by eros.com, most gentlemen will peruse a lady's website five times before they actually contact her."

Once a client contacts her, Maddy does her due diligence. "I never see clients I haven't screened," she says. "I find out where they work, and I can verify that they actually are who they say they are."

This evening, Maddy will meet her gentleman caller at the boutique hotel where she is staying and spend two hours with him (for a set fee of $1,200), fulfilling any fantasies he might have. Going to a sex worker, she says, "is a safe place for [clients] to explore their desires, such as cross-dressing or getting fucked in the ass. I use a strap-on with a lot of my clients." (A strap-on is a dildo that Maddy can strap around herself.)

Many married men choose to go to an escort rather than risk endangering their marriages with an affair. "We're not going to call them, we're not going to disrupt their marriage or their family," Maddy says. "They love their wives, but they have physical needs."

After her business engagement, Maddy plans to have a late dinner and a "foursome with two men and another woman," all three of whom she is friendly with. "These are all people I enjoy," she says. They know what she does for a living and are not at all bothered by it, she adds.

Even though she has been working as an escort (on and off) for nine years, Maddy has never come close to being arrested. "I'm very careful. I never discuss money and I never count my money. I just leave it there until after the appointment is over," she says. "I won't compromise my safety."

As a stylishly dressed white woman catering to upper-class clients whom she has carefully screened, Maddy does in fact face little risk of being arrested. She herself is acutely aware that there is a double standard in the United States when it comes to enforcing the laws against prostitution. While the D.C. police routinely arrest streetwalkers and raid massage parlors in poor and mixed-income neighborhoods, they tend to leave high-end independent escorts like Maddy alone. Abolishing laws against prostitution would benefit streetwalkers the most, if only because they bear the brunt of law enforcement. "The practice is not to prosecute what isn't seen," Maddy says. "It's economically advantageous to have [high-end sex work] going on."

Maddy believes that many companies and government agencies are less likely to hold major conferences in places where prostitution laws are strictly enforced. And indeed, several gentlemen's clubs (a euphemism for private clubs where men can drink, obtain lap dances, and meet sex workers) are openly advertised right next to the restaurant listings in *Where* magazine, one of the free publications on display in my Marriott Hotel room.

"[Going to an escort] is so prevalent among the upper level of government that if they really prosecuted it, it would collapse the government," Maddy says, giggling. "My client list alone would be enough to put the country on hold for a few days."

The woman sitting at the table next to us is staring at her; it's likely that she has overheard parts of our conversation. Maddy feels the intensity of her gaze and flushes. "I'm going to have to talk more quietly," she says. "I have a loud voice."

Like many other sex workers, Maddy doesn't understand the distinction that society makes between men like Donald Sterling (the former owner of the Los Angeles Clippers) who have a trophy girlfriend and pay all their expenses and then some, and men who spend a few hours with an escort like herself in exchange for compensation. "That is the only thing where two consenting adults can engage in something, but because money is involved, it's suddenly illegal," she says, her eyebrows drawn together into a dark-blond line. "What's the difference between this and maintaining your younger girlfriend in an apartment?"

Four blocks to the west of Kramer's, the sex industry assumes a decidedly different cast. A passerby would never know that on the fourth

floor of a narrow building on Connecticut Avenue hides the office of
FAIR Girls, the nonprofit organization that serves sexually exploited girls
and young women. There are no signs outside or in the lobby announc-
ing the organization's presence. A prearranged appointment is required,
and the door to the suite is locked. When the door is opened, I walk
into a brightly lit room buzzing with young women; there are no men
on the premises. Three young African American women are sitting
around a conference table; they look up and smile at me brightly. A
twenty-something woman rushes over and introduces herself as Teresa,
the director of FAIR (Free, Aware, Inspired, and Restored) Girls. Teresa
guides me through another room, containing a blanket-strewn sofa, a
chair, and a small refrigerator, to a back office where Executive Director
Andrea Powell is typing intently on her laptop. She looks up briefly and
asks me to wait a few minutes until she finishes. She too looks young and
is slender, with long blonde hair and bare legs under a short skirt. Two
necklaces of brightly colored beads hang around her neck, made (I later
learn) by the girls her organization helps.

FAIR Girls provides services to girls and young women, age eleven to
twenty-four, who are "survivors of sexual trafficking and labor exploitation," Powell explains. "The average age of our clients is sixteen, and the
average number of years they've been trafficked is four years." FAIR Girls
provides emergency housing, clothes, and food, along with counseling
and legal support. It also helps its clients find jobs or schooling and
teaches them the skills they need to become independent.

Powell founded FAIR Girls in 2004, a few years after she first stumbled across the problem of sexual exploitation, while doing a junior year
abroad in Germany. In a German class, she met a sixteen-year-old Bos-
nian Muslim girl who had been sold by her family into servitude as the
fourth wife of a much older man. The relationship had become abusive,
and Powell and her new friend made plans for her to escape, but before
they could put the plan in motion, the girl disappeared. "I traveled to
Bosnia to find her, and while I was there I saw a lot of girls and young
women engaging in what you could call survival sex—this was not
long after the Yugoslav war," which followed the breakup of Yugoslavia,

Powell says. "I also saw what I think was some trafficking." She never did find her friend.

After Powell returned to the United States and graduated from Texas State University, she started FAIR Girls in Boston, initially working with young women who had been trafficked to the United States from abroad. But when she moved to Washington, D.C., she started hearing more about domestic youth being exploited. "We now serve upwards of 125 to 150 girls a year," Powell says. "Over 90 percent are American citizens." Most of the girls have run away from abusive situations at home or in foster care. The work Powell and her employees do involves everything from helping their charges get their records expunged—laws in many states now allow sex workers to get convictions expunged from their records if they can prove they have been trafficked—to getting them back home or into school.

FAIR Girls also runs an "empowerment" program that teaches the girls how to make jewelry. "They earn a small amount of money, but more importantly, their self-esteem goes through the roof," Powell says. "We have an annual gala, and the girls sell the jewelry they made. Fesha, the young woman from Kenya, made a necklace that Rose [DeLauro], the congresswoman from Connecticut, bought. That made her feel so great."

Powell works closely with local police, since they are the ones who often refer clients to her organization. But she doesn't think sex workers of any age should be arrested, and her organization (along with others that work with exploited youth) is currently pressing for the passage of a bill, known as Safe Harbor, that would prohibit the arrests of minors involved in commercial sex in Washington, D.C. Safe Harbor laws have already been passed in other states, including New York, Washington State, and Illinois. "Criminalizing those who are being sold is just re-traumatizing the victims and pushing them further underground," Powell says.

Like other nonprofits, FAIR Girls finds that working with law enforcement can be a double-edged sword, since many teenagers from dysfunctional families have had run-ins with the law and don't trust the police. Powell, who is now thirty-four and married, says she can also do without the teasing from some cops. "I have a standing fight with one detective, who calls me 'Rescue Barbie,'" she says. "I tell him I know how to tweet and he doesn't, and one of these days something I say about him is going to go viral."

Unlike some antitrafficking proponents, Powell recognizes the difference between trafficking and prostitution. "Prostitution is a crime in which a person is selling sex on their own and there's not any force, fraud, or coercion," she says. But then she adds, "If the majority of our clients were between thirteen and twenty-four when they first got coerced into [sex work], the concept of choice gets pretty blurry." For that reason, she supports laws that would criminalize buyers, particularly those who have sex with underage girls and boys. "Someone who buys sex from a sixteen-year-old and does it more than once, that's not a john, that's a serial child pedophile," Powell says. "They need to be held accountable."

Sex workers' rights advocates agree that it should be illegal to buy or sell sex involving underage prostitutes. However, several studies have found that blanket laws criminalizing the buyers of sex from adult prostitutes only expose sex workers to greater violence and make it more difficult for them to practice safe sex.[1] For that reason, many academics who study the sex industry are opposed to overly broad laws that make it illegal to buy or sell sex.

Researchers, antitrafficking groups, and sex worker advocates all agree that sanctions against violent pimps and coercive traffickers should be increased but diverge widely on the definition of a trafficker and on the question of who should be subject to criminal penalties. Many states currently criminalize anyone who lives off the earnings of a prostitute, which means that a nonabusive boyfriend or husband or even a roommate can be arrested and charged with pandering, pimping, or trafficking. Some researchers say such overly broad laws should be repealed because they make it more difficult for sex workers to work safely with people who know when and where they are selling sex and who can be summoned if help is necessary.

"Punishment should be restricted to those who are violent or coercively exploitative—for example, forcing a person to work at certain times, to earn a certain amount of money before she or he can leave work, to perform disliked sex acts, and so on," says Ronald Weitzer, the sociology professor at George Washington University who has studied the sex industry for years.[2]

Weitzer and other respected researchers favor a relatively open system that decriminalizes sex work but also subjects it to some restrictions, akin to New Zealand's approach. Such a hybrid system of semiregulation would permit the licensing of both large, corporate-run brothels (like Sheri's Ranch in Nevada) and smaller, cooperative brothels, where a number of sex workers could band together, rent an apartment, and hire a manager to screen calls and make appointments for them. The brothels themselves would be licensed and taxed, but individual workers would not be required to register.

"Escorts want to be able to work just like any other business, but they don't want to go through any kind of licensing," says Barbara Brents, the sociology professor at the University of Nevada, Las Vegas, who has written several books about prostitution. "And when you're working the streets to escape an abusive husband and feed your kids, who wants to register?"

In countries where prostitution is legal and individual sex workers are required to register (for example, Germany), many refuse to do so and continue to work illegally, which defeats the purpose of decriminalization. Instead of a requirement that individual sex workers register (and be exposed to public stigma), researchers who study the issue say that brothels and other venues (for example, massage parlors and private clubs) should be licensed, taxed, and inspected regularly, like any other business. And if such businesses violate the law (by hiring minors or illegal immigrants or exploiting their workers), they should be shut down. Even though independent sex workers like Maddy should not have to get licensed, they should still be required to pay taxes and could list their occupation as escort. (Maddy already pays taxes now, but on tax forms, she lists her occupation as a model and translator.)

Like many other sex workers, Maddy supports decriminalizing prostitution but is adamantly opposed to a legal approach that permits only the kind of heavily regulated prostitution found in Nevada's brothels. "If it's heavily regulated, we'll be targeted and further marginalized," she says. "We'd be relegated to red-light districts, to strip clubs that are in the poorest, most crime-ridden areas." Or to brothels in the desert that are an hour away from any urban centers.

Some researchers agree. As Weitzer notes in his 2012 book, "the less onerous and costly the regulations, the smaller the illegal sector [of sex workers]," and he points out that the latter is virtually nonexistent in New Zealand.[3]

Taking another page from New Zealand's bold experiment, researchers suggest that policy makers take into account the voices of sex workers themselves as well as the views of local residents, who know what may be best for their neighborhoods. "The fear is that the politically savvy men who make the laws are listening to the voices of people with a lot of capital and resources instead of listening to people who actually do the work," Brents says.

If federal and state prohibitions against adult consensual prostitution were removed, it would be up to local municipalities to decide how they want to regulate the commercial sex trade. "Every area might come up with something a little different," Brents says, again echoing the approach in New Zealand and the Netherlands of putting control in the hands of local counties or municipalities. All municipalities would probably prohibit sexually oriented businesses from locating near schools and playgrounds, and some might also ban street prostitution, as Amsterdam has done.

Adopting New Zealand's hybrid approach to regulating prostitution would bring millions of dollars into local government coffers in licensing fees and taxes from brothels, massage parlors, and escort services. Much as the legalization of marijuana in a growing number of states has done, it would take money away from the criminal element (in this case, exploitative pimps and traffickers) and put it into the hands of sanctioned businesses, individual women, and regulatory agencies. A recent study in Britain suggests that legalizing and taxing brothels and other places of prostitution would boost that country's gross domestic product by at least $8.9 billion.[4]

When New Zealand removed prohibitions against adult consensual prostitution, the same legislation officially recognized sex work as legitimate work, thus according its participants the rights and protections available to workers in other occupations. As a result, sex workers Down Under can sue brothel owners for harassment or exploitation, and have done so successfully. Weitzer suggests that the United States remove such prohibitions as well, so that sex workers can better protect themselves from exploitation and the pressure to practice unsafe sex.[5] Indeed, during the period when Rhode Island unintentionally decriminalized indoor prostitution, the state saw a steep decline in reported rapes and cases of gonorrhea.[6]

Experts also suggest that local government encourage safe sex practices and regular health exams, but not mandate them (as currently required in Nevada's brothels). "Compulsory testing for sexually transmitted infections stigmatizes sex workers, tests are not always accurate, and testing clean on a certain day may give the false impression that a person is sexually healthy afterward," Weitzer says.[7] Instead, he recommends that local health officials conduct safe-sex outreach education with sex workers and clients and encourage regular exams and free testing, as they do in the Netherlands and New Zealand, which don't mandate testing and have very low rates of HIV infection.

Mandatory testing may actually increase the danger of sexually transmitted disease transmission, according to some. As Lenore Kuo, the professor of women's studies and philosophy at California State University, Fresno, writes:

> In reality, medical exams simply force prostitutes who are infected to work in an illegal venue, where they are often more likely to infect their clients due to the related difficulties of practicing "safe" sex. In Nevada, as in other jurisdictions, there is a common tendency for many men to offer prostitutes bribes not to use condoms. Regulations requiring medical testing of prostitutes are only likely to increase this tendency because they

lead to the false expectation that the prostitute is disease-free. It is quite possible that a prostitute has been exposed to an STD [sexually transmitted disease] since her most recent test. . . . There is therefore no clear value in such tests but significant danger in encouraging clients to believe that prostitutes are disease-free.[8]

Both Weitzer and Kuo make persuasive arguments that criminalizing prostitution is a failed and dangerous strategy. It doesn't reduce the prevalence of sex work, and it clearly harms the women who do it. Arresting prostitutes heightens their isolation and estrangement from family and friends and makes it very difficult for them to seek other types of employment. Kuo notes that "criminalization also strengthens the prostitutes' dependence on pimps, who will post bail, arrange child care, and obtain legal counsel when they do get arrested."[9]

Women who are not sex workers are also threatened by a culture that allows sexual predators to kill with impunity and views prostitution as something dangerous and forbidden. Kuo argues that "women will never be normalized, will never cease being 'other' until sex and sexual activity are normalized. And sex and sexual activity will never be normalized until the sale of sexual activity is normalized (and vice versa)."[10]

On a more pragmatic level, decriminalizing adult consensual prostitution would allow law enforcement to focus on violent crimes and what both sex worker advocates and antitrafficking proponents consider a priority: prosecuting pimps who exploit underage youth and traffickers who force illegal immigrants into the sex trade. Many researchers argue that decriminalization would make it easier for victims and clients to report abuse to the police without the fear of being arrested themselves.

"Sex workers would be much more likely to come forward if you just talk to them than if you arrest them," says John Lowman, the criminology professor at Simon Fraser University in British Columbia. "If there's an adversarial relationship between prostitutes and the police, they're not going to solve anything."

BACK AT KRAMER'S BOOKSTORE, Maddy is getting restless. Earlier in the interview, watching me scribble away in a notebook, she admitted, "I'm a little nervous talking to you." Now, in response to my questions about her future, she says she won't be doing sex work for much longer. "The work I do is a wonderful fit, but it's not forever," she says. "It's like modeling or sports."

At the time of the interview, Maddy was about to complete a bachelor's degree and had already been accepted into several M.B.A. programs. She tells me that when she starts graduate school, she will probably stop doing sex work. "The economy has tanked, so there's less of a demand for luxury goods," she says, implying that this may be a good time for her (as a luxury item) to get out of the business. She bends over and changes back into her flats. Then she abruptly stands up. "I really have to go," she says and, with a quick wave of her hand, flies out the door.

# EPILOGUE

## *Silent No More*

Two years have passed since I last visited Julie Moya's brothel in Manhattan, and only one of the sex workers I met then is still working there: "Paris," the slender New Jerseyite who attended Rutgers University. She is slated to graduate at the end of 2015, Julie says, and plans to become a nurse. Sarah, the tiny spitfire from Israel who was also in school, studying art history, left for a higher-end escort service, which made Julie sad. "She got great reviews," Julie says. "The men loved her." Sarah's friend, Natasha, the buxom blonde from Russia who overstayed her visa, recently got married (solving her visa problem) and is now pregnant. Another of Julie's regulars, an attractive brunette whose work name was Taylor, also escaped into matrimony. "She met a client, and they ended up getting married," Julie says. "They are doing real well together."

Julie especially misses Sarah and Taylor. "They were such sweet girls," she says wistfully. But in the next instant, her mood brightens. "We've got some really nice new girls now," she says. "You should come and visit again."

Julie herself has turned over daily management of the brothel to friends now that she is the primary caregiver for her grandson. She received full custody of him in July 2014, and he has been out of foster care and living with her for more than a year. "The courts decided I was the best with him," she says. "As long as I don't bring him near the business, they're basically going to let it be."

Her grandson, who turned eight in May 2014, is still acting up in school, but he refuses to take psychoactive drugs. "He doesn't like the way they make him feel," she says. "He's a handful, but I'll never give him up."

At one point, Julie had talked of moving back to Cincinnati and opening up a nightclub there with her older son, now that gambling is legal in Ohio. But for now, she is focused on raising her grandson and trying not to repeat the mistakes she made with her own children as a young single mother. "I understand things much better now," she says.

Gambling has also come to Massachusetts, and Elle St. Claire, who turned forty-four in 2014, is hoping it will give her business a much-needed boost. While she continues to do sex work, phone sex, and adult webcams, she and Jessica, her longtime fiancée, are perennially strapped for cash. In 2013, Jessica took a part-time job as an electronics equipment technician, working out of the apartment doing customer service and diagnosing DVR equipment malfunctions. "It's been a stable source of income while the economy has been up and down," Elle says.

Elle says there are plans to build a casino in the Springfield area (one of three now permitted in Massachusetts). MGM recently received the license for the Springfield casino and resort. "Once the casino is built, a lot of people will come to Springfield to have fun, whether it's gambling or shows, and I think my phone will ring more," she says.

In the meantime, Elle has gone back to driving a cab, which she did as a single parent in the 1990s. She is trying to save up enough money to renew her real estate license and pay off the debt she and Jessica incurred when they had to move out of their Holyoke house. Elle says the company that managed their duplex found out she and Jessica were in the adult entertainment business and told them point blank that it didn't want "our kind here," she says. So after several years of battling the company in court, in May 2014, Elle and Jessica moved to a new apartment in Chicopee, a few miles away. "The new place is really perfect for us," Elle enthuses in an email. "The location is convenient and suits our lifestyle; our neighbors are very accepting and supporting. In fact, the community has been treating me as 'completely normal,' which I am not used to. Things are amazing, absolutely wonderful!"

Jillian, the activist-escort from western Massachusetts, is also still doing sex work. At age thirty-three, she says she's more organized and efficient than she used to be. "When I was younger, I'd do five calls in a day, and then I wouldn't work for a week," she says. "Now I decide what days I'm working, and I'm sort of on the clock from noon until 10 p.m. I usually work three to four days a week, although right now I'm working five or six days because I really need to make the rent on August 4."

Jillian often works with another woman (they share clients and sometimes do threesomes), and she prefers regulars to new clients, particularly new clients who are younger men with an entitled attitude. Recently, she says, one twenty-year-old client got hysterical at the sight of her menstrual blood and made such a fuss that she returned some of his money. But he soon texted her again and asked if he could see her that same day and pay her a few days later. Jillian texted back, "No escorting on the layaway plan." Then there was the doctor who booked a threesome with Jillian and her friend. As she describes the session on her blog, he "wanted to bend 'D' and me into acrobatic positions and, after asking whether we were on drugs or had diseases before giving me the money, had the audacity to be annoyed about switching condoms between us — a doctor!" She concludes, "Sorry for kvetching at such length, but these people are unbelievable sometimes."

Jillian, however, has also met some very nice clients. She describes two of them on her password-protected blog:

> The two clients I saw today, one hour right after the other, were both exceptions to my usual rule about guys in their late twenties being jackasses. The first was a polite analytical chemist in his late 20s. He was even good looking, which usually spells disaster because that type tend to be arrogant, but despite being somewhat laconic he was the soul of courtesy. The second was a nerdy, sweet bearded heating and air worker. He showed me some hilarious pictures of himself skiing in a kilt and horned head gear, and we laughed about him freaking out everyone on the slopes. We talked sci fi novels and role playing games. He even gave me a ride to the bank and then dropped me off at 7–11 afterwards. (I didn't feel comfortable with him dropping me off at home, so I just walked the block back from the store.)

Many of Jillian's best clients are regulars, which is why she was so upset when one of her favorite regulars, a married man in his midsixties, emailed her recently to say he was going to stop seeing her because a death in his family made him realize he needed to be more financially responsible and attentive to his wife. The man had started seeing Jillian and her partner because, as she puts it, "His wife was his second sexual partner ever, and since she was very traditionally Catholic sexually, he regretted all the sexual experience he'd missed throughout his life." He was very generous, paying double for sessions, bringing Jillian chocolate, and taking her out for Indian food on occasion. As she wrote wistfully in her blog, "I should have remembered the general pattern that holds that when a client seems to have fallen in love with you and starts to spend a whole bunch of cash on you, it's not going to last forever."

While Jillian still volunteers with Arise for Social Justice, the non-profit that advocates for the rights of poor and low-income people, she has devoted much of her spare time over the past two years to another unpaid activity: writing and editing for *Tits and Sass,* the blog for and by sex workers. She says she devotes "maybe twenty hours a week to it; I tend to work slowly and am somewhat obsessive." When the famous poet and writer Maya Angelou died, *Tits and Sass* published a blog about Angelou's foray into sex work as a young single mother. *Gawker* picked up the blog, the *Huffington Post* did a segment on it, and it was widely shared on Facebook.

Jillian plans to continue doing sex work for the foreseeable future. "I have no specific exit plan," she says. "I don't feel like I'm ready to go back to school yet. So I will continue writing and try to put myself out there more as a freelancer." When she first began doing sex work, she thought the demand for her services might dry up by the time she hit thirty or thirty-five. But now she sees women in their forties and early fifties who are still doing well in sex work. "Age isn't as much of a barrier as I originally thought," she says. "A lot of sex workers don't have an exit plan. In this unstable economy, you tend to stick with what you know."

By contrast, Anna, "the girl next door" whom I'd met at Sheri's Ranch in Nevada, did have a definite exit plan. She stopped doing sex work when she left the Nevada brothel in October 2013. Her husband had finished graduate school in Las Vegas, so they had moved back to Florida, and Anna commuted by air. But after a month of that, she decided she'd had enough. She says she and her husband spent weeks repairing the damage renters had done to their central Florida house, and then Anna found out that she was pregnant. Now the mother of a baby girl, Anna has put off her plans to go to graduate school for the time being. "I wanted a family," she says.

Anna loves being a mother, but there are days when she misses the high life at Sheri's Ranch and all her friends there. Before she left, her co-workers gave her two goodbye parties. "It was a beautiful send-off," she says. "The girls made me cry. My last two weeks there, there were two send-off cakes and people signed cards. It was very sweet. [Sheri's] definitely was my second home for four years. I loved it and do miss it."

Anna and many of the other young women I profiled in this book never considered sex work a permanent career. Like many women in the late nineteenth and early twentieth centuries, they viewed it as a short-term economic choice, a way to pay off debt, get through school, or support a family. For some, like Elle, who had already sampled the 9-to-5 life, it remains a conscious career choice. For others, like Julie and those with a criminal record, it is a trap with no easy exit. And for still others, particularly women like Maxine Doogan, Carol Leigh, and Jillian, it has become a lifelong political and socioeconomic statement. Yet whether these sex workers are in the profession by choice or under duration, for the short or long haul, they share common ground in the challenge of living with criminal laws that make it difficult for them to live safe, financially secure lives.

Consider, for example, what recently happened to Joi Love. She left Rhode Island in 2013 to move in with her mother in Richmond, Virginia, and help her deal with some pressing personal issues. "My little brother had been terrorizing my mom and my sister," Joi says, referring to her half-brother, her mother's son from a second marriage. "Helping my brother was a useless cause, but I got him out of the house." She and her longtime boyfriend, Lucky, then moved to Atlanta, where Joi began working again as an escort. In the spring of 2014, they met a younger woman who was also interested in doing sex work and they began traveling around with her. In July 2014, Joi and Lucky were visiting her mother in Richmond, and their acquaintance was staying at a nearby hotel when she got caught in a prostitution sting. To save herself, the young woman claimed that Lucky was forcing her into sex work—in essence, trafficking her. Richmond police immediately arrested Lucky and Joi.

"They told me I could also be a [trafficking] victim witness against him," Joi says. "But that would be a lie. Clearly, I'm not a victim of anything, and we've lived as husband and wife forever." When Joi refused to play ball, she was charged with two felonies: conspiracy to pander and conspiracy to receive the earnings of a prostitute, even though she says she was not getting any money from the younger woman and had nothing to do with her decision to sell sex. She was also charged with a prostitution-related misdemeanor. Joi's boyfriend, Lucky (no longer so lucky), was charged with more serious crimes, including kidnapping, pandering, transporting, and receiving money from a prostitute.

After spending fifteen days in the Henrico County jail, Joi was finally able to post bond. It cost her $1,500; Lucky had to pay $2,400. They were released only after agreeing to wear GPS monitors on their ankles (for which each had to pay $75 a week.) The woman who turned on them was released on her recognizance and will not be charged, Joi says. While Lucky managed to scrape together the funds to hire a private attorney, Joi did not have enough money to hire a lawyer for herself. Instead, she was given a court-appointed attorney, who pressed her to say she was a trafficking victim so she could avoid jail time.

"When I met with my attorney, he was basically making the case for the prosecutors," she says. "He didn't even have a defense he was going to present." Joi herself collected the evidence to show that she was innocent of the felony charges and convinced her attorney to mount a defense. On October 20, she pleaded guilty to the misdemeanor, and her lawyer convinced the Henrico County prosecutors to drop the felony charges.

At Lucky's trial, the woman who claimed she was trafficked kept changing her story. In the end, Lucky was convicted of only one felony, transporting a sex worker. Joi says her boyfriend is currently on "home incarceration" at her mother's house in Richmond while he appeals his conviction.

After Joi was arrested, her middle daughter, who had been accepted at a North Carolina college on a full scholarship, had to delay her enrollment in school because Joi could not afford the remaining school fees. Her ex-husband had died of stomach cancer in June of 2014, and her youngest daughter, who was supposed to come stay with Joi in Atlanta, had to go live with her ex-husband's sister in North Carolina instead.

Joi is hoping her middle daughter will be able to start college in the spring. And she is looking forward to becoming a grandmother. Her oldest daughter, who finally graduated from Wake Forest University in 2013, is pregnant and living in Virginia with her boyfriend, a basketball player whom she met in college.

Even so, Joi remains bitter about what happened to her. "The prosecutors don't care what the facts are," she says. "They just want a number they can add to their [crime-fighting] stats."

This is as true today as it was in the 1960s, when Miss Major Griffin-Gracy, an African American transgender woman, walked the stroll on 42nd Street and Eighth Avenue every evening. Now a seventy-year-old transgender woman who walks with a cane and has to be helped up to the stage, Miss Major is the keynote speaker on the first day of the Desiree Alliance conference in Las Vegas. One of the organizers introduces her briefly as a transsexual gay rights activist, but it is very clear that the audience knows who she is. As many as a hundred women and men have crowded into the main ballroom to hear her speak, and they hoot and holler in admiration, pound the tables, and clap loudly as she lumbers to the podium. Looking around, I am struck by the sheer diversity of the people in the room, women and men of every conceivable color, shape, and age, gathered here from all over the United States. Many sport tattoos, nose rings, and other piercings, and a smattering show off Mohawk-style haircuts. Others are dressed much more conventionally in revealing dresses, flowing skirts or shorts, and tank tops. Some of the women are strikingly beautiful, but most of the people in the room look like you and me, with all the quirks of body and face one would find at any large gathering. For a Monday morning, however, this is an unusually joyous, high-energy bunch. I hear laughter and lots of conversation floating in the air around me.

Miss Major, as she is known, a huge woman who is wearing a stylish black wig and has no front teeth, begins by talking about the racism and sexism that still permeate U.S. society. She cites the case of George Zimmerman, who killed an unarmed black teenager in Florida and was acquitted. Despite the risks of being black or brown, gay or transgender in a culture that can seem unforgiving, she tells the crowd that they don't need to follow "the white man's rules"; they should do what feels right for them.

Women, she says, have always used sex to survive in difficult circumstances, to get what they needed. "My mother was doing the same thing I'm doing," she says. "She needed a stove, so she gave a little honey. It's the same thing."

New York in the 1960s used to be a fun and exciting place for a hooker, Miss Major says — "42nd Street was heaven. The men all wore nice suits, the women in nice dresses. You could afford to live in New York City back then. Now it's become a place for the extremely rich and extremely poor, and there's no place for people in between."

In 1969, Miss Major was partying at Stonewall Inn, a favorite watering hole for gay, lesbian, and transgender people, the night police raided the place. While New York's finest often harassed and arrested the patrons there, that June evening the regulars had had enough. The four days of riots that resulted became known as the Stonewall uprising, which gave rise to the modern LGBT (lesbian, gay, bisexual, and transgender) civil rights movement.

A year later, Miss Major was arrested for robbing a white john. "I thought I was a female Robin Hood, and then I would go shopping," she says, with a sly smile that exposes her toothless pink gums. Sent to Attica, she was incarcerated there during the riots in 1971, a four-day uprising that claimed the lives of ten correctional officers and thirty-three inmates. "I met one of the organizers of the riots, they called him Big

Black, and he politicized me," she says. "I'm a proud black, transgender ex-con."

For the past decade, Miss Major, as founder of TGI Justice in San Francisco, has tried to help transgender women in the prison system make better lives for themselves when they get out. "We try to make sure they have support so they don't end up back in prison," she says. "If you want to hook and walk the street, that's fine on you. But if you want a different life, we try to help you have that."

Miss Major looks out over the audience. "You know, there was a time when we couldn't have met like this," she says. "At least now we can do this. So you have to make sure you enjoy this, laugh a lot, and share your uniqueness with each other."

For a few seconds, there is quiet and then the crowd erupts, giving Miss Major a standing ovation. In this room, at this time, a self-selected sample of America's sex workers are silent no more.

# ACKNOWLEDGMENTS

This book could not have been written without the assistance of the sex workers whose lives I chronicle in these pages. I owe an enormous debt of gratitude to Margo St. James, Julie Moya, Jillian, Elle St. Claire, Joi Love, Madeleine Colette, Amy Lebovitch, Valerie Scott, Maxine Doogan, Carol Leigh, and the many other sex workers I spoke to in the course of doing research for this book. I am especially grateful to Julie Moya and Jillian, who gave me so much of their time and who generously put me in touch with others in the sex work community. I am also grateful to the researchers, community health professionals, human rights advocates, and law enforcement officials who helped me see the larger picture.

My heartfelt thanks to the friends and colleagues who took the time to read parts of my manuscript and offer feedback, including John Temple, Jim Harms, Benyamin Cohen, Daleen Berry, Lois Raimondo, Mary Kay McFarland, Shula Reinharz, and Karen Osborn.

I would also like to thank my editor, Phyllis Deutsch, whose incisive comments and support kept me focused and moving forward, and the excellent editing team at the University Press of New England.

Finally, I would like to thank my husband, Jim Palmer, whose love and support keep me smiling, and my two sons, David and Jake, who make me proud and show me what really matters.

# NOTES

## Preface

1. Barbara G. Brents and Teela Sanders, "Mainstreaming the Sex Industry: Economic Inclusion and Social Ambivalence, *Journal of Law and Society* 37, no. 1 (March 2010): 44.

2. Ronald Weitzer, *Legalizing Prostitution: From Illicit Vice to Lawful Business* (New York: New York University Press, 2012), 3–4.

3. Gregor Gail, "Sex Worker Collective Organization: Between Advocacy Group and Labour Union?" *Equality, Diversity and Inclusion: An International Journal* 29, no. 3 (2010): 293.

4. Ibid.

5. Ibid.

## Prologue

1. Weitzer, *Legalizing Prostitution*, 63.

## 1. The Madonna-Whore Divide

1. Anne Seagraves, *Soiled Doves: Prostitution in the Early West* (Hayden, Idaho: Wesanne Publications, 1994), 104.

2. Deborah Mellon, *The Legend of Molly b'Dam* (Kellogg, Idaho: Maple Street Publishing, 1989), 6–7.

3. Timothy Gilfoyle, *City of Eros: New York, Prostitution and the Commercialization of Sex, 1790–1920* (New York: W.W. Norton, 1992), 106.

4. Ibid., 60.

5. Ibid., 59.

6. Nickie Roberts, *Whores in History* (London: Grafton Press, 1993), 23.

7. Ibid., 236.

8. Gilfoyle, *City of Eros*, 84.

9. Ibid., 87.

10. Ibid., 91.

11. Roberts, *Whores in History*, 240.

12. Gilfoyle, *City of Eros*, 64.

13. Ibid., 65.

14. Seagraves, *Soiled Doves*, 106.

15. Mellon, *The Legend of Molly b'Dam*, 13–14.

16. Seagraves, *Soiled Doves*, 106.

17. Ibid., 107.

18. Carl B. Glasscock, *Lucky Baldwin: The Story of an Unconventional Success* (Indianapolis: Bobbs-Merrill, 1933), 223.

19. Ibid., 225.

20. Ibid.

21. Mellon, *The Legend of Molly b'Dam*, 24.

22. Barbara Brents, Crystal A. Jackson, and Kathryn Hausbeck, *The State of Sex: Tourism, Sex and Sin in the New American Heartland* (New York: Routledge, 2010), 46.

23. Sandra Dallas, *Fallen Women* (New York: St. Martin's Press, 2013), 342.

24. Ibid., 343.

25. Brents, Jackson, and Hausbeck, *The State of Sex*, 50.

26. Dee Brown, *The Gentle Tamers: Women of the Old Wild West* (New York: Bantam Books, 1974), 67.

27. Ibid., 66.

28. Ibid., 67–8.

29. Seagraves, *Soiled Doves*, 109.

30. Ibid., 110.

31. Ibid., 45.

32. Ibid.

33. Ibid., 47.

34. Kingsley Davis, "The Sociology of Prostitution," *American Sociological Review*, 2, no. 5 (1937): 747.

35. Gilfoyle, *City of Eros*, 271.

36. Ibid., 290.

37. Jan MacKell, *Brothels, Bordellos and Bad Girls: Prostitution in Colorado, 1860–1930*, (Albuquerque: University of New Mexico Press, 2004), 204–5.

38. Gilfoyle, *City of Eros*, 303–4.

39. Seagraves, *Soiled Doves*, 45.

40. Roberts, *Whores in History*, 267.

41. Gilfoyle, *City of Eros*, 312.

42. Roberts, *Whores in History*, 268.

43. Polly Adler, *A House Is Not a Home* (New York: Rinehart Books, 1953), 21.

44. Ibid., 25.

45. Ibid., 44.

46. Ibid., 92.

47. Ibid., 97.

48. Ibid., 126.

49. Ibid., 130.

50. Ibid., 164.

51. Ibid., 217.

52. Elizabeth Clement, *Love for Sale: Courtship, Treating and Prostitution in New York, 1920–1945* (Chapel Hill: University of North Carolina Press, 2006), 245.

53. Ibid.

54. Ibid., 243.

55. Ibid., 215.

56. Adler, *A House Is Not a Home*, 268.

57. "Polly Adler Dead: Wrote 'A House Is Not a Home,'" obituary, *Washington Post*, June 10, 1962.

## 2. The Modern Sex Workers' Rights Movement

1. "Polly Adler Dead: Wrote 'A House Is Not a Home.'"

2. Polly Adler, *A House Is Not a Home*, 48.

3. Ibid., 113.

4. Ibid., 110–1.

5. Jennifer Thompson, "The Greening of Margo St. James," *San Francisco Magazine*, June 1974, 26.

6. Margo St. James, afterword to *Prostitutes—Our Life*, by Claude Jaget (Bristol, United Kingdom: Falling Wall Press, 1980), 197.

7. Ibid.

8. Wayne Ellis, "The Other Side of Sexuality," *Every Other Weekly*, March 9–22, 2000, 8.

9. Ibid.

10. St James, afterword to *Prostitutes, Our Life*, 197.

11. Ibid., 198

12. Roberts, *Whores in History*, 283.

13. Ibid., 320.

14. Ibid., 290–1.

15. Ellis, "The Other Side of Sexuality," 11.

16. Ibid.

17. "Transcript of Evidence and Proceedings," *United States of America v. Marshall Clay Riddle, Ralph Louis Bernius, Jacqueline Riley, Malcolm Britton Wooton,* vol. 8, U.S. District Court, Eastern District of Kentucky, July 25, 1978, 1554.

18. Ibid., 1637.

19. "Transcript of Evidence and Proceedings," *United States of America v. Marshall Clay Riddle,* 1560–1. Bob Fogarty, "Prostitute Reveals Ring's Operation," *Cincinnati Enquirer,* July 14, 1978.

20. "Transcript of Evidence and Proceedings," *United States of America vs. Marshall Clay Riddle,* 1594.

21. Nancy Allen and David W. Reid, "13 Indicted on Prostitution Ring Charges, *Cincinnati Enquirer,* May 5, 1978. "Prostitution Case," *Cincinnati Enquirer,* May 6, 1978.

22. Ellis, "The Other Side of Sexuality," 11.

23. Jerry Seltzer, "Hooker's Ball" (blog), http://rollerderbyjesus.com/tag/hookers-ball/.

24. "Hookers Win Case Oakland vs ACLU," *Coyote Howls,* June/July 1975, 1.

25. Ellis, "The Other Side of Sexuality," 11.

26. Elizabeth Bernstein, *Temporarily Yours: Intimacy, Authenticity and the Commerce of Sex* (Chicago: University of Chicago Press: 2007), 11.

27. Roberts, *Whores in History,* 291.

28. Devon D. Brewer et al, "Extent, Trends and Perpetrators of Prostitution-Related Homicide in the United States," *Journal of Forensic Sciences,* 51, no. 5 (September 2006), 1101–8.

29. St. James, afterword to *Prostitutes, Our Life,* 192.

30. Frederique Delacoste and Priscilla Alexander, eds., *Sex Work: Writings by Women in the Sex Industry,* 2nd ed. (San Francisco: Cleis Press, 1987), 145–6.

31. "Transcript of Evidence and Proceedings," *United States of America v. Marshall Clay Riddle,* 1595–6.

32. Bob Fogarty, "Outburst at Lawyer Cross-Examination," *Cincinnati Enquirer,* July 27, 1978.

33. Bob Fogarty, "9 Persons Enter Guilty Pleas in Interstate Prostitution Case," *Cincinnati Enquirer,* July 12, 1978.

34. Bob Fogarty, "Defendants Found Guilty in Interstate Prostitution Case," *Cincinnati Enquirer,* Aug. 2, 1978,

## 3. Sex Work Goes Online and Indoors

1. Bernstein, *Temporarily Yours*, 30.

2. Barbara Brents and Kathryn Hausbeck, "Marketing Sex: us Legal Brothels and Late Capitalist Consumption," *Sexualities*, 10. no. 4 (2007): 425–9. Weitzer, *Legalizing Prostitution*, 39.

3. Robert Kolker, "The New Prostitutes," *New York Times*, June 29, 2013.

4. Bernstein, *Temporarily Yours*, 122.

5. Ibid., 172.

6. Ibid., 174.

7. Neil Postman, *Technopoly: The Surrender of Culture to Technology* (New York: Alfred A. Knopf, 1992), 179.

8. Bernstein, *Temporarily Yours*, 120.

9. Ibid., 121.

10. Weitzer, *Legalizing Prostitution*, 35.

11. Christine Milrod and Ronald Weitzer, "The Intimacy Prism: Emotion Management among the Clients of Escorts," *Men and Masculinities*, 15, no. 2 (2012): 454, DOI: 10.1177/1097184X12452148.

12. Ibid.

13. Bernstein, *Temporarily Yours*, 134.

14. Milrod and Weitzer, "The Intimacy Prism," 465.

15. Bernstein, *Temporarily Yours*, 80.

16. Fred Contrada, "Council Tables Panhandler Rule," *Springfield Republican*, February 7, 2009.

## 4. Why Women and Men Do Sex Work

1. Weitzer, *Legalizing Prostitution*, 10.

2. Lenore Kuo, *Prostitution Policy: Revolutionizing Practice through a Gendered Perspective* (New York: New York University Press 2002), 173.

3. John Lowman, "Taking Young Prostitutes Seriously," *Canadian Review of Sociology and Anthropology*, 24, no. 1 (1987): 103.

4. Ric Curtis et al., "The Commercial Sexual Exploitation of Children in New York City," report submitted to the National Institute of Justice, U.S. Department of Justice (vol. 1, September 2008): 46, http://www.courtinnovation.org/sites/default/files/CSEC_NYC_Volume1.pdf.

5. Ibid., 47.

6. Ibid., 105.

7. Ibid., 51.

8. Ibid., 50.

9. Weitzer, *Legalizing Prostitution*, 14.

10. Tamara O'Doherty, "Victimization in Off-Street Sex Industry Work," *Violence Against Women*, New York: Sage Publications (June 10, 2011), DOI: 10.1177/1077801211412917.

11. Private online journal by "Jillian," May 22, 2006.

12. Weitzer, *Legalizing Prostitution*, 25.

13. Ibid., 14.

14. Kuo, *Prostitution Policy*, 95.

15. Ronald Weitzer, "New Directions in Research on Prostitution," *Crime, Law & Social Change*, 43, (2005): 218, DOI: 10.1007/s10611-005-1735-6.

16. Kuo, *Prostitution Policy*, 173.

17. Weitzer, "New Directions in Research on Prostitution," 216.

18. Kuo, *Prostitution Policy*, 97.

19. Gillian Abel et al., eds. *Taking the Crime Out of Sex Work: New Zealand Sex Workers' Fight for Decriminalization* (Bristol, United Kingdom: Policy Press: 2010), 254.

20. Rochelle Dalla, *Exposing the Pretty Woman Myth* (London: Lexington Books 2006), 77.

21. Ibid., 77.

22. Abel et al., *Taking the Crime Out of Sex Work*, 251.

23. Ibid., 255.

24. Weitzer, "New Directions in Research on Prostitution," 218.

25. Ibid.

26. Ibid.

27. Ibid.

28. Weitzer, *Legalizing Prostitution*, 9.

29. Davis, "The Sociology of Prostitution," 748–9.

30. Ibid., 749.

31. Donna M. Hughes, *The Demand for Victims of Sex Trafficking*, research report (June 2005): 7, http://www.uri.edu/artsci/wms/hughes/demand_for_victims .pdf.

32. Andrea Dworkin, *Life and Death* (New York: Free Press, 2002), 145.

33. Melissa Farley, "Prostitution and Trafficking in Nine Countries," *Journal of Trauma Practice* 2 (2003): 34.

34. Melissa Farley, "Prostitution, Liberalism, and Slavery," *Logos*, 12, no 3, (Fall 2013): 12, http://logosjournal.com/2013/farley/.

35. Bernstein, *Temporarily Yours*, 51.

36. John Money, *Lovemaps* (New York: Prometheus Books, 1986), 29.

37. Ibid., 29.

38. Ibid., 58.

39. Ibid., 169.

40. Dwight Garner, "Not Tonight, or Any Other Night," review of *How to Think More about Sex*, by Alain de Botton, *New York Times*, August 15, 2013.

## 5. The Truth about Sex Trafficking

1. Donna M. Hughes, "The 'Natasha' Trade: The Transnational Shadow Market of Trafficking in Women," *Journal of International Affairs* 53, no. 2 (Spring 2000): 625–51.

2. Ibid., 650.

3. Kari Lerum et al., "Using Human Rights to Hold the US Accountable for Its Anti–Sex Trafficking Agenda: The Universal Periodic Review and New Directions for US Policy," *Anti-Trafficking Review* no. 1 (June 2012): 87, http://www.antitraffickingreview.org/index.php/atrjournal/article/view/24/26.

4. *Human Trafficking: Better Data, Strategy, and Reporting Needed to Enhance U.S. Antitrafficking Efforts Abroad*, U.S. Government Accountability Office (July 2006), 10, http://www.gao.gov/new.items/d06825.pdf.

5. *Human Trafficking: A Crime That Shames Us All*, Global Report on Trafficking in Persons, U.N. Office on Drugs and Crime (February 2009): 48, http://www.unodc.org/documents/Global_Report_on_TIP.pdf.

6. *Human Trafficking: Better Data, Strategy, and Reporting Needed*, 12.

7. Duren Banks and Tracy Kyckelhahn, *Characteristics of Suspected Human Trafficking Incidents, 2008–2010*, Special Report, U.S. Department of Justice (April 2011), 1, http://www.bjs.gov/content/pub/pdf/cshti0810.pdf.

8. Amy Farrell, Jack McDevitt, and Stephanie Fahy, "Where Are All the Victims? Understanding the Determinants of Official Identification of Human Trafficking Incidents," *Criminology and Public Policy* 9, no. 2 (2010): 215.

9. Curtis et al., "The Commercial Sexual Exploitation of Children in New York City," 3.

10. Martin Cizmar, Ellis Conklin, and Kristen Hinman, "Real Men Get Their Facts Straight," *Village Voice*, June 20, 2011, 4. Laurel Kirchner, "Darts & Laurels," *Columbia Journalism Review*, May 26, 2011.

11. Kimberly J. Mitchell, David Finkelhor, and Janis Wolak, "Conceptualizing Juvenile Prostitution as Child Maltreatment: Findings from the National Juvenile Prostitution Study," *Child Maltreatment* 15, no. 1 (February 2010): 18–36.

12. Michelle Stransky and David Finkelor, *Sex Trafficking of Minors: How Many*

*Juveniles Are Being Prostituted in the US?* University of New Hampshire Crimes against Children Research Center, May 2008 (revised June 2012): 3, http://www .unh.edu/ccrc/pdf/cv279_Revised_Sex_Trafficking_Bulletin.pdf.

13. Curtis et al., "The Commercial Exploitation of Children in New York City," 47.

14. Anthony Marcus et al., "Conflict and Agency Among Sex Workers and Pimps: A Closer Look at Domestic Minor Sex Trafficking," *ANNALS of the American Academy of Political and Social Science* 653 (2014): 241–242; DOI: 10.1177/0002716214521993.

15. Curtis et al., "The Commercial Exploitation of Children in New York City," 74.

16. Ibid., 76.

17. Ibid., 73.

18. Ibid., 37.

19. Sex Workers Project, *Behind Closed Doors: An Analysis of Indoor Sex Work in New York City*, Urban Justice Center, March 30, 2005, http://swp.ujcprd.vshift .net/sites/default/files/BehindClosedDoors.pdf.

20. *Impact Report 2013*, Coalition to Abolish Slavery and Trafficking (CAST), 7, http://www.castla.org/impact-report, 7.

21. Farrell, McDevitt, and Fahy, "Where Are All the Victims?," 201 and 203.

22. Carol Leigh, "Prop 35, Youth, Sex Trade and Sex Trafficking—Interview with Alexandra Lutnick, Researcher," Indybay.org, Nov. 2, 2012, https://www .indybay.org/newsitems/2012/11/02/18724988.php.

23. Curtis et al., "The Commercial Sexual Exploitation of Children in New York," 120.

24. Farrell, McDevitt, and Fahy, "Where Are All the Victims?," 223.

25. Michelle Chen, "Are New York's Sex Workers Getting Their Fair Day in Court?," *Nation*, October 6, 2014, http://www.thenation.com/blog/181861/are -new-yorks-sex-workers-getting-their-fair-day-court#.

26. Christie Thompson, "Escorted to Jail," *Chicago Reporter*, November 1, 2012, http://www.chicagoreporter.com/escorted-jail#.VCHU1RYAWmQ.

27. G.W. Rasopsoff, "Kenai's 'Gifted Hands Massage' Owner Found Guilty on Six Felony Prostitution and Sex Trafficking Charges," *Alaska Native News*, August 1, 2013, http://alaska-native-news.com/kenai-s-gifted-hands-massage -owner-found-guilty-of six-felony-prostitution-and-sex-trafficking-charges-8497.

28. Mark Billingsley (assistant public defender) "Motion to Dismiss Complaint," State of Alaska v. Celestine Theisen, District Court for the State of Alaska, Fourth Judicial District, October 24, 2013.

29. Leigh, "Prop 35, Youth, Sex Trade and Sex Trafficking—Interview with Alexandra Lutnick."

30. Henry Lee, "19 Charged in Alameda County Massage-Parlor Crackdown," *San Francisco Chronicle,* May 2, 2014, http://www.sfgate.com/crime/article/19 -charged-in-Alameda-County-massage-parlor-5449576.php.

31. Amanda Milkovits, "Hunting Houses of Ill Repute: Law Enforcement Sex Trafficking," *Providence Journal,* May 27, 2014.

32. Helen Peterson, "Madam Trafficked in Teen Girls, DA Says," *Daily News,* February 15, 2005.

## 6. From Bad Laws to Bad Cops and Violence against Women

1. Devon D. Brewer et al., "Extent, Trends, and Perpetrators of Prostitution-Related Homicide in the United States," *Journal of Forensic Sciences* 51, no. 5: 1101.

2. John J. Potterat et al., "Mortality in a Long-Term Open Cohort of Prostitute Women," *American Journal of Epidemiology* 158, no. 8 (2004): 778–85, http://aje .oxfordjournals.org/content/159/8/778.full.

3. Ibid.

4. Weitzer, *Legalizing Prostitution,* 26.

5. O'Doherty, "Victimization in Off-Street Sex Industry Work," 13.

6. Abel et al., *Taking the Crime Out of Sex Work,* 223.

7. Annie Sprinkle, "Remembering Our Dead and Wounded," in *Hos, Hookers, Call Girls and Rent Boys,* David Henry Sterry, ed. (New York: Soft Skull Press, 2009), 12.

8. C. Gabrielle Salfati, Alison R. James, and Lynn Ferguson, "Prostitute Homicides: A Descriptive Study," *Journal of Interpersonal Violence* 23 (March 2008): 538.

9. Delacorte, *"Sex Work: Writings by Women in the Sex Industry,* 205.

10. Weitzer, *Legalizing Prostitution,* 198.

11. Bernstein, *Temporarily Yours,* 58.

12. Steven D. Levitt and Stephen J. Dubner, *SuperFreakonomics* (New York: Harper Collins, 2009), 45.

13. Celia Williamson et al., *Domestic Sex Trafficking in Ohio,* Research and Analysis Sub-Committee of the Ohio Human Trafficking Commission, August 8, 2012, 16–18, http://www.ohioattorneygeneral.gov/getattachment/2ff15706–77ad -4567-b1aa-d8330b5c4005/2012-Domestic-Sex-Trafficking-in-Ohio-Report.aspx.

14. Robert Kolker, *Lost Girls: An Unsolved American Mystery* (New York: Harper Collins, 2013), 111–28.

15. Ibid., 129–33.

16. Ibid., 330.

17. Ibid., 333.

18. Ibid., 260.

19. Joseph Goldstein and Al Baker, "For Prostitutes, the Discovery of Bodies on Long Island Is Stoking Fear," *New York Times*, May 30, 2011, http://www .nytimes.com/2011/05/31/nyregion/prostitutes-fears-grow-as-remains-on-long -island-are-identified.html?pagewanted=all&_r=0.

20. Scott J. Croteau, "Detective Work Led to Scesny; 'Person of Interest' in Deaths of Women," *Worcester Telegram & Gazette*, May 4, 2008, A1.

21. Gary V. Murray, "Scesny Gets Life in Woman's Murder," *Worcester Telegram & Gazette*, March 31, 2012.

22. Scott J. Croteau, "Profiling Team Upgrades Scesny's Status in Deaths of Prostitutes," *Worcester Telegram & Gazette*, April 2, 2012.

## 7. Busted in Sin City

1. Brents et al., *The State of Sex*, 81–82.

2. Ibid., 84.

3. Ibid., 143.

4. Weitzer, *Legalizing Prostitution*, 88.

5. Seagraves, *Soiled Doves*, 86–87.

6. Brents et al., *The State of Sex*, 52.

7. Ibid., 55.

8. Ibid., 63.

9. Ibid., 65.

10. Ibid., 74.

11. Weitzer, *Legalizing Prostitution*, 88.

12. Brents et al., *The State of Sex*, 92.

13. Melissa Ditmore, "Sex and Taxes," the *Guardian*, April 16, 2009, http:// www.theguardian.com/commentisfree/cifamerica/2009/apr/03/nevada -prostitution-tax.

14. Brents et al., *The State of Sex*, 124.

## 8. Misguided Laws and Misuse of Resources

1. Helen Peterson, "Madam Trafficked in Teen Girls, DA Says," *New York Daily News*, February 15, 2005.

2. Barbara Ross and Bill Hutchinson, "Madam on Hook for 5 Yrs," *Daily News*, July 28, 2005.

3. Julie Pearl, "The Highest Paying Customers: America's Cities and the Cost of Prostitution Control," *Hastings Law Journal*, 38 (April 1987): 784.

4. Bernstein, *Temporarily Yours*, 57.

5. Arrests for Prostitution Offenses 2013, New York State Division of Criminal Justice Statistics, *2013 New York State Statistical Yearbook*, 37th ed., http://www.rockinst.org/nys_statistics/.

6. Drake Hagner, ed., "Criminal Law Chapter: Prostitution and Sex Work," Tenth Annual Review of Gender and Sexuality Law, *Georgetown Journal of Gender and the Law* 10, no. 2 (2009): 10.

7. Kuo, *Prostitution Policy*, 74–75.

8. Arrests for Prostitution Offenses 2013.

9. *Criminal, Victim, or Worker? The Effects of New York's Human Trafficking Intervention Courts on Adults Charged with Prostitution-Related Offenses*, report by the Red Umbrella Project, October 2014. http://www.redumbrellaproject.org/wp-content/uploads/2014/09/RedUP-NYHTIC-FINALweb.pdf.

10. David Kepler, "New York Bill Would Bar Condoms as Proof of Prostitution," *Associated Press*, April 27, 2014, http://news.yahoo.com/ny-bill-bar-condoms-proof-prostitution-125545358.html.

11. Hagner, "Criminal Law Chapter: Prostitution and Sex Work," 3.

12. Ibid., 3.

13. Pearl, "The Highest Paying Customers," 772.

14. Ibid., 772.

15. Laurie Becklund, "Prostitution Arrests Cost $2,000 Each, Study Finds," *Los Angeles Times*, July 10, 1987.

16. Pearl, "The Highest Paying Customers," 769.

17. Ibid., 775.

18. Ibid., 782.

19. Ronald Weitzer, "Sociology of Sex Work," *Annual Review of Sociology*, 35 (August 2009): 213–34.

20. Arrests for offenses, New York State Division of Criminal Justice Statistics, *2011 New York State Statistical Yearbook*, 37th ed., http://www.rockinst.org/nys_statistics/.

21. James Bovard, "The Legalization of Prostitution," *Freedom Daily*, September 1998, http://fff.org/explore-freedom/article/legalization-prostitution/.

22. Kuo, 125.

23. Ibid., 125–6.

## 9. The Rhode Island Story

1. Lynn Arditi, "How Rhode Island Opened the Door to Prostitution," *Providence Journal-Bulletin*, May 31, 2009,

2. Ibid.

3. Ibid.

4. Karen Lee Ziner and Tom Mooney, "14 Nabbed for Prostitution Under New Law" *Providence Journal*, December 12, 2009.

5. Editorial, "Progress against Prostitution," *Providence Journal*, February 16, 2011.

6. Weitzer, *Legalizing Prostitution*, 76.

## 10. Sex Work Overseas

1. Sandra Ka Hon Chu and Rebecca Glass, "Sex Work Law Reform in Canada: Considering Problems with the Nordic Model," *Alberta Law Review*, 51. no. 1 (2013): 104.

2. Ibid.

3. Ibid., 106.

4. Susanne Dodillet and Petra Östergren, "The Swedish Sex Purchase Act: Claimed Success and Documented Effects," paper delivered at the International Workshop on Decriminalizing Prostitution and Beyond: Practical Experiences and Challenges, the Hague (March 3 and 4, 2011), 22–23, http://chezstella.org /docs/etude-suede-2011.pdf.

5. Ibid., 23.

6. Ibid., 24.

7. Jay Levy and and Pye Jakobsson, "Sweden's Abolitionist Discourse and Law: Effects on the Dynamics of Swedish Sex Work and on the Lives of Sweden's Sex Workers," *Criminology and Criminal Justice*, 14, no. 5 (2014): 603, DOI: 10.1177/1748895814528926.

8. Petra Östergen, "Sexworkers Critique of Swedish Prostitution Policy," *Bildernaar tagna av Orlando G Bostrom, Webb av Sphinxly, CMS* (2010), 5, http:// petraostergren.com/pages.aspx?r_id=40716.

9. Jane Scolar, "What's Law Got to Do with It? How and Why Law Matters in the Regulation of Sex Work," *Journal of Law and Society*, 37, no. 1 (March 2010): 19. Levy and Jakobsson, "Sweden's Abolitionist Discourse and Law," 598.

10. Scolar, "What's Law Got to Do with It?," 19

11. Ibid., 19.

12. Levy and Jakobsson, "Sweden's Abolitionist Discourse and Law," 599.

13. Samuel Lee and Petra Persson, "Human Trafficking and Regulating Prostitution," *Law and Economic Research Paper Series,* New York University School of Law, Working Paper no. 12–08, June 2012, 25–26.

14. Ibid., 4.

15. Östergren, "Sexworkers Critique of Swedish Prostitution Policy," 5.

16. Östergren, "Sexworkers Critique of Swedish Prostitution Policy," 5. Levy and Jakobsson, "Sweden's Abolitionist Discourse and Law," 599.

17. Levy and Jakobsson, "Sweden's Abolitionist Discourse and Law," 600.

18. Chu and Glass, "Sex Work Law Reform in Canada," 107.

19. Ibid., 123–24.

20. Laura Agustin, "The Sex Worker Stigma: How the Law Perpetuates Our Hatred (and Fear) of Prostitutes," *Salon,* August 17, 2013, http://www.salon.com /2013/08/17/the_whore_stigma_how_the_law_perpetuates_our_hatred_and_fear _of_prostitutes_partner/.

21. Bernstein, *Temporarily Yours,* 159.

22. Ibid., 160.

23. Dina Siegel, "Human Trafficking and Legalized Prostitution in the Netherlands," *Temida,* 1. no. 12 (March 2009): 10.

24. Annalise L. Daalder, *Prostitution in the Netherlands since the Lifting of the Brothel Ban,* Summary, Wetenschappelijk Onderzoeken Documentatiecentrum (WODC), Ministry of Justice (the Hague: BJU, 2007), http://english.wodc.nl /onderzoeksdatabase/1204e-engelse-vertaling-rapport-evaluatie-opheffing -bordeelverbod.aspx?cp=45&cs=6798.

25. Weitzer, *Legalization Prostitution,* 163.

26. Bernstein, *Temporarily Yours,* 142–3.

27. Ibid., 143–4.

28. Ibid., 165.

29. Daalder, *Prostitution in the Netherlands since the Lifting of the Brothel Ban,* 14.

30. Weitzer, *Legalizing Prostitution,* 201.

31. *Trafficking in Human Beings, Visible and Invisible (2012): A Quantitative Report 2007–2011,* National Rapporteur on Trafficking in Human Beings and Sexual Violence against Children (2012), http://www.dutchrapporteur.nl/reports /trafficking-visible-invisible/.

32. Siegel, "Human Trafficking and Legalized Prostitution in the Netherlands," 8.

33. Weitzer, *Legalization Prostitution,* 200.

34. Dina Siegel, "Mobility of Sex Workers in European Cities," *European Journal on Criminal Policy and Research,* 10: 1007 (December 27, 2011): 2–3, DOI: 10.1007/s10610–011–9168–5.

35. *Trafficking in Human Beings, Visible and Invisible (2012)*, 39.

36. Anna G. Korvinus et al., *Trafficking in Human Beings*, Third Report of the Dutch National Rapporteur (2004): 91, http://www.dutchrapporteur.nl/reports /third/.

37. Daalder, *Prostitution in the Netherlands since the Lifting of the Brothel Ban*, 47.

38. Ibid., 79.

39. Ibid.

40. Ibid., 47.

41. Siegel, "Human Trafficking and Legalized Prostitution in the Netherlands," 12.

42. Andrea Di Nicole et al., *Study on National Legislation on Prostitution and the Trafficking in Women and Children*, (Brussels: European Parliament, 2005), x, http://lastradainternational.org/doc-center/1073/study-on-national-legislation -on-prostitution-and-the-trafficking-in-women-and-children.

43. Weitzer, *Legalizing Prostitution*, 122–3.

44. Ibid., 118–20.

45. Ibid., 118.

46. Ibid., 97.

47. Abel et al., *Taking the Crime Out of Sex Work*, 220.

48. DML v. Montgomery, Human Rights Review Tribunal of New Zealand, vol. 6 (February 12, 2014), http://www.nzlii.org/nz/cases/NZHRRT/2014/6.html.

49. Abel et al., *Taking the Crime Out of Sex Work*, 228.

50. Christine Harcourt et al., "The Decriminalization of Prostitution Is Associated with Better Coverage of Health Promotion Programs for Sex Workers," *Australian and New Zealand Journal of Public Health* 34, no. 5 (2010): 482.

51. John Godwin, *Sex Work and the Law in Asia and the Pacific*, United Nations Development Programme (October 2012): 6, http://www.undp.org/content/dam /undp/library/hivaids/English/HIV-2012-SexWorkAndLaw.pdf.

52. Ibid., 1.

53. Ibid., 24–25.

54. Anne Elizabeth Moore, "Here's Why It Matters When a Human Rights Crusader Builds Her Advocacy on Lies," Salon.com, May 28, 2014, http://www .salon.com/2014/05/28/heres_why_it_matters_when_a_human_rights_crusader _builds_her_advocacy_on_lies/.

55. Simon Marks, "Somaly Mam: The Holy Saint (and Sinner) of Sex Trafficking," *Newsweek*, May 21, 2014, http://www.newsweek.com/2014/05/30/somaly -mam-holy-saint-and-sinner-sex-trafficking-251642.html.

56. Gerry Mullany, "Activist Resigns Amid Charges of Fabrication," *New*

*York Times*, May 29, 2014, http://www.nytimes.com/2014/05/30/world/asia /anti-trafficking-activist-quits-amid-charges-stories-were-fabricated.html.

57. Melissa Gira Grant, "The Price of a Sex-Slave Rescue Fantasy, *New York Times*, May 29, 2014, nytimes.com/2014/05/30/opinion/the-price-of-a-sex-slave -rescue-fantasy.html.

58. Weitzer, *Legalization Prostitution*, 100.

59. Gillian Abel and Lisa Fitzgerald, "Risk and Management in Sex Work post-Prostitution Reform Act," in *Taking the Crime Out of Sex Work*. Gillian Abel et al., eds. (Bristol, United Kingdom: Policy Press: 2010), 234.

60. Gillian Abel and Lisa Fitzgerald, "Decriminalisation and Stigma," in *Taking the Crime Out of Sex Work*, 239.

## 11. Canada's Public Health Experiment

1. *The Challenge of Change: A Study of Canada's Criminal Prostitution Laws*, report of the Standing Committee on Justice and Human Rights and the Subcommittee on Solicitation Laws, December 2006, 13–14, http://www.parl.gc.ca /Content/HOC/Committee/391/SSLR/Reports/RP2610157/391_JUST_Rpt6_PDF /391_JUST_Rpt6-e.pdf.

2. O'Doherty, "Victimization in Off-Street Sex Industry Work," 1.

3. Kate Shannon et al., "Prevalence and Structural Correlates of Gender Based Violence among a Prospective Cohort of Female Sex Workers," *British Medical Journal* 339:b2939 (August 11, 2009): 4.

4. Press release, "Canadian Laws on Prostitution Shown to Increase Violence against Sex Workers," British Columbia Centre for Excellence in HIV/AIDS, August 12, 2009, http://www.cfenet.ubc.ca/news/releases/canadian-laws-prostitution -shown-increase-violence-against-sex-workers.

5. L. Lazarus et al., "Risky Health Environments: Women Sex Workers' Struggles to Tind Safe, Secure and Non-exploitative Housing in Canada's Poorest Postal Code," *Social Science & Medicine* 73 (October 4, 2011): 1602–3.

6. Ibid., 1605.

7. Ibid., 1606.

8. Ibid., 1601.

9. Bernstein, *Temporarily Yours*, 186.

10. Kuo, *Prostitution Policy*, 131.

11. Suzanne Fournier, "'Sixties Scoop' Victims Seek Compensation," *Windsor Star*, June 2, 2011, A8.

12. Lori Culbert, "Pickton Murders: Bloody Knife Fight Left One Victim

Barely Alive," *Vancouver Sun*, August 10, 2010, http://www.vancouversun.com
/news/Bloody+knife+fight+left+victim+barely+alive/3360157/story.html.

13. Sandro Contenta, "Canada to Legalize Prostitution?," *Global Post*, June 15,
2011, http://www.globalpost.com/dispatch/news/regions/americas/canada/110615
/canada-legalize-prostitution.

14. John Lowman, "Crown Expert-Witness Testimony in *Bedford v. Canada*:
Evidence-Based Argument or Victim-Paradigm Hyperbole?" in *Selling Sex:
Experience, Advocacy, and Research on Sex Work in Canada*, Emily van der Meulen,
Elya M. Durisin, and Victoria Love, eds. (Seattle: University of Washington
Press, 2013), 241.

15. *The Challenge of Change*, 89.

16. Sean Fine, "Supreme Court Strikes Down Canada's Prostitution Laws,"
*Globe and Mail*, December 20, 2013, 1.

17. John Lowman, *Tripping Point*, brief to the Standing Committee on Justice
and Human Rights on The Protection of Communities and Exploited Persons
Act, http://184.70.147.70/lowman_prostitution/HTML/SCJHR/Tripping_Point
_Lowman_Brief_to_the_SCJHR_on_Bill_C36.pdf.

18. O'Doherty, "Victimization in Off-Street Sex Industry Work." Melissa
Farley et al., "Prostitution and Trafficking in Nine Countries: An Update on
Violence and Posttraumatic Stress Disorder, *Journal of Trauma Practice* 2, no.
3/4): 35.

## 12. California

1. *What Is Human Trafficking? Exploring the Scope and Impact of the CASE Act*,"
draft report, San Francisco Human Rights Commission, 2014, 17.

2. Jeordan Legon, "Supervisors Diversify: S.F. Appointee Stands Out as
White, Straight Male," *San Jose Mercury News*, February 7, 1997.

3. *What is Human Trafficking?*, 16.

4. "Solicitation of Minors for Prostitution," analysis of Senate Bill 1388, Senate
Committee on Public Safety, April 22, 2014.

5. Lewis Kamb and Eric Nalder, "Conduct Unbecoming: Cases under Review,"
*Seattle Post-Intelligencer*, August 3, 2005,

6. Ibid.

7. Ibid.

8. Drew Joseph, "Prop. 35 Gets Tough on Traffickers," *SF Gate*, September 17,
2012, http://www.sfgate.com/politics/article/Prop-35-gets-tough-on-human
-traffickers-3872843.php.

## 13. A Saner Approach to Prostitution

1. Chu and Glass, "Sex Work Law Reform in Canada," 107, 117. Dodillet, "The Swedish Sex Purchase Act: Claimed Success and Documented Effects," 22–23. Östergen, "Sexworkers Critique of Swedish Prostitution Policy," 2.

2. Weitzer, *Legalizing Prostitution*, 210.

3. Ibid.

4. "Prostitution: A Personal Choice," *The Economist,* August 9, 2014, 9.

5. Weitzer, *Legalizing Prostitution*, 207.

6. "Prostitution: A Personal Choice," 9.

7. Weitzer, *Legalizing Prostitution*, 211.

8. Kuo, *Prostitution Policy*, 130.

9. Ibid., 125.

10. Ibid., 169.

# SELECTED BIBLIOGRAPHY

Abel, Gillian et al., eds. *Taking the Crime Out of Sex Work: New Zealand Sex Workers' Fight for Decriminalization*. Bristol, United Kingdom: Policy Press, 2010.

Adler, Polly, *A House Is not a Home*. New York: Rinehart Books, 1953.

Albert, Alexa, *Brothel: Mustang Ranch and Its Women*. New York: Ballantine Books, 2001.

Bernstein, Elizabeth, *Temporarily Yours: Intimacy, Authenticity and the Commerce of Sex*. Chicago: University of Chicago Press, 2007.

Brents, Barbara G., Crystal A. Jackson, and Kathryn Hausbeck, *The State of Sex: Tourism, Sex and Sin in the New American Heartland*. New York: Routledge, 2010.

Clement, Elizabeth, *Love for Sale: Courtship, Treating and Prostitution in New York, 1920–1945*. Chapel Hill: University of North Carolina Press, 2006.

Dallas, Sandra, *Fallen Women*. New York: St. Martin's Press, 2013.

Delacoste, Frederique, and Priscilla Alexander, eds., *Sex Work: Writings by Women in the Sex Industry*, 2nd ed. San Francisco: Cleis Press, 1987.

Gilfoyle, Timothy, *City of Eros: New York, Prostitution and the Commercialization of Sex, 1790–1920*. New York: W.W. Norton, 1992.

Glasscock, Carl B., *Lucky Baldwin: The Story of an Unconventional Success*. Indianapolis: Bobbs-Merrill, 1933.

Grant, Melissa Gira, *Playing the Whore: The Work of Sex Work*. New York: Verso Books, 2014.

Jaget, Claude, *Prostitutes, Our Life*. Bristol, United Kingdom: Falling Wall Press, 1980.

Kolker, Robert, *Lost Girls: An Unsolved American Mystery*. New York: HarperCollins, 2013.

Kuo, Lenore, *Prostitution Policy: Revolutionizing Practice through a Gendered Perspective*. New York: New York University Press, 2002.

Leigh, Carol: *Unrepentant Whore: Collected Works of Scarlot Harlot*. San Francisco: Last Gasp, 2004.

MacKell, Jan, *Brothels, Bordellos and Bad Girls: Prostitution in Colorado, 1860–1930.* Albuquerque: University of New Mexico Press, 2004.

Mellon, Deborah, *The Legend of Molly b'Dam.* Kellogg, Idaho: Maple Street Publishing, 1989.

Money, John, *Lovemaps.* New York: Prometheus Books, 1999

Nagle, Jill, ed., *Whores and Other Feminists.* New York: Routledge, 1997.

Roberts, Nickie, *Whores in History.* London: Grafton Press, 1993.

Seagraves, Anne, *Soiled Doves: Prostitution in the Early West.* Hayden, Idaho: Wesanne Publications, 1994.

Sterry, David Henry, ed. *Hos, Hookers, Call Girls and Rent Boys.* New York: Soft Skull Press, 2009.

Weisberg, D. Kelly, *Children of the Night: Adolescent Prostitution in America.* Lexington, MA: D.C. Heath, 1985.

Weitzer, Ronald, *Legalizing Prostitution: From Illicit Vice to Lawful Business.* New York: New York University Press, 2012.

# INDEX